An Introduction to Painting and Sculpture

UNDERSTANDING ART

An Introduction to Painting and Sculpture

UNDERSTANDING ART

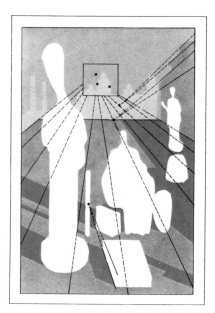

The Mitchell Beazley Library of Art

Editor-in-Chief and Editor of Volume 1
Jack Tresidder
Senior Executive Art Editor
Michael McGuinness
Senior Editor and Editor of Volumes 2 and 3
Paul Holberton
Editor of Volume 4
Jane Crawley
Editors
Ian Chilvers
Jane Cochrane
Katharine Kemp
Jean McNamee
Roslin Mair
Judy Martin
Susan Meehan
Senior Designer
Marnie Searchwell
Designers
Paul Bickerstaff
Alan Brown
Peter Courtley
Gerry Douglas
Jane Owen
Chief Picture Researcher
Flavia Howard
Picture Researchers
Celestine Dars
Tessa Politzer
Sandy Shepherd
Researchers
Julian George
Andrew Heritage
Tony Livesey
Julian Mannering
Kate Miller
Robert Stewart
Editorial Assistants
Barbara Gish
Amber Newell
Proof Reader
Gillian Beaumont
Indexers
Hilary and Richard Bird
Production Controller
Suzanne Semmes

THE MITCHELL BEAZLEY LIBRARY OF ART
was edited and designed by
Mitchell Beazley Publishers, Mill House,
87–89 Shaftesbury Avenue, London W1V 7AD

© Mitchell Beazley Publishers, 1981

ISBN 0 85533 177 1 Slipcased set

ISBN 0 85533 355 3 Volume 1

Composed by Filmtype Services Limited, Scarborough, England
and Tradespools Ltd, Frome, England

Origination by Gilchrist Bros, Leeds, England
and Scala Istituto Fotografico Editorale, Florence

Printed in the Netherlands
by Koninklijke Smeets Offset b.v., Weert

The Mitchell Beazley Library of Art

VOLUME 1: UNDERSTANDING ART

Looking at Art
Variations on Twelve Themes
The Language of Painting
Materials and Methods of Painting
The Language and Methods of Sculpture

STRUCTURE AND ORGANIZATION

This book is the first of four independent but interrelated volumes designed to provide a wide range of knowledge about painting and sculpture in a compact but comprehensive library of art. The exceptionally high proportion of illustrations reflects the importance given to visual information. Words about art lose much of their impact when they cannot be related directly to the works they describe, and it has been one aim of this project to bring together words and pictures more closely than ever before. In general, if a work of art is mentioned in the text it is also illustrated – and described in further detail – on the same page.

VOLUME 1

The first volume covers both the formal and the technical sides of painting and sculpture, providing a basic course of art appreciation that leads the reader into the following two volumes of history. A survey of some of the great themes of art and of the different ways in which they have been treated sets the scene for these differences of approach to be examined in detail. The formal language of painting – the structure of style itself – is first analysed not merely by giving examples of works that illustrate principles but also by using original diagrams and reconstructions which reveal the artist making choices and engineering his effects. An artist's use of colour or light, perspective or viewpoint, texture or pattern, movement or proportion, often works on us in ways that are by no means obvious, and by understanding these underlying factors we are better able both to appraise and enjoy paintings and to recognize what is going on in them. The achievement of an artist is also more understandable if we know something of the materials and methods of painting and sculpture, each of which has its own possibilities and limitations. This volume is not a technical guidebook, much less a course in how to paint or sculpt, but anyone who reads it will arrive at a good working idea of the characteristics of each medium of art – vital to appreciation. Above all, the aim is to generate interest and enthusiasm.

VOLUME 2: GREAT TRADITIONS

Ancient Worlds
Medieval and Early Renaissance Art
The Sixteenth Century
The Baroque Era

VOLUMES 2 AND 3

These two volumes of history cover the entire span of painting and sculpture from Palaeolithic images to modern art as it looked in 1980. First, the development of the Western tradition is traced from Egypt, Greece and Rome through medieval art to the Renaissance and the era of Baroque before the French Revolution ushered in the modern world. Then, in Volume 3, the arts of Islam, Asia and Japan are introduced before continuing with Western art of the nineteenth and twentieth centuries. Half of this entire volume is devoted to an extended treatment of modern art, which undeniably can present difficulties to the general public. A particular aim of the book has been to give a clear exposition of the main trends throughout the century.

In general, the organization of the history is geographic and chronological, but the art of a particular school or movement is usually followed through to its final development, not treated piecemeal. Though enough context is given to orientate the reader, the aim is not to provide a socio-cultural history but to keep the focus of interest on the paintings and sculptures themselves; the issues and preoccupations of the day, the conditions under which the works were produced, are discussed not for their own sake, but in order to throw light on the form and content of the art.

As in Volume 1, particular subjects, or aspects of them, are usually encapsulated within a single two-page "spread". This allows the reader either to begin at the beginning in the conventional way or to enter the book at any point, finding each spread more or less self-contained, though it connects with the others to build up a coherent whole. In the history volumes, the spread system makes possible a double approach. The broad development of art is unfolded in "narrative" spreads, which begin usually with background information and then cover a particular period, movement or region. In the course of the story some artists arrive of such stature that they have

VOLUME 3: NEW HORIZONS

Eastern Art
The Age of Revolutions, 1789–1917
Art since 1915

VOLUME 4: ART AND ARTISTS

Biographies of 3,000 Artists
Techniques and Methods
of Painting and Sculpture
Groups, Movements and Critical Terms
Portraits and Self-Portraits

one of these spreads to themselves. An alternative kind of spread, a "focus", is recognizable by a large-scale illustration. Here, the opportunity is taken to pause and contemplate a single work of art. Whether a stupendous Michelangelo or a painting in quieter key, such as Chardin's *House of cards*, the aim is to convey the essential flavour of the work, sometimes to show why it was specially significant or influential, sometimes to trace out the process of its creation, always to make the reader look at it again, with deeper understanding.

VOLUME 4
The final volume, arranged in alphabetical sequence, is primarily a biographical dictionary which supplements and complements the first three volumes. In addition to giving succinct accounts of the lives and works of more than 3,000 artists, it contains entries on art movements, terms, techniques and sites. The illustrations take the form of portraits (or photographs) of artists, many of them self-portraits, providing an intriguing visual commentary on the changing image of the artist through the ages.

HOW THE BOOKS WORK TOGETHER
All four volumes are both self-contained and interrelated. By using the cross-references provided at the foot of Volume 4 entries, the reader may approach Michelangelo, for example, from several different viewpoints. One of his masterworks, *David*, is discussed and illustrated as an archetypal theme of art in the first section of Volume 1. Subsequent sections look at his formal use of colour and articulation, his technique of fresco-painting and his methods of drawing and of stonecarving. In Volume 2 he appears in the artistic context of the High Renaissance, his protean range and influence is studied in a commentary on his life's work, and more detailed attention is focused on his most famous work, the ceiling of the Sistine Chapel. Finally, the Volume 4 entry assembles concisely the essential facts about his life and work, and shows a self-portrait.

EDITORIAL AND INDEXING METHOD
The locations of works of art shown in the first three volumes are not given in the captions but can be found, together with the dimensions and medium, in the list of illustrations that precedes the index of each volume. These lists are headed, as are the captions themselves, by the name of the artist or, if this is unknown, by the place of origin or original location of the work. This may be different from the present location; thus "*The Virgin of Vladimir*" appears under the heading CONSTANTINOPLE, where it was made, though it is kept in the Tretyakov Gallery in Moscow.

Titles of works of art are given in italics, but if translation is inappropriate or the title is a popular one which may not properly describe the image, it is also placed in inverted commas and captitalized – thus "*Totes Meer*", "*The Embarkation for Cythera*" (an appropriate translation is provided in brackets after the title). The names of monuments or buildings, notably churches, are usually the local names – thus Ste Madeleine, the Residenz. "S." is used for all the Italian variants, San, Santa, Sant', Santo. For Chinese words, the pinyin rather than the Wade-Giles system is used (though the Wade-Giles spelling is cross-referenced to the pinyin in the indexes to Volumes 2 and 3 and in Volume 4). The Latin form of an ancient Greek name has been used except in the historical section on ancient Greek art; thus Hercules in Renaissance art, Herakles in Greek art.

Full indexes are included in each of the first three volumes and the Volume 1 index also cross-refers forward to the main entries on artists in the history. In addition, Volume 4 forms a cumulative index, carrying cross-references to illustrations or main text in all volumes. Cross-references to other volumes are also provided within the body of the text where appropriate.

Specialized art terms, when they cannot be avoided altogether, are usually explained in Volume 1, or where they first appear. Alternatively, a fuller definition can be found under the alphabetical listing in Volume 4.

Contents: UNDERSTANDING ART

LOOKING AT ART

by David Piper

THE WOMAN IN RENOIR'S PAINTING, looking negligently out at us, is herself a spectator, half-dreamy perhaps in the heady murmur rising like incense from a theatre audience below. As she surveys the scene, waiting for the lights to go down and the lights on the stage to come up and illusion to begin, she is watched no doubt in turn by many inquisitive eyes in the audience, taking bearings, noting unexpected alliances, generating gossip. So her companion, too, surveys the auditorium with his opera-glasses in search of recognized faces, of friends, of desirable unknowns perhaps as possible conquests – though what more he could want than the enchanting creature at his side, it is hard to imagine.

It may well be familiar to you, this painting. It is one of the best-known and most popular of Renoir's works, reproduced in countless books whether on Renoir himself, or on Impressionism, or on the general history of painting in the West. In part, its almost instantaneous appeal depends simply on the woman's beauty. Then, too, the painting breathes of leisure, of pleasure. Through it we participate in a world of well-being – the splendour of physical youth, the nonchalance of wealth. It seems to pervade almost all the senses; at least I sense in it the excited buzz of the expectant audience below, the warm fragrance wafted from their expensive persons; I almost feel the padded plush of the rim of the box on which her hand, holding the glasses, rests. But the real impact of the picture is most directly on the sense of sight. The dominants in the composition are black and white, but everywhere kindled and broken by the shifting lights, whites flushing with the subtlest pinks. The image is fused on to the canvas with a succulence of touch and texture in the oil-paint characteristic of certain French painters (Renoir very much amongst them) which seems to translate into matter the very essence of colour, almost a visual equivalent of *haute cuisine*.

It all seems so easy, so happy, no less relaxed in execution than in subject. But most people, when it was first shown, did not find it so at all. Renoir signed and dated this canvas 1874, and in that year it was shown in an exhibition in Paris which was at first notorious and derided, though it has now long become famous as marking a decisive turning-point in the history of Western art. A group of young painters, rejected by or spurning the official exhibitions of the art establishment, opened a show at the former studio of the famous photographer Nadar. Among the paintings shown was Monet's *Impression: sunrise,* from the title of which the Impressionist movement took its name, though it was applied derogatively by a hostile critic. Virtually all the artists involved were assailed with ridicule, nor was Renoir himself spared. The critic of *Figaro* wrote: "Try to explain to M. Renoir that a woman's torso is not a mass of flesh decomposing in the green or purplish

RENOIR: *The theatre box* (La loge), 1874

blemishes that indicate that a corpse is in full putrefaction. . . ."

Thus for many, used to the polished finish of Salon work, even Renoir's painting was incoherent and unintelligible, an insult to cultivated taste, and yet of all the Impressionists Renoir was the most traditional. Even today we may misconstrue this canvas. Certainly it has now the look of an impression – a spontaneous reaction to a passing moment glimpsed on the spot in a theatre. It was in fact worked out in an entirely traditional studio manner, deliberately and calculatedly posed. The couple are Renoir's brother Edmond, and a Montmartre model called Nini. A sharp French eye would detect that the girl is palpably not of the high social class which her position in the box, her superb dress, her jewels, might lead one to expect, but a woman of the people, a girl such as Renoir indeed loved to paint all through his career.

THERE IS, THEN, MORE THAN MEETS THE EYE even in a picture apparently so direct and immediately seductive as *The theatre box*, and so it is with almost any painting or sculpture of high quality. It is the function – and privilege – of books such as this to bring out some of the resonances that might otherwise pass in works of art assembled from the four corners of the world, many of them less familiar and less accessible than Renoir's, but no less enjoyable. Very few, if any, will have the opportunity to devote in tranquillity to each of the originals reproduced in this library the necessary minutes – or, more likely, hours – that it takes to enter and to explore, to commit to visual memory, a masterpiece. Indeed, the individual viewer at a major loan exhibition, or the diligent tourist in the holiday months, may find it difficullt, in a jammed picture gallery, to contemplate uninterrupted any one object for even a few seconds. The collection of reproductions that anyone can build up on private bookshelves – André Malraux's "Museum without walls" – can never displace the need to become familiar with the originals, the pleasure of confronting the works themselves. Yet books do act as reminders to fallible memory no less than as stimulants to the pursuit of the originals. They also set them in a context that can be profoundly enriching, offering comparison with other works of the same artist or the same period, and with works far distant in time or place.

Our ability to respond to a painting is often affected by its cultural context if only because, until the move away from figurative art in the twentieth century, many paintings had for subject matter some figure or event from myth, sacred writ, legend or idealized history. While a picture of a young man with a blue skin talking to a beautiful girl by a pool may seem bizarre to Westerners, a Hindu would have no difficulty recognizing the Lord Krishna conversing with a milkmaid. Even within a single historical tradition, common references may quickly become puzzling: a painter in seventeeth-century Rome, Madrid, Antwerp or London could expect his audience to know who Apollo was, what happened at Thermopylae, how Jacob treated Esau, what Zacchariah said to Mary or Christ to the Woman of Samaria – knowledge that cannot necessarily be assumed today. As well as such references, the political, social and economic forces that have in more or less degree conditioned works of art can be explained in a book; so too the technical constraints that have shaped them, and it seems axiomatic that the fuller the understanding of the original the richer and more satisfying the enjoyment of looking at it is likely to be.

It is, in fact, only by experience, by comparison, that an awareness of art can be tuned to its finest pitch of sensitivity. Certainly, just as there are those gifted with perfect pitch in music, some are born with an unerring eye for quality, but they are rare and for them, too, instinctive pleasure in quality is enlarged enormously by knowledge. One purpose of these volumes is to make available a store of information and to present it in a way that can be understood by anyone interested in art. But the object always is to increase enjoyment, and discussion is based not upon theoretical aspects of art but upon individual works – the concrete objects themselves. The same principle is followed in sections of this book in which my colleagues discuss the formal language of painting and sculpture – the calculated or intuitive decisions artists make about tone or colour, viewpoint or proportion – as well as the physical means by which art achieves its effect, the media of paint, ink, pencil, of stone or wood or metal, with their various creative limitations and possibilities. The two volumes of history which follow constitute a commentary, roughly chronological, of the ever-expanding and diversifying course of art, from prehistoric times to the late twentieth century. The final volume provides a biographical index of artists and an explanation of art terms; here the entries are in summary form but are designed to yield basic information for the reader. The work as a whole is, however, conceived less as an exhaustive encyclopaedia than as a commentary, a companion, which I hope will inform, stimulate but above all open the reader's eyes to further pleasures, heightening awareness and enhancing life. Where matters of selection were involved I have tried to bear in mind the interests and needs of the gallery-goer, which do not always correspond with those of art historians. This means not only that the overall balance of the history to some extent reflects my own tastes, but also that the quality, preservation and accessibility of what has survived is taken into account.

THROUGHOUT, WE REFER BACK CONTINUALLY to specific works of art, for my part inevitably, as I am no aesthetician nor philosopher. Definitions of art have modulated through the centuries and across the world, according to the functions it has had to serve. By a modern European, paintings may be regarded as portable commodities bought for prestige or pleasure. In other times and places they have been magical signs, focuses of ritual, embodiments of myth or legend or aids to spiritual contemplation. They have also provided environments for escapist fantasy and instruments of education or propaganda to enhance the power and status of institutions, social classes or prominent and wealthy individuals. For St Bonaventura in the Middle Ages a picture was "that which instructs, arouses pious emotions and awakens memories", and we will look soon at a picture that is a call to prayer. For Zola, the nineteenth-century realist, a picture was "a bit of nature filtered through an individual temperament" ("un coin de la nature vu à travers un tempérament"). Only a few years after Zola, the twenty-year-old painter Maurice Denis, in 1890, formulated a tenet that was to be widely approved (though by no means universally) through the succeeding century: "A picture – before being a war-horse or a nude woman or some little genre scene – is essentially a flat surface covered with colours assembled in a certain order". Twenty years later, Kandinsky, followed rapidly by others, demonstrated that the war-horse, woman or genre scene could be dispensed with entirely, and in the West for a time it seemed that figurative or representational art, whether in painting or sculpture, was being obliterated in the flood of non-figurative or "abstract" art. It has now become clear that traditional forms are not so easily dispensed with, and they re-emerge, their horizons enlarged by the explorations of the abstractionists.

IF ONE IS TO SPEAK IN GENERAL TERMS OF ART, the analogy of music seems to become more and more relevant. Already Michelangelo claimed that "finally, good painting is a music and a melody which intellect only can appreciate". The suggestion implicit here recurred again and again, from Goethe's famous definition of architecture as "frozen music" to Walter Pater's scarcely less celebrated contention that "all art constantly aspires towards the condition of music". As the twentieth-century emphasis on the formal content of painting and sculpture increased, it began to seem that music was indeed the only viable analogy by which to describe or attempt to analyse the quality of much abstract painting. In the early years of abstract art there seemed (to the majority of the general public) no point of recognition from which to start an exploration. Time has brought its own solution to this, partly in a somewhat incestuous way, as the prolific expansion and diversification of abstract art has created its own internal body of reference and its own standards of quality, of good and bad, but also because it has gradually become clear that many of these standards relate very closely to those of traditional figurative art – to its basic ingredients of line and shape, rhythm and pattern, mass and space, light and shade, colour and texture. Even so, abstract art still evokes a less rich response from most viewers than does figurative art of comparable distinction, and it is indeed deprived of the immediate relationship to the life and flesh and blood that figurative art offers. Henry James, writing about Whistler's *Nocturnes* and *Arrangements* (to which he did not respond), asked that "a picture should have some relation to life as well as to painting". James had in fact earlier responded with delight to Whistler's portrait of his mother, but as "a masterpiece of tone, of feeling, of the power to render life", whereas Whistler, anticipating Maurice Denis, was to forbid assessment of the painting in terms of a portrait of a specific person and demand that it be known as *Arrangement in grey and black*.

The danger that threatens some non-figurative art is that it seems, and is often indeed asserted to be, art about art. To the public, even that part of it genuinely and sympathetically concerned with art, an obsessive concern among painters and sculptors with intellectual problems is frustrating, at least when that obsession leads to the sincerely held (but one hopes false) conclusion that figurative art is obsolete. When even the art object, the painting or sculpture itself, is jettisoned, artists' activities may come to seem to others mere narcissistic behaviour, posturing. The effective channels of communication available to the visual artist are sensual rather than conceptual, above all the sense of sight, but also, in sculpture, that of touch.

The ultimate feedback, however, from the exploratory investigations of the avantgarde to the mainstream of art is unpredictable; it has recently become increasingly evident that all kinds of art are pursued in all kinds of traditions, by dedicated men and women indifferent, sometimes heroically so, to the changing tides of fashion. The present uncertainty about the nature and function of art may derive from our inability, even after almost a century and a half, to come to terms with the consequences of one technical invention – photography. Its full effect on our attitude to man-made images is difficult to assess but has certainly been fundamental; for instead of being unique and finely-crafted objects, owned by few, or relatively costly engravings reproduced for wider dissemination, visual images now bombard us daily, reproduced by photographic techniques in colour and – in film and television – in motion as well. The devalued potency of the man-made image is felt at the most basic level: primitive amazement at the sight of reality's double has evaporated, and artistic illusion, which once could seem positively magical, supernatural, is commonplace and so ceases to be illusion.

PHOTOGRAPHY HAS INVADED THE TERRITORY of whole branches of art, of not only traditional, anecdotal, narrative painting but also, in films and television, the art of visual satire and social comment; few would now hang today's equivalent of Hogarth's savage "comic-history" engravings on their walls, and reproductions of Hogarth have been turned into picturesque decorations for pub interiors. The artist seems to have lost his most immediately obvious practical function as a unique recorder – whether of topography, human events or individual likenesses – a function now answered more quickly and cheaply by the camera. At the same time, many of the great traditional themes which have stirred artists to masterpieces are abandoned in a crisis of patronage: the Church is no longer a major patron, and the great works it commissioned in the past now turn many churches into museums. Visitors to the little chapel of Vence in the south of France come not to pray but to see Matisse's decorations, and so too, in the great old shrines of the West, it is to admire the architecture, or to pay homage to Giotto, to Michelangelo and Raphael, to Bernini, that the visitors come. In the museum and art gallery, twentieth-century art finds a purpose-built home but one that seems, to some artists, rather too final a shrine for their work, separated from life and no longer offering the satisfaction of creating a work for a particular person, or place, or purpose, as most artists have done throughout the history of painting and sculpture.

Photography, however, has not shrunk the possibilities of art; rather it has been the order of release from the slavery of imitation. Without it, the experiment of abolishing subject matter in abstract art might never have taken place. Photography has not only greatly extended our knowledge of the artistic traditions of the past, but also helped indirectly to change our approach to them – instead of dogma we look for humanity, instead of dwelling on subject matter we look for what makes it great art. The greatest artists have always been able to add something to life, a pattern or order, an emotion, a vision.

Major movements during the twentieth century have widened the freedom of artists to convey emotion through distortion, to re-create the landscapes and sensations of dreams, as well as to create abstract works that answer only to their own logic of shape, line, texture or colour. If it seems that artists today are still often caught off-balance by this revelation of imaginative freedom, and do not know what to do with it, it is also true that we, the observers, are still constrained by the expectations of lifelike imitation. In looking at traditional Renaissance art, we know the conventions and instant, if superficial, recognition allows us to respond and – if we have will enough and time – to become increasingly involved with its profounder depths. Each age selects from the past the art most relevant to its own needs, and it is only too true that we mostly like what we already know, simply because it is easier that way. Yet great art, even of the traditional kind, is not easy. To come to grips with it can mean the application of one's entire sensory, mental and imaginative faculties, and with a concentration suspiciously like that involved in hard work.

LIFELIKE IMITATION has never, in fact, been the only style of figurative art, and treatments by different artists of the same subjects vary enormously, even within a shared tradition. By way of illustrating this, and as visual intro-duction to the more technical and formal aspects of understanding art, we begin this book with a discussion of twelve great themes of painting and sculpture to which artists have consistently turned. Each discussion starts from contemplation of one single work, with a following commentary on just a few of the countless variations on the theme. As the commentary is necessarily brief, whereas the themes have produced not only a vast range of art but also a vast literature of criticism, the section is intended primarily as a picture gallery, an opportunity to compare and contrast paintings and sculptures of different eras in a manner impossible in a chronological history – though some will be discussed later, and in detail, in their own historical context in the volumes that follow.

We begin with the visible world – the individual, society, the material fabric of life – and end with the world of the spirit and the imagination. The thematic organization does not mean that the subject matter of pictures is the most important thing about them. Similarities between works on the same subject often reflect the fact that art is itself raw material for art – sometimes rather more so than the world of natural appearances. Yet it is the differences that are perhaps more striking, and these arise not only from variations of design, technique or medium but from fundamental differences of function. An art of emotion or persuasion is unlike that of sober, literal record, and each of these is different from the kind of art in which the wish to establish a formal order of shapes, colours, patterns for purely aesthetic ends overrides any attempt to imitate appearances. For the artist, a painting or sculpture usually has a personal function; it expresses a view of the world, an individual vision.

ARTISTS TURN TO PAINTING AND SCULPTURE because what they have to express is inexpressible in words; in spite of the superficial resemblances between photography and art it is equally inexpressible in photographs, which are products of a different creative process. What the camera records in the split second of the shutter opening is limited to the scene gathered in by the lens at that instant, and the range of choices the photographer can make about viewpoint, aperture and timing are necessarily limited; so too, in scale, colour and texture, the final positive image that can be produced is limited by the mechanical processes of printing. Artists stand between us and their subject matter in a different way, selecting at will the elements they feel are essential and transmuting them, often over weeks or months, into materials that record the mark of their hand and mind and which have a surface texture that can itself engage our feelings. The sterility of much academic art usually lies in the fact not that it is figurative but that it copies other art. What great paintings and sculptures have in common with great works of literature, with any form of great art, is their ability to create a fresh order from the flux of life. The pleasure we are given from looking at them is primarily that of having our view clarified, distilled, detached from the distractions that condition our everyday way of seeing. We are able to share a perception of the world different from our own, and more penetrating, to see a pattern that was not evident, or an attraction in things not ordinarily thought beautiful, or even a dimension in life that may be called spiritual.

Visual artists work with gross physical matter which, even when the medium is of stone or metal, is perishable, yet the greatest of them can transcend it, asserting the existence of a reality impervious to time and death. Years ago, a phase from the conclusion of E.M. Forster's novel "*A Room with a View*" lodged in my mind. The heroine is expressing thanks to her mentor, an old man of experience and forthright wisdom: "It was as if he had made her see the whole of everything at once". Art, at that level of vision, can be a stimulus, a challenge, an inexhaustible enjoyment. The resonance of a dozen or so lines scratched by Rembrandt with pen and ink on a piece of paper may fill one with an astonishment different but no less intense than the wonder of his painting "*The Jewish Bride*", with all its elaboration of scale and colour.

Everything that follows is designed as aid to such enjoyment. I close this

introduction with a little-known painting that has always delighted me. It may not be the greatest work of art among the thousands we will show, but it contains within its small frame – only about the size of our reproduction – an unexpected richness. It demonstrates also the capacity of a book such as this to give access to branches of art that the ordinary gallery-goer can never be sure of being able to see – far less to handle, as this miniature was intended to be handled. It is one of the illuminations of a prayerbook, a so-called Book of Hours, painted for one of the great heiresses of Europe, Mary of Burgundy. The name of the artist is unknown, "the Master of Mary of Burgundy", but he is comparable in quality with any of the great followers of Jan van Eyck.

It is Mary herself who is shown here, gazing downwards on to a book in her lap – contemplative counterpart to her worldly sister in Renoir's *The theatre box* four hundred years later. The book she holds is perhaps the very same Book of Hours of which this is one page. To left and right, casement windows open – not on the outdoors but upon the interior of a great Gothic church in the centre of which Mary's namesake, the Virgin Mary, sits with the Child in her arms. Though the supernatural has entered into the scene in the choir it is painted with no less realism than the pensive lady whose vision it is. In a bewitching double-take she reappears, kneeling in front of the Madonna with her court ladies, and that red accent under her arm may be the same Book of Hours. The Mother of God is depicted as if she had just looked in on the church one silvery Flemish afternoon. There is a subtle play with illusion and reality in this image, and to scholars, a wealth of symbolic meanings in the objects and flowers displayed. The blue iris soaring from the vase is a flower sacred to the Madonna; it was also *gladiolus*, the sword-lily, and its prophetic presence alludes to a traditional representation of Mary after the Passion, her heart transfixed by a sword. It is the one dark note in the composition. The significance of the two carnations is less certain, but pinks or carnations were often allusions to betrothal – and if so the little painting should be of 1477, the year Mary married Maximilian of the great Hapsburg house of Austria. The illuminated initial at which the Book of Hours is opened is an "O", which has suggested to scholars that she is engaged with the popular prayer *Obscero te* ("I beseech thee"). If so, for Mary, invocation soon proved vain: she died in 1482, from a riding accident, only 25 years old. Yet the pervasive quality of the picture is serenity and peace, and to experience its mood we need no arcane knowledge, simply the time to look – to join Mary there in meditation on and within that beautiful synthesis of the natural and the supernatural, the human and the divine, the ephemeral and the eternal.

VARIATIONS
ON TWELVE THEMES

"The art of the Greeks, of the Egyptians, of
the great painters who lived in other
times, is not an art of the past; perhaps
it is more alive today than it ever
was. Art does not evolve by itself; the
ideas of people change and with them their
mode of expression." – PICASSO

(left) TITIAN: "*The Concert Champêtre*", detail, *c.*1510; (above) LEONARDO: *A woman pointing*, after 1513

The Human Figure

Through all the changing styles and themes of art, painters and sculptors seem to return to one fundamental point of departure, the study of the nude human figure. Michelangelo's *David* is only one of a myriad variations following from the Renaissance rediscovery of the Greek belief that perfection of the spirit should be expressed in physical perfection of the body. Yet it has become one of the best-known images in art, almost universally available not only in photographs but in small-scale casts. In such reproductions, the subtlety and vitality of the original are inevitably softened and diluted, and one forgets an essential quality of the original: it is colossal.

Michelangelo was only 26 when he began carving the statue, as a civic commission from the city of Florence in 1501, using a block of marble more than four metres (nearly 15ft) high. The block was to hand, ordered years before for a proposed giant statue of a prophet to adorn a buttress of Florence Cathedral, but abandoned after an earlier sculptor had started to rough out the figure. From these botched beginnings, it became in Michelangelo's hands the first free-standing colossal nude male statue of the Renaissance, an ideal self-portrait, perhaps, of the youthful genius confronting his personal and artistic destiny and, for his fellow-citizens, a proud assertion of the independence of Florentine democracy. Though it was moved indoors, to conserve it from erosion, in 1873, the rather harsh, weather-stained copy that occupies its site outside the Palazzo della Signoria in the centre of Florence makes its original impact more intelligible and its huge scale even more telling than in the less sympathetic setting of the Accademia, where the original now stands.

David, the Jewish shepherd boy who saved his people by slaying the giant Goliath with a stone cast from a sling, has proved an irresistible subject in Christian art. Many of the great artists who have represented him have chosen to show the moment of triumph – the boy poised with one foot on the giant's severed head – or of action, as in Bernini's superb study of David drawing a bead on his target with the unerring eye of the natural athlete. Michelangelo's moment is of confrontation; the pose is easy, relaxed, the beautifully-handled torso electric with intent of action. One side of the body is open, the sling lying easily on the shoulder. Resting on the thigh is David's right hand, the executive hand, carved, like the head, aggressively larger in scale than the rest.

In pose and torso, in the bold insistence on nakedness, Michelangelo has adapted classical Hellenistic example. In that magnificent, precisely carved head, however, in the relation of head to body, he has realized at its finest the specifically Florentine ideals of the harmony of physical, spiritual and intellectual beauty. The image is less of the historical David, complex in his human strengths and frailties – still less of the slightly-built shepherd boy defying apparently overwhelming odds – than of an ideal hero, a personification of all that Michelangelo himself felt about the physical glory of the male nude body and the courage of the human spirit.

MICHELANGELO: *David*, 1501–04

The Human Figure

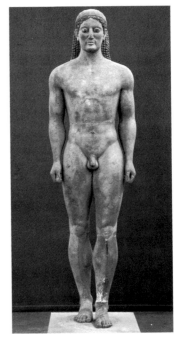

TANZANIA: *Rock-painting*

EGYPT: *Fowling in the marshes,* 1400 BC

GREECE: *Kouros, c.* 540-515 BC

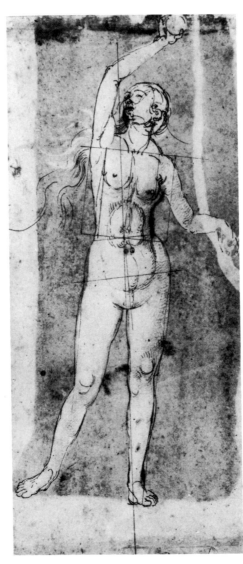

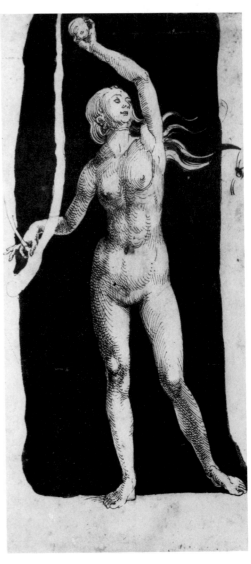

DURER: *Nude woman,* 1493

DURER: *Eve, c.* 1506

DURER: *Eve, c.* 1506

KHAJURAHO, INDIA:
The Kandarya Mahadeva temple, detail, c. 1000

GREECE (left): "*The Venus de Milo*", c. 100 BC

Among the earliest representations of man are the matchstick figures of prehistoric cave-paintings, shorthand diagrams of the human physique, like those still to be found in the art of the South African Bushman and in the drawings of young children everywhere. Many cultures elaborated their own conception of the human figure from such elementary beginnings, the Egyptians introducing into their essentially linear portrayals a sense of movement by showing the body both frontally and in profile. Archaic Greek sculpture demonstrated a similar stiffness and stylization, but it is from the originally rigid and impersonal *Kouroi* that the classic Greek figure developed, based upon ideal proportions and quickening into life. For the Greeks discerned divinity in the harmony of the perfect naked body.

During the first millennium of Christianity reaction to the pagan celebration of physical form meant that the body again became a cypher, an expendable mortal shell whence the essential element, the soul, would soon escape to the true reality of life after death. When, after long estrangement and unease, European artists began to focus more closely on the body, it was at first not revivals of the Greek ideal they produced but much less flattering transcriptions from the actual configurations of normal – and fallible – human figures. The transition between medieval and Renaissance art is illustrated vividly in the development of Dürer, whose early drawing at Bayonne (1493) of a stocky peasant girl is entirely credible. Thirteen years later, in Italy, studies, one on each side of the paper, record a fundamentally different conception of woman. In one a geometric armature is traced within the figure. The second, more fully worked-out, image based on these calculated proportions becomes an enchanting compromise between real and ideal.

Dürer's slimly elegant figure refers back to classical interpretation of the human body as a module of proportion which could be related geometrically to the basic forms of square and circle – to the proposal of the Roman Vitruvius that architecture itself should be based upon the ratios of the human body. Greek sculptors of the Hellenistic period had already shown that such ideal proportions could be relaxed in more flexible and sensuous solutions, as in the famous "*Venus de Milo*" of about 100 BC. Almost comparably fluent expressions of the religious impulse in human form are found in Eastern art, never more enthusiastically celebrated than in the sculpture of India – the Hindu temple of Khajuraho teems with the voluptuous delights of Heaven. It was in the humanist culture of the West, however, that the nude would assume a central significance in art from the time of the Renaissance onwards. *The three Graces*, Raphael's study of the female body from three different angles, was painted at a time when it was still not permissible to draw naked women from the life. Yet it shows a confident assimilation of classical models in an idealized but sensuous image of physical perfection, a harmony that does not appear to proceed from calculation and which is both flawless and utterly convincing.

RAPHAEL: *The three Graces*, 1504-05

The Human Figure

Since the rediscovery of the human figure in the fifteenth century, Western artists have used the nude in enormously varied ways, as a theme on which to develop the original variations of their own time, their own interests, their individual styles. The range extends from the classical ideal to the literal recording of particular physical form, both traditions being aided by the developing science of anatomy and by the rapidly established academic tradition of drawing from life.

The delicacy of Raphael's *The three Graces* is far from the voluptuous, ripe radiance that Tintoretto was to infuse, later in the century, into *Susannah and the Elders*, an overtly erotic subject in which we, the spectators, are implicated as we spy with the old men upon Susannah's nakedness. In the large exuberance of her flesh, Tintoretto's nude is not classically proportioned but she is still idealized, a tendency which seems to diminish as one goes northwards: fascination with the reality of the flesh in all its imperfections increases from Umbria (Raphael) to Venice (Tintoretto) and then to Holland and the greatest master of the unideal, Rembrandt. His *Bathsheba* conveys, as perhaps no other nude in all art, the vulnerability of all mankind, not only woman, in the body. It is an image that is certainly erotic, but which rebukes the *voyeur*-spectator and demands love rather than lust; this nude is very far from being a sex object.

The great Baroque decorative painters of the seventeenth century, above all Rubens, must be open to the accusation of presenting women principally as objects for male desire, but the physical exuberance of Rubens' golden Amazons seems more accurately to be a natural outcome of the inexhaustible energy of his style. Eighteenth-century Rococo painters, such as Boucher and Fragonard, emphasized the erotic element above all else – Boucher's *Miss O'Murphy* seems overt invitation – and in much nineteenth-century academic art classical references became hardly more than a veneer of respectability over the eroticism of nymphs at play. Courbet, arch-enemy of academic classicism, used the nude more forthrightly as the focus of his allegory of modern life in *The artist's studio* – radiant at the centre of the canvas.

Only with the revolution against figurative art, signalled by Cubism in the first decade of the twentieth century, did the nude, and indeed the human figure, seem to lose its status as the centre of the world. First disintegrated by Picasso, it became in the hands of Boccioni a collection of planes moving through space, more a machine than an organism; it was abstracted to a study of pure cylinders by Brancusi. It vanishes entirely in the austere constructions of Mondrian – and yet it persists. From the formless welter of action painting in the 1950s there emerged, battling their way into ferocious presence, those elemental females, vital as Neolithic fertility figures, of De Kooning. The tradition of the human figure, of the nude in particular, has in fact never been lost; Picasso himself, in the midst of experimentation with light, form and line in *Nude in an armchair*, was able to reconcile non-literal representation with a voluptuous awareness of the body's opulence.

TINTORETTO: *Susannah and the Elders*, c. 1550

RUBENS: *Bathsheba reading David's letter*, c. 1636-38

REMBRANDT: *Bathsheba at her toilet*, 1654

BOUCHER: *Miss O'Murphy*, 1732

BOCCIONI: *Unique forms of continuity in space*, 1913

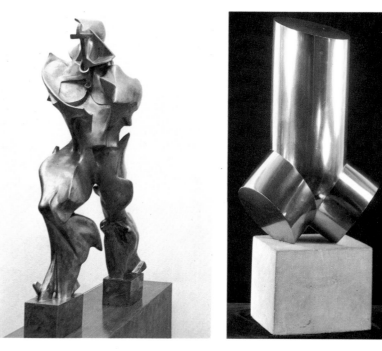

COURBET: *The artist's studio*, detail, 1854-55

BRANCUSI: *Male torso*, after 1924

PICASSO: *Nude in an armchair*, 1932

DE KOONING: *Woman IV*, 1952-53

The Human Face

A prime difficulty with Leonardo's *Mona Lisa* is simply that of seeing it clearly. The most famous painting in the world, it is so besieged by crowds in the Louvre as to be often almost invisible. It is still further set apart by the armoured-glass-fronted shrine wherein it dwells in the dusk acceptable to scientists as a safe level of light – a submarine dimness in which, nevertheless, the eye observes that the painting is further obscured by old and discoloured varnish. On the other hand it is over-exposed in countless reproductions – postcards, posters, illustrations in books and periodicals all over the world. The spray of words that began to accumulate about it, from critics and writers through the centuries since Leonardo painted the lady while (they say) musicians sang to her, often mists rather than clears our view of the image.

Mona Lisa was the otherwise unremarked wife of Francesco del Giocondo, an influential merchant of Florence, yet not all agree that she was indeed the subject of this portrait. If, as seems probable, she sat for a portrait drawing Leonardo made in 1503 or 1504, the completeness and perfection of the final painting make it likely that he worked on it, as on all his important paintings, over a considerable period, and put into it more than could be discovered in the person of the Giaconda herself.

In revealing the formal potentialities of portraiture, the *Mona Lisa* is central to the whole development of that art. There are Flemish precedents for the beautiful, half-turned pose, but previous portraits had been in terms of a closed characterization – the sitter defined within a clear contouring line. By "melting" the contour so that the eye is led round it in imagination, Leonardo introduced new qualities – ambiguity of character and mood, the illusion of movement, and so of time passing – in short, the breath of life. The soft play of light and shade over the features, the hazy blending of the figure with an alpine landscape that suggests an organic unity of water, rocks and living things, the enigma of that famous, lop-sided smile, half lost in shadow, all create an elusiveness that is analysable to some degree in purely visual terms. At first it was the painting's technical mastery that awed observers – the delicacy of the chiaroscuro, the exquisite modelling of the lips, eyes, hands, the compositional harmony of it all.

The mysterious power of the portrait, its magical hold over the imagination of the viewer, is not finally explicable by formal means, however. Walter Pater's celebrated invocation: "She is older than the rocks among which she sits; like the vampyre she has been dead many times, and learned the secrets of the grave . . .", his equation of her with Leda, the mother of Helen of Troy, and with St Anne, the mother of Mary, may seem far from the reaction of Duchamp who, in our own century, drew a moustache on a postcard of her, subscribed by an obscene inscription. Yet both – Pater for a Romantic age, Duchamp for a sceptical one in which her defacement was the ultimate artistic sacrilege – acknowledged her as a lay icon, an image which remains, as it perhaps was for Leonardo himself, all things to all men.

LEONARDO: *Mona Lisa*, c. 1503–06

The Human Face

JOSEPH WRIGHT:
The Corinthian maid,
detail, 1784

AMMAN: *Jericho skull, c.* 6000 BC

RUBENS: *Susanna Lunden, c.* 1622-25

AFTER POLYEUKTOS:
Demosthenes,
original *c.* 280 BC

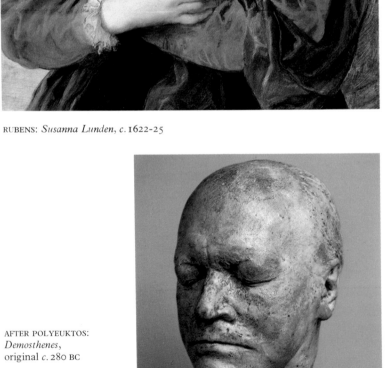

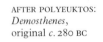

J.S. DEVILLE: Life-mask of William Blake, *c.* 1825

DAVID:
Napoleon in his study, 1812

GILLRAY: *Maniac ravings*,
detail, 1805

DIX (below): *Sylvia von Harden*, 1926

BRAQUE: *Man with a guitar*, 1911

Of all subjects of art, portraiture represents perhaps the most poignant attempt to retain something that cannot be retained, to deny the mortality of a unique human being. In a Greek myth (which later fascinated Joseph Wright), the Corinthian maid Dibutade, knowing her lover was about to leave her, traced his shadow on the wall. The same enduring concern reveals itself in primitive decoration of skulls, their skin rehabilitated with clay, their eyes with cowrie shells – from the Jericho skulls of 6000 BC to those of twentieth-century New Guinea. Such works seem intended to capture not only the likeness but also the spirit of the departed.

Aristotle distinguished between three kinds of portraiture – the idealized image of formal state portraits, the naturalistic mapping of the sitter's features and the satirical portrait. Yet Greek artists also attempted a psychological penetration that went beyond a mere likeness; the statue of the orator Demosthenes shows a remarkable introspective sensitivity. In its suggestion of a living presence this is not far from the force of personality inherent in the life-mask of the poet William Blake.

Christianity, with its emphasis on the spirit rather than on its mortal container, almost lost sight of portraiture for many centuries; only with the humanist and classical revival of the Renaissance did portrait painting revive and spread, growing in confidence and complexity. The range could extend from Netherlandish realism of an almost photographic fidelity to the ennobling idealism of Italian masters for whom dignity and decorum were tenets of artistic faith. In the wake of Leonardo's experiments with tonality and the capture of movement in human expression came seventeenth-century masters such as Rubens, who could make an informal record of a friend as affectionate, as perceptive, as glowing with life as his portrait of Susanna Lunden, whose sister he was later to marry.

At the other end of the scale from this freely-handled portrayal of a woman in the bloom of sensual youth is the official state portrait, didactic, clear-cut, with the sitter shown emblematically in the regalia of office, his bearing and surroundings projecting his authority. David's Neoclassical portrait of Napoleon splendidly answered his sitter's demand for portraits of great men in keeping with their greatness – an artistic licence that cartoonists carried to the opposite extreme.

The twentieth century has presented new variations, among them the use of portraiture as a foundation for formal experiment, hardly different in function from a still life. In the Cubism of Picasso or Braque the ever-present conflict between artist and sitter is won entirely by the artist, who, in disintegrating and reconstituting his subject, swallows his identity as ruthlessly as some spiders devour their mates. Expressionist portraiture offers another alternative to photography, using distortion to capture the human condition *in extremis*, as in Otto Dix's study of a German journalist, her features deformed by the violence, cynicism and isolation of our era.

The Human Face

Many artists have been praised for their ability to paint not only the face but the soul, though one of the finest of portrait painters, Reynolds, avowed that the artist could catch only so much of the inner character as was betrayed by the lineaments of the sitter. And as most people know to their cost, "face value" is not always reliable.

One form in which one might hope for a more than superficial assessment of character is the self-portrait, though most artists of the second rank in fact have tended to show themselves as vain as anyone else – if not more so – and as prone to paint their mirror-image in terms of the constraining fashions of their time. Self-portraiture can, however, provide artists with their most accessible and consistent source of personal and pictorial research. The narcissism essential to personal expression can here be focused most revealingly, whether to project an image of the artist in a certain guise for public view or to undertake an honest analysis for the artist's own satisfaction.

A startling example of honesty is the bleak, uncompromising account of his own person by Dürer, who seems to convey the sensation of the night of the soul in his own unidealized physique. Dürer was one of those few major artists who have left something approaching a pictorial autobiography (from which vanity was not always absent, as in one depiction of himself apparently as Christ). The broadest of all such autobiographies is that of Rembrandt – a life-long sequence of images of himself, sometimes role-playing but finally, in the last decade of his life, revealing through his own person the tragic destiny of all mankind, emerging from darkness into the light of life before receding into the final darkness. No one has rivalled Rembrandt in his ability to kindle the flame of the spirit on gross flesh.

Other formidable autobiographies include that of Courbet, boisterously extravagant compared with Rembrandt but aggressively asserting his artistic genius. Hokusai asserted himself unquenched at the age of 82: "At a hundred I shall have become truly marvellous". Van Gogh, in a whole series of concentrated head-and-shoulders studies, seems to attempt to establish his own identity, his precarious sanity; often they look like police photographs of suspects, if not of convicted criminals. Cézanne, too, scrutinized his features, not in search of spiritual essence but rather to crystallize a solid structure out of his own stubborn skull, foreshadowing the Cubists' concern with establishing a formal order. In contrast, the Expressionist Kokoschka's violent brushwork, proportional exaggerations and jarring colours display an almost accusing self-appraisal.

While photography has taken over much of the recording function of art, its own peculiarities have themselves become subjects for art. Chuck Close's gigantic self-portrait, nearly three metres (more than 9ft) high, embellishing in meticulously applied acrylics the camera's eye for detail, retains the impersonal neutrality of his source photograph and, in so doing, reveals its limitations – the extent to which it fails to represent form naturalistically and to capture the sitter's true character.

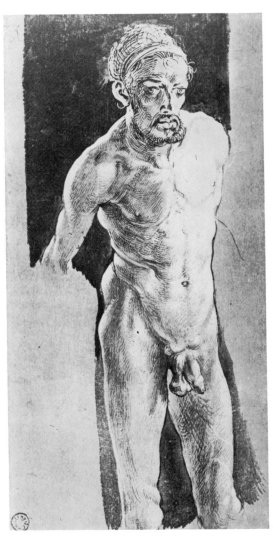

REMBRANDT: *Self-portrait*, 1669

HOKUSAI: *Self-portrait, c.* 1843

DURER: *Self-portrait, naked, c.* 1510

COURBET (below): *The meeting*, 1854

VAN GOGH: *Self-portrait*, 1890

CLOSE: *Self-portrait*, 1968

CEZANNE: *Self-portrait*, 1880

KOKOSCHKA: *Self-portrait*, 1913

Couples

Individual portraits establish a direct, one-to-one confrontation between viewer and image. The situation becomes much more complex when the artist has to present not an isolated image but figures involved in a subtle relationship within the space of the painting or sculpture. The difficulties – and the risks – of attempting to convey human emotions at their most intense and fleeting are exemplified in a work almost as famous as the *Mona Lisa* itself – Rodin's *The kiss*.

Like many of Rodin's most famous images, this statue developed from an element sketched out for incorporation into his monumental and never-completed masterpiece, the Gates of Hell. The two figures – very differently posed – were originally perhaps of Dante's doomed lovers, Paolo and Francesca, from *The Inferno*, though the theme of two lovers intertwined was one on which Rodin played many variations. The earliest version, in 1886, was half-life-scale; the first rather larger-than-life marble, commissioned by the French state, was shown early in 1898, alongside Rodin's *Balzac*, and it was the latter – interpreted as an insult to one of France's great writers – rather than *The kiss* which then drew the virulent attacks provoked by nearly all of Rodin's greatest works.

The version which Rodin himself thought the best (now in the Tate Gallery, London) was finished in July 1904 for a commission from the Anglo-American antiquarian Edward Perry Warren. It was originally lent to the Town Hall of Lewes, a small English country town; there it had to be railed off and draped with a sheet, and after two years it returned to its owner. Though prudery is no longer a reason for hostility, it does not now attract the learned attention given to those other visions with which Rodin startled the late nineteenth century – the *Balzac* statue, *The burghers of Calais*, or even *The thinker*. Those for whom the artist's direct involvement with his medium is an article of faith question the validity of a work carved – as were all the marble versions of *The kiss* – by an assistant, a practice common to most sculptors in stone in the nineteenth century. Yet Rodin was profoundly aware of the material qualities of marble, closely supervised the whole operation, and was actively involved in bringing the final surfaces to that translucent quality of which he was the master. The contrast between the surfaces left rough-hewn and those finished was fascinating to Rodin; he exploited them deliberately to produce a romantic impression of unformulated chaos yielding up finished and finite but elemental images, an echo of the Creation.

The central problem of *The kiss* may simply be that its theme is so basic, so archetypal, that, to some, Rodin's treatment of it seems blatant, sentimental, even vulgar. As an ideal expression of romantic love it nevertheless captures as nobody quite had before both its sensual and its spiritual essence. From whatever angle it is viewed, the two figures seem indissoluble and oblivious, linked in a movement of such sudden intensity that nobody can intrude upon it. Perhaps only Rodin could have lifted an image of such private tenderness into the realm of heroic public statuary.

RODIN: *The kiss*, 1901–04

Couples

EGYPT: *Rahotep and Nofret*, c.2550 BC; panel of Tutankhamun's throne, before 1361 BC

DURER: *Adam and Eve*, 1507

VAN EYCK: *"The Arnolfini Marriage"*, 1434

IRAN: *Salaman and Absal reach the shore of the sea*, 1556-65

REMBRANDT: *"The Jewish Bride"*, detail, c. 1665

DOGON: *Male and female principles*, undated

MOORE: *King and Queen*, 1952-53

GROSZ: *A married couple*, 1930

WOOD (right):
American Gothic, 1930

Doubtless from the very beginnings of human society, ritual and ceremony have attended the mystic union of male and female, whence all life continues, for even most animals and birds have established procedures at least in courting. So the story, in Christian art, of Adam and Eve tends towards the ceremonial; one of the most beautiful versions is Dürer's, classically perfect in body, serene in spite of the attending snake. Adam and Eve as a model of the union of any couple are translated into bourgeois terms in van Eyck's celebrated *"Arnolfini Marriage"*; though decorously clothed the couple are surrounded with the trappings of an earthly Paradise, inventoried in the lovingly detailed domestic setting, lucidly defined by the fall of light and by the exquisite symmetries of the picture's structure.

In a very different context, the twin Egyptian statues of Rahotep and Nofret confront eternity in their motionless four-square immobility, conveying to modern sensibilities perhaps a poignant impression of loneliness in togetherness. Yet Egyptian art could also capture tenderness, as witnessed in the delicate scene on the back of Tutankhamun's throne showing teenage royalty in playful intimacy. The dream of young love is apparently irrepressible, and not only in the culture of the West, influenced by the troubadour conventions of courtly love – the woman on a pedestal adored from afar. Persian and Mughal courtesies of wooing are amongst the most enchantingly poetic ever recorded, often enacted in gardens of exquisite artifice, where the lovers, dallying among flowers and shade coaxed from arid desert, seem woven into a decorative pattern of mystical beauty. The jewelled perfection of the example shown here reflects a cultivated society with sophisticated courtship rituals, but the innocent animation of the couple is entirely human.

Rembrandt's portrayal of love perhaps captures its sacramental essence more movingly than any other, in the tenderness of a simple yet profound gesture; the touch of hands and the downcast eyes of husband and wife in *"The Jewish Bride"* speak overwhelmingly yet with exquisite restraint. A similar universally understood gesture of affinity – a slight inward inclination of head or body – can be found in works of art utterly removed from European tradition, as in the culture of the Sudan, where male and female principles are figured with hieratic dignity, befitting a seminal mystery. The same movement may be discerned again in Moore's not so different *King and Queen*, whose regal status, conveyed in the upright, almost comic dignity of their figures, is underpinned by a private bond, hinted at in the closeness of arms, the merest tilt of heads.

Romantic or passionate love is not the only kind portrayed in art; Grosz views his squat, amiable couple with satirical good humour while not denying the strength of their relationship, and a subtle irony seems to pervade the title and whole composition of *American Gothic*, in which the prosaic pair yet emerge immortalized, as if hewn out of living timber, the very essence of frontier tenacity and rectitude.

Couples

If the ceremonies of love offer a subject on which art can most elegantly devise endless formal solutions, unbridled passion presents more thorny problems – at least, in the general tenor of Western conventions, even in the permissive society of the late twentieth century. The conventions of other cultures can be less inhibited, most remarkably in Hindu sculpture, in which the sexual appetite finds frank expression. In contrast, the sensuality of some of even the greatest Western artists may seem a little prurient – literally so for example in Titian's *Venus and the organ player*. Even though it is a superb celebration of the pleasure of the senses – rich in the sensation not only of colour and mass, but of almost audible music – the conventions of depicting love in terms of a ceremony are here gravely at risk; why is the decorously clothed gentleman playing thus to the naked lady? To render the actuality of physical love is even trickier for Western artists, tending to verge on the obscene or the merely ridiculous. The genius of Titian could, however, encompass passion itself in action, as in his formidably tumultuous drawing of Jupiter's assault on Io. Many other major artists have also executed erotic drawings but concealed them from public view. Few are so explicit as the art of the Japanese "pillow books", manuals of sexual instruction in which the act of love is depicted in graphic and elegant detail as a leisurely, sophisticated pleasure. Shame or melancholy as the consequences of the sexual act seem to be themes exclusive to Western art; the satirical eye of Hogarth caught the ludicrous and pathetic aspects of passion, the exhausting discrepancy between desire and satiation, in his *Before* and *After* – the seducer's eagerness turned to indifference, his coy victim now beseeching.

Courbet, however, with characteristic defiance, in *The sleepers* painted satisfaction without inhibition; his female lovers lie in a slumber as deep and abandoned as the passion (we can only assume) that went before. Taste has indeed changed since he painted this as a private commission – it has since become one of the most celebrated and exhibited of all his works. Less explicit and literal styles than Courbet's have been used by Romantic and Expressionist artists who wished to convey the turmoil of physical love. The erotic work of earlier artists may have been confined to sketches partly because oil-painting required a deliberation and finish inappropriate to the subject. The release of style from finish in the dynamic brushwork of Delacroix opened the way for the still more energetic methods of Munch and the Expressionists, who embodied in rich, jarring colours and savage brush-strokes desolate visions of the psychological relationship of man and woman. Munch's lover in *Vampire* appears the helpless victim of his mistress, merged with her predatory form as if the surrender of love meant the surrender of himself to an enemy. Indeed, remarkably few twentieth-century artists have portrayed the act of love without some undertone of violence or fear. In Schiele's painting, the naked couple huddling together in a storm of agitated lines seem, even in passion, desperately alone.

KHAJURAHO: *The Kandarya Mahadeva Temple*, detail, *c.* 1000

TITIAN: *Venus and the organ player, c.* 1550

TITIAN: *Jupiter and Io, c.* 1560

KORYUSAI: *Shunga*, detail, second half of 18th century

COURBET: *The sleepers*, 1862

MUNCH: *Vampire*, 1895-1902

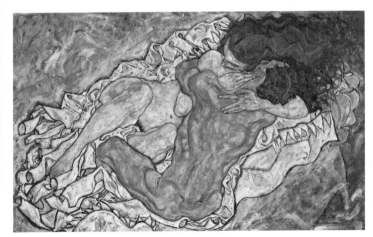

HOGARTH: *Before the seduction* and *After*, 1731

SCHIELE: *The embrace*, 1917

Life and Work

According to the legends that recur in many cultures there was a Golden Age, the lost Garden of Eden, in which the only work needed to produce a continual harvest of life-giving food (vegetarian) seems to have been a little genteel gardening. The reality of taming and working the soil – laborious, dirty, unglamorous – has, however, always been the privilege of the poor, of the peasantry. Scenes of such humdrum agriculture are found in ancient art, and the theme received increasing attention from the fourteenth century on, in the medieval Books of Hours. These prayerbooks, codifying a practice of devotion within a framework of ordered time, began with a Calendar tabulating saints' days and church festivals, and illustrating, month by month, the cycle of community life and work in a standard sequence of twelve themes.

In the great masterpiece of the genre, the *Très Riches Heures* of the Duc de Berri, begun by the Limbourg brothers in Burgundy in the early fifteenth century, a medieval innocence of conception, but also certain medieval formal conventions, fuse with that intense interest in the depiction of the natural world typical of Renaissance art to produce crystalline visions of a world strange as a dream yet sharply real as the waking from a dream. These twelve miniatures are, amongst other things, a major step in the evolution of landscape painting – they show an empirical understanding of perspective if not of the mathematical perspective of the Florentines, and, in some, sophistications adopted by later artists appear for the first time – the observation of the cast shadow, for instance. They illustrate two main facets of life, the courtly pleasures of the aristocracy, and then, as counter-theme, the peasants at their labours – both themes marking the changing rhythms of the seasons. In the semi-circles above each one, the relevant phases of the Zodiac are calibrated and imaged.

In February – incidentally one of the first, if not the first, snow-clad landscapes in art – peasants sit about the fire, holding up their tunics to the grateful warmth (in a gesture that had sometimes to be modified for nicer tastes when reproduced later), while men are at work, cutting wood or slogging through the bitter cold outside. Some summer months show the elegant aristocracy at their pleasures, but March, June, October notably have accurately detailed accounts of labourers in the fields, ploughing and pruning the vines, then haymaking, then, in the autumn, harrowing and sowing as the cycle proceeds. These mundane activities are shown without overt comment, observed simply for what they are; yet the modern observer may diagnose an intrinsic irony. The foreground fields in which the peasants toil are set against a backcloth of turrets, pinnacles, castellations fretting the clear sky like story-book fairy castles. But they were real, the fantastic palace-castles of the fifteenth-century Burgundian aristocracy, and the foundations on which they rested were the labours of the peasants of the fields, here shown for the first time in such accuracy, establishing a theme of humble toil to be elaborated by many later artists.

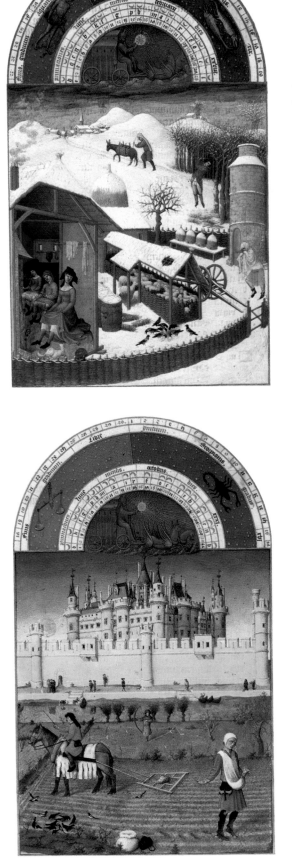

THE LIMBOURG BROTHERS:
February

THE LIMBOURG BROTHERS:
October

THE LIMBOURG BROTHERS: *June*, page from *Les Très Riches Heures du Duc de Berri*, 1413–16

Life and Work

DELLA QUERCIA: *Labours of Adam and Eve*, c. 1428

ANTELAMI: *June* and *September*, c. 1200

THEBES (left):
The tomb of Menna:
Harvesting, c. 1450 BC

CRETE (right):
The Harvesters' Vase,
c. 1550 BC

BRUEGEL (below): *August* (The corn harvest), detail, 1565

STUBBS (below): *The reapers*, 1795

MILLET: *The reaper, c.* 1866-68

VAN GOGH (below): *The reaper,* 1889

The biblical concept of labour as punishment for disobedience has profoundly affected its representation in Christian art, which frequently portrays it as painful thraldom. Jacopo della Quercia's powerful relief sculpture shows Adam and Eve reaping the fruits of their sin, Eve clutching her distaff and shackled by two squalling children – the infant Cain and Abel – while a grim-faced Adam, every muscle straining, tries to break the unyielding ground. A similar melancholy clouds the faces of labourers in the Baptistery in Parma; the garnering of bread and wine, staples of both physical and sacramental life, brings no flicker of joy to these earnest, stumpy figures, although their labour has a naive and touching dignity.

Other cultures were less inhibited and agricultural work is treated more lightly, even with humour, in Egyptian and Minoan art. A frieze from a tomb at Thebes depicts harvesting with vivacity and grace, while as early as around 1550 BC the famous late Minoan Harvesters' Vase from the Palace of Hagia Triada in Crete records an exultant harvest-home.

In Western art, agriculture was to remain a continuing theme especially, as we have seen on the previous page, in medieval Books of Hours. The calendar convention was to find its finest expression in Bruegel's series, *The Seasons of the Year* (see vol. 2 pp. 162–163). *August* is a wonderful evocation of sweltering summer heat, corn bleached by the sun, the spread-eagled figure of the worker expressing utter physical exhaustion. In marked contrast with this realistic portrayal of toiling peasantry is Georges Stubbs' view of eighteenth-century rural England, in which the workers are disposed across the foreground like figures in an antique frieze. Though the overseer on his horse reflects the notion of manual labour as being beneath a gentleman, his workers have a dignity of their own. Their clothes, seemingly quite unsuited to the dust and sweat of harvest, are hardly plainer than their master's and they stand or bend with a grace that derives partly, perhaps, from Neoclassical principles of composition – but only partly, for the landscape, though idyllic, is unmistakably English, and the unselfconscious harmony of the pictures seems rooted in acceptance of the natural and social order.

In the nineteenth century, with the awakening of a more sensitive social consciousness, labour began to be celebrated with a reverence once reserved for religious subjects. The noblest and most consistent painter of this theme was Millet, some of whose most famous images – *The Angelus* for example – reflect the romantic, pantheistic idea of a deep spiritual communion between man and nature. Others are of labour very much in action, like his *Sower* or *The reaper*; the latter captures back-breaking effort expressively but without comment. But the images of van Gogh, who copied several Millets and felt deeply for the sufferings of both industrial and peasant workers, are more overt in their fierce, heavy contours and distortions of feature into brutish near-deformity; his *Reaper* speaks without restraint of lives relentlessly exhausted in the battle for survival.

Life and Work

Memorable pictures of those kinds of work that do not involve muscular labour so much as skills of hand or mind are relatively rare. Apart from lacking the elemental drama of working the soil, such subjects present a difficult challenge simply because they often involve internal mental rather than external physical action.

In the materialist society of seventeenth-century Holland, business of all kinds provided subject matter for occasional anecdotal pictures, often of a fairly trivial kind. But there were also startling visions of intellectual discovery, among them *The anatomy lesson of Dr Tulp*, in which Rembrandt orchestrates the drama in strong contrasts of light and shade, the intent faces expressing the excitement of scientific investigation. The American Thomas Eakins later used chiaroscuro for similar ends in his *Gross Clinic*. The gruesome element was thought shocking at the time, yet it is the high tension of the operation that now compels our attention – the face of the surgeon rather than his bloodied hands.

In settled societies the traditionally feminine skills have been shown not as arduous labour (though arduous they often were) but as images of serene contentment. Vermeer, quietest of painters, was the master of such patient domesticities. In his hands a maid pouring milk becomes a profound, inexhaustible meditation on life itself, an everyday gesture taking on an almost sacramental quality, the mood evoked through a matchless handling of light, glowing like a pearl.

Except in the work of Chardin it was not until the nineteenth century that such subjects were again treated seriously, in Degas's scenes of women ironing. With an eye quick as a camera shutter in catching a momentary pattern in everyday life, Degas also succeeded in animating the traditional group portrait; his remarkable *Cotton Exchange at New Orleans* is the first to catch the flavour of a modern office at work. Its activity is suggested not by atmospheric lighting but by the seemingly random disposition of figures in a tightly organized design; within an asymmetrical perspective of steeply converging lines, workers are caught in mid-gesture, as in a photograph.

Reynolds, too, used an unconventional composition to revitalize the way in which intellectuals had traditionally been portrayed, eyes cast heavenwards, pen poised to write. He posed Dr Johnson with deliberate awkwardness, not simply for a true likeness of an ungainly man, but to convey the fact that great mental achievements come from human effort, not divine inspiration.

More recently, the idea of physical labour as heroic activity has been celebrated by Mexican painters such as Rivera and Orozco, and by the socialist-realist artists of the communist states. In the West, Expressionist artists have produced perhaps the most potent images of work, as in Ferdinand Hodler's stupendously emphatic *Woodcutter*. The artist, however, who has found the most satisfactory solution for a social and political philosophy is Léger – his workmen, integrated into a design of scaffolding and ladders, give a hieratic dignity to machine-age labour.

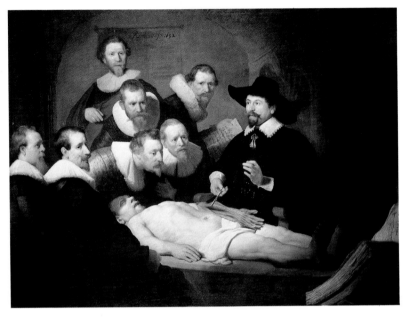

REMBRANDT: *The anatomy lesson of Dr Tulp*, detail, 1632

EAKINS: *The Gross Clinic*, 1875

VERMEER: *Servant girl pouring milk*, detail, *c.* 1663

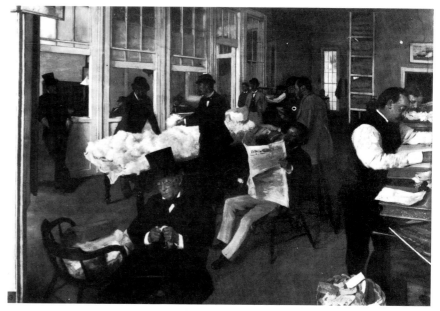

DEGAS: *The Cotton Exchange at New Orleans*, 1873

REYNOLDS (left): *Dr Johnson*, 1756

LEGER (right): *The builders*, 1950

HODLER (below): *The woodcutter*, 1910

Life and Leisure

The summer afternoon is perfect. The Sunday lunch party is just beginning to break up; dessert and wine are still on the table. Utterly relaxed, well-dined, friends linger together; a desultory sparkle of gossip, of badinage, of flirtation, is almost audible. Soon, some decisions about what to do next through the long afternoon will have to be arrived at – but not just yet.

Renoir captured this moment, this eternity, of pure *joie-de-vivre* at the Restaurant Fournaise on the isle of Chatou on the Seine near Paris in 1881. This was one of the favourite weekend resorts for Parisians in the summer months – poets, artists, patrons; they came from the bourgeoisie and the fashionable world to enjoy themselves. Boating was in high fashion (hence the men in their singlets, though one landsman, Baron Barbier, retains the full formality of the top hat). Pretty women, as always, were also in fashion. That ripe pouting profile on the left under the hat is the first sight in Renoir's work of Aline Charigot; their love-affair was to consolidate into marriage. The girl raising a glass is "La belle Angèle", a witty and provocative professional model, and the enchanting figure leaning on the balcony rail Alphonsine Fournaise, daughter of the proprietor (Renoir painted her three times). The men, too, are mostly identifiable – Gustave Caillebotte, friend of Monet and Renoir, artist himself, and collector of their works, is the young man so casually, hat tip-tilted, astride his chair; seated next to him is an actress, Ellen Andrée, and the other young man, leaning over him but focused obviously on Ellen, is a journalist friend, M. Maggiolo.

The setting is a wooden dining-terrace built out from the restaurant, overlooking the river. It is high summer, not too hot, just right, the fringe of the terrace awning moving gently in the air. When he painted this idyll Renoir was 40, not in first youth but in the early maturity of his prime, beginning to enjoy the confidence of hard-won professional success. The picture is pervaded by his relaxed assurance; we sense that the artist is as much at ease as are his subjects.

Renoir had been foremost among Impressionists in experimentation with divisionist technique, juxtaposing strokes of pure, intense colour, eliminating black from his palette and contouring outline from his design. Yet he had already shown himself interested less in optical effects than in achieving the sensuous feeling of light and of fresh, moving air. In this painting, his later development is foreshadowed: theoretical considerations yield to his pleasure in his subject matter, in the pleasure of life itself. Foliage and background are handled in Impressionist technique but the foreground figures are fully solid in the flower of their flesh and the rich texture of his paint; his work would soon become ever more strongly a celebration of human happiness in the human form. As here, he could indeed paint idylls, but unlike the dreams of Watteau (whom he adored) it is the now – present laughter – that he recorded, not as a detached observer but as one sharing the tastes and sounds of that summer afternoon, its immediacy sharpened by the individual portraits of his friends.

Raoul Barbier

Alphonsine Fournaise

Ellen Andrée

Aline Charigot

Gustave Caillebotte

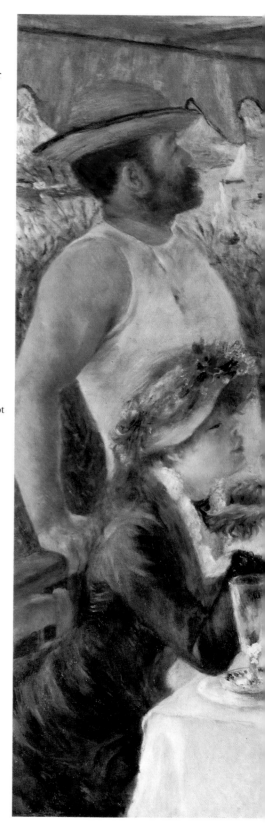

RENOIR: *The luncheon of the boating party*, 1881

Life and Leisure

EXEKIAS:
Dionysos sailing, c.550 BC

BELLINI: *The feast of the gods*, 1514

HARUNOBU: *Girl viewing plum-blossoms at night*, c.1768

BRUEGEL: *The peasant wedding*, c.1567

WATTEAU (right): *Les Champs-Elysées*, detail, 1717

FRITH: *Derby day*, detail, 1856–58

KIENHOLZ: *Barney's beanery*, detail, 1965

MATISSE: "*La Joie de Vivre*", 1905-06

One of the most complete, or replete, solo counterparts in all art to Renoir's orchestration of relaxed pleasure in *The luncheon of the boating party* is provided by the Greek potter Exekias in about the mid-sixth century BC. The wine-god, Dionysos, reclines on his barque; sea and sky have merged indissolubly into an infinite heaven in which dolphins sport. The ship's mast is also the support for a luxuriant grapevine. Form and decoration answer function perfectly (even the flaking of the white from the sail cannot spoil the harmony), for the composition is contained within the rim of a shallow drinking-bowl.

Pleasure is celebrated no less consummately, and with almost equal control of line and design, more than 2,000 years later and on the other side of the globe in Harunobu's exquisite print of a *Girl viewing plum-blossoms at night*. From classical Greece to eighteenth-century Japan – and since – the depiction of pleasure has been a constant theme, as if the ephemeral intoxication of the senses could be answered, renewed and even to some degree endowed with immortality by the rhythm of line and gloss of colour. Conviviality heightens pleasure, and feasts, parties, processions have all proved irresistible subjects for art. In one of the supreme masterpieces of the genre, *The feast of the gods*, painted by the aged Bellini and finished by the young Titian, gods and men, satyrs and beautiful girls consort in a picnic that seems both supernatural and real, set in one of the most idyllic landscapes ever painted. A little later, Bruegel recorded carousel of a more earthly kind; the stamp and huff of the dancers is all but audible, the movement of line and swirl of dress as vivid as if one were there. How different from the gusto of his cut-out shapes and emphatic colour contrasts is the approach and style of Watteau, who was painting with a different intention for a different social order. The airy, melting harmonies of his Rococo idyll capture the indolent sophistication of aristocratic eighteenth-century France – an eternal summer time of wine, lovely women and music in which leisure seems not something seized from life but its perpetual condition.

Beside the dreams of Watteau, Frith's view of a Victorian day out seems as matter-of-fact as a photograph, mere industrious craftsmanship. Yet documentary record has always been an important strand of art, and the pleasure Frith's panorama offers is close to that of sightseeing. We are sightseeing indeed in Edward Kienholz's surreal *Barney's Beanery*, a walk-in environment re-creating, in a mixture of ghostly plaster casts and real, assembled trappings of bottles and glasses, the artist's own rueful nostalgia for a particular bar. The tyres and clocks and dingy clothes offer at the same time a commentary on the reality of plebeian urban leisure in the pressured twentieth century. It may be Matisse who, in an idiom of art far from this, abstracted not the reality but the spirit of leisure – Matisse who, after all, wished art to be, amongst other things, the mental equivalent of a comfortable armchair. In the suppleness of his linear rhythms he evokes an ideal leisure – one that is entirely relaxed and yet refreshingly vital.

Life and Leisure

Leisure, no less than work, becomes tedious if unorganized and without apparent aim. Sport is the work-out of leisure, first emerging clearly and becoming ritualized as one would expect in the context of the Greek culture of physical perfection and beauty. For sculptors, the body of the naked male athlete in action has been a supreme challenge – answered most famously by *The discus thrower*, modelled originally for bronze by Myron about 450 BC, though now known only in marble.

The controlling of the competitive aspects of sport, the imposition of order codified by often mysterious laws, proceeded in more settled and sophisticated cultures until, in Pieter de Hoogh's *Skittle-players in a garden* of the 1660s, it slows down into a social ritual as stately and ceremonious as a quadrille. The pattern of the play is answered by de Hoogh's assured grasp of the interrelationships of the standing figures (as if a free variation on the regimentation of the skittles) and of the tall verticals of house and trees.

It is more difficult for art to find a formal equivalent for the swifter, more violent outdoor sports: the attempts of the Italian Futurists, who made a fetish of movement, are not very convincing. Surely the most entrancingly absurd attempt at catching the spirit – or anyway, a spirit – of modern sport in motion is the Douanier Rousseau's vision, *The ball-players* of 1908, admirably self-satisfied, striped like technicolor, mustachioed tigers, gallivanting with a rather round rugby ball apparently in the depths of a thicket. One of the delightful attributes of so-called Naive art is its freedom from the constricting need to represent life with any kind of objective accuracy. The more successful literal attempts to show people at play tend to emphasize the ritual elements. A haunting example, *Memories* by the Belgian Symbolist Khnopff, 1889, is a very early salute to lawn-tennis, but the figures of these seven women, waiting perhaps for the nets to be raised before a game, evoke in their hieratic stillness something mysterious, as though each one, solitary, were in communion with some unseen elemental force. A more hostile presence seems to bear down on the awkward boys in Ben Shahn's *Handball*, accurately frozen by an artist whose eye is that of a social realist.

Indoor pastimes and games naturally captured the attention of many Dutch painters in the seventeenth century, and the best of them – Vermeer or Terborch, say – were able to catch in this stillness an echo of music: the music lesson, with its often slightly erotic overtones, was a favourite theme. Card-playing is another favourite, treated in almost as many ways as there are styles. In the anticipation of boys playing cards, a French follower of Caravaggio sensed explosive movement, and expressed it in the characteristic Baroque drama of contrasted light and shade. Cézanne, obsessed by the theme over some years, conversely painted two rather dour peasants into an elemental immobility; their individual feelings about the game are much less important than the part they play in building up a purely pictorial, almost monumental, structure.

AFTER MYRON: *The discus thrower*, original *c*.450 BC

DE HOOGH (below): *Skittle-players*, *c*.1663-66

ROUSSEAU: *The ball-players*, 1908

KHNOPFF: *Memories*, 1889

TERBORCH (left):
The concert, after 1675

SHAHN: *Handball*, 1939

AFTER CARAVAGGIO: *The card-players*, detail, 17th century

CEZANNE (above): *The card-players*, 1890–92

Narration

In 1528 Duke William IV of Bavaria commissioned eight large paintings of great battles of classical antiquity. The commission was entirely in key with the Renaissance discovery of antiquity; in Italy comparable projects were the series of *uomini famosi* (famous men) painted for state apartments. Just as these served as examples and inspiration to fame, so too legendary conflicts could serve as spurs to heroism and conquest. They had a narrative purpose, as much religious art had done, but the story was of human affairs and ambitions; the theme of each painting was probably laid down by the Duke's learned court historian, Aventinus. One of the painters employed was Albrecht Altdorfer, the most remarkable and genial of German painters after Dürer and Grünewald, and the most original landscape artist of his time.

Altdorfer's contribution was not just outstanding, it proved to be one of the most spectacular battle-pieces ever painted, with hundreds, or perhaps thousands, of warriors clashing in furious action within a frame only a little more than 1.5 metres (5ft) high. Its grandeur, however, does not rest on considerations of scale and detail but on an intensity of vision unique in his work. The battle portrayed is Alexander the Great's crucial defeat of the Persians under Darius III in 333 BC, but presented in terms of the massed clash of armies in Altdorfer's own time. Though Darius appears in an antique chariot, the armour and weapons, the splendid banners and pennanted lances, are those of sixteenth-century Europe, and there may be echoes here of the great battle of Pavia of 1525, only a few years before the artist was painting.

In the foreground the swaying tides of conflict are marshalled with extraordinary coherence, the lances like corn in the wind, the helmet plumes like foam on the sea. A surging rhythm pervades the entire composition, thrust and counter-thrust of armoured phalanxes subsiding in winding curves to the encamped tents, the turreted town at peace at the water's edge, only to pick up again, at first frozen in the alpine ranges and then galvanized into cosmic action in the vast turbulence of the heavens. Here, the symbolism becomes overt: the sun, signifying Alexander and Greece, rises through a vortex of cloud while the crescent moon, signifying Darius, Persia and perhaps, anachronistically, Islam fades. The lapidary inscription, miraculously but credibly afloat in the sky, suspends its tasselled cord over the press and shock of troops at the centre of action – Alexander on horseback, lance outthrust, tramples through a cleared ring of fallen bodies in hot pursuit of Darius, whose chariot is turned for flight. It is the turning point of the battle itself.

Human conflict here becomes as much a manifestation of the elemental force of Nature as the geological tumult that heaved up the mountains or the storm-tossed sky. As exultation of battle it has not been surpassed, and its quality was clearly grasped by Napoleon, who abducted it to hang in his bathroom at St Cloud, where he could contemplate over and over again its splendour, and no doubt identify satisfactorily with Alexander.

ALTDORFER: *The battle of Alexander and Darius on the Issus*, 1529

Narration

CANTERBURY: The Bayeux Tapestry, *c.* 1080

LICHTENSTEIN: *Whaam!*, 1963

GIOVANNI DI PAOLO:
*St John entering the
wilderness, c.* 1450

HOGARTH: *The arrest* and *The prison*, from *The Rake's Progress, c.* 1733

RUBENS: *The marriage,*
from the Médicis cycle, 1622-25

RIVERA (right): Detail from
a mural at the National School of
Agriculture, Chapingo, 1924-27

GREECE: Stela, 5th century BC

HUGHES: *Home from the sea*, 1862

Narration, story-telling, implies a series of events and hence a dimension of real time with a beginning, middle and end, a dimension that paintings or sculptures may seem to lack by comparison with moving pictures. Yet artists who wish to tell a story may, as we have seen in Altdorfer's painting, choose an historical moment so crucial that its implications extend both before and after the event depicted, and concentrate the action so fiercely that the whole scene becomes impossible to take in at once, involving the viewer in minute exploration of the unfolding battle. Chinese scrolls provided a more ingenious method of presenting a pictorial sequence, so that even an unrolling landscape could become the story of a voyage down the length of a winding river to the sea. An early episodic example in Western art is the story of the Norman conquest of England told in the Bayeux Tapestry, ancestor of the comic strip and, in turn, of Roy Lichtenstein's *Whaam!* Here the brazen graphic energy of a mass medium is treated as art in two huge canvases placed side by side, so that we identify first with the pilot taking aim, then with his exultation.

Sequential narrative was common in medieval art – in manuscript illuminations, in the little predella panels showing the lives of saints at the bottom of altarpieces and, on a larger scale, in the fresco cycles and radiant stained glass of churches, the "Bibles of the poor", illustrating the Christian story in terms of a sequence of key events. Frequently, however, painters and stained glass illuminators felt under no constraint to observe the unities of time, place and action, and instead showed two or more stages of the narrative within a single frame. An enchanting example of such "continuous representation" is *St John entering the wilderness*, where the saint is seen emerging from the gate of a town and again halfway up the hill beyond it. By the sixteenth century this convention had given way to great, ambitious cycles of paintings by Baroque masters such as Rubens, whose allegorical evocation shown here of the marriage of Marie de Médicis is one of a sequence of 21 paintings depicting incidents from the life of the widow of Henry IV commissioned for her new Luxembourg Palace. Hogarth turned the method to satirical account in a number of narrative cycles including *The Rake's Progress*.

Equally with historical events, basic human emotions can have implications beyond the expression of a single moment; thus an austere relief of two figures in a Greek grave-marker can convey the echo of lost joys as well as a desolation shadowing the future. The popularity of Victorian narrative painting depended on a more explicit rendering of context and on titles which themselves told the story, as in Arthur Hughes' vision of a sailor boy prostrate on his mother's grave in a sunlit churchyard. In the twentieth century, narrative painting, where it survives at all, has been used mainly as an instrument of political persuasion or exhortation: Diego Rivera's vivid accounts of the history of the Mexican Revolution provide rare modern examples of the older tradition of fresco cycles.

Narration

Of all narrative topics, few have gripped the imagination of the artist so consistently and ubiquitously as battle, the struggle for survival. Men have always found in war a mixture of glory and horror, terror and exultant exhilaration. The visual dynamics of the subject – the hard, diagonal lines of flags, lances, brandished swords – can give even pictures of hand-to-hand combat a powerful urgency and realism, as in the detail from the Graeco-Roman mosaic of Alexander the Great; or again, the medieval manuscript illumination of the same hero, as if in ballet, unrelated to ground or sky but ferociously potent, painted with an astonishing energy and directness.

Some artists seem to have been born to paint the turbulence of full-scale battle; Rubens, for all his diplomatic efforts in the cause of peace, appears to have found in scenes of rape and pillage huge satisfaction for his copious vigour. Artists have been noble and persuasive propagandists, too, in the cause of freedom, of rebellion against tyranny – so the sculptor Rude, whose "*La Marseillaise*" is a call to arms as stirring as the anthem it interprets in stone on the Arc de Triomphe. The momentum of the winged figure is carried forward irresistibly by the wheel of figures turning below it.

From time to time, compassionate awareness of the pity and tragedy of war appears – in the etchings of Callot early in the seventeenth century, for instance – yet it is an awareness of a suffering implied to be inevitable. Stronger protest is first registered in great art in the paintings and etchings of Goya, whose horrific visions of the Napoleonic Wars are diametrically opposed to those of Rude or of Napoleon's own favourite painter, David. Goya spells out the full physical brutality of war, piling huddled figures together to suggest the helplessness of ordinary men, women and children against it. Nineteenth-century artists more often romanticized the subject, as in Leutze's vast canvas *Washington crossing the Delaware*, in which the privations of the American Army are subsumed in a dramatic image of Washington, posed in precarious, fully-accoutred glory on the gunwale of a pitching longboat.

It took the massacres of World War I for a more general admission of the unacceptable cruelty of war to materialize. Picasso's famous *Guernica*, painted in outrage at the bombing of a civilian town in the Spanish Civil War, shows the expressive power of his formal inventiveness, his capacity to take reality to pieces and construct an alternative reality from the splinters. In the great *Surrender of Breda* Velazquez had painted the magnanimity, the ceremonious stateliness of the humane victor, the battle over, all passion spent; the inclination of victor and vanquished towards each other is one of the most beautifully observed and rendered moments in art. In scathing contrast is the vision of Georg Grosz, satirizing the survival of militarist sentiment in the Germany of the 1920s. His mutilated manikins *Republican automatons*, faceless veterans in a sterile urban landscape but still wearing medals, waving the flag, offer eloquently dumb contradiction to Velazquez's view of the aftermath of battle.

POMPEII: The Alexander mosaic, detail, original *c*. 300 BC

GERMAN MANUSCRIPT: *Alexander the Great in single combat*, 13th century

RUBENS: *The battle of the Amazons*, c. 1618

RUDE: "*La Marseillaise*", 1833-36

LEUTZE: *Washington crossing the Delaware*, 1850

PICASSO: *Guernica*, detail, 1937

GOYA: *The same*, from *The Disasters of War*, 1810-15

VELAZQUEZ: *The surrender of Breda*, detail, 1634-35

GROSZ: *Republican automatons*, 1920

Landscape

The curve of Mount Fujiyama starts long and slow from the left, almost accelerating to the climax of the peak on the right. The orangeish cone of the volcano, lifted clear of the stubble of the tree-line, is only just veined with snow at its peak. A flock, a shoal, of fleecy clouds moves horizontally from left to right across the deepening blue of the sky. Suspended in the sky on the left, the title – *Southerly wind and fine weather (Gaifū Kaisei)* – also suggests springtime or early summer, perhaps at dawn when the upper slopes, catching the rising sun, can glow red, suggesting the fierce inner life that once carried the volcano upwards in that matchless sweep.

No human being intrudes. The vision seems pure landscape, distilled to its essence. Yet it is preserved in one of the most fragile of mediums: coloured inks on a sheet, a mere 35 centimetres (14in) or so across, of that famous soft, almost transparent Japanese paper made from the fibre of mulberry tree bark – a woodblock print, in the "brocade" tradition, which reproduced, for the popular middle-class market of Edo (Tokyo) ephemeral images of *ukiyo*, the "floating world" of leisure. It dates from the late 1820s, and one of the inscriptions hung in the sky is its designer's signature: *Hokusai Aratame Iitsu Hitne.*

Hokusai (1760-1849) was then working at about the same time as his rather younger contemporaries, Constable and Turner, were revolutionizing the concept of landscape in the West. His own treatment was no less revolutionary, but very different, in terms of an abstraction from natural forms into a clarity that would have astonished and perhaps baffled them. It is only twentieth-century painting and printmaking that have accustomed Westerners to such grand simplicities of colour and design. This print is at one level a brilliant exercise in formal values. The symmetry of Fuji, set asymmetrically within the rectangle of the block, is balanced with the most delicate precision against the echoing shape, inverted, of the sky, and tuned to vibrant life by the subtlety of the contours, by the rhythmic shoaling of the cloud, and the modulation of the extraordinarily restrained range of colour. It is one of the most famous of Hokusai's most famous sequences, the *Thirty-six views of Mt Fuji.* They occur late in the development of a highly sophisticated tradition, though they are also a radical innovation.

Japan was at this time still a country forbidden to Europeans, but Hokusai was aware, through engravings, of Western traditions in art, and took something from them (shocking his compatriots) – thus the single, low viewpoint here is a departure from Japanese tradition, and Hokusai's devotion to landscape as such was also new. Yet the image – so superb in grandeur, so lyrical in its solitude – is wholly and quintessentially Japanese, and its intensity must owe much to the artist's obsession with Fuji as a sacred shrine, symbol almost of the Japanese national identity, even as Constable's intensity of vision of English landscape was fired by his Wordsworthian empathy with Nature, or as Cézanne's obsession with Mont Ste-Victoire answered some deep necessity of his imagination.

HOKUSAI: *Southerly wind and fine weather*, from *Thirty-six views of Mt Fuji, c.* 1823-29

Landscape

LI CHENG?: *Temple in the mountains after rain, c.* 1000?

GIOVANNI DI PAOLO: *Madonna and Child in a landscape, c.* 1432

POMPEII (left):
Landscape with villa,
detail, *c.* 50 BC

DURER (right):
The piece of turf, 1503

JAN VAN EYCK: *The Madonna with Chancellor Rolin*, detail, *c.* 1435

BRUEGEL: *The hunters in the snow*, 1565

JACOB VAN RUISDAEL: *Wheatfields*, *c.* 1670

Landscape as the prime subject for a painting occurs perhaps earliest in China, during the Tang dynasty, and by Song times (tenth and eleventh centuries) the theme was being expressed in variations that would prove endless – dreamlike visions of the world emerging from mist, fantastic crags, rivers as long as time itself, and the dreamer man the poet, a minute figure almost invisible in the vastness of his imagination.

Such absorption in nature comes much later in the West; in the fourteenth century the poet Petrarch is recorded as the first European to climb a mountain for the sake of the view. Glimpses of landscape survive from the paintings of classical antiquity, treated relatively naturalistically, but strictly as background material. When landscape began to reappear in medieval art it was highly stylized and used for symbolic or decorative effect. The elements of landscape in Giovanni di Paolo's beautiful *Madonna and Child*, for instance, are clearly treated as decorative pattern, and are far removed from the remarkable study of botanical reality shown in Dürer's watercolour *The piece of turf*. Here, a single clump of grass is scrutinized with an intensity that seems to summarize a whole landscape. Dürer's studies were, however, closer to still life than to that interest in sheer space and the wonder of the natural world revealed in all its detail by light which was to characterize the great landscapes of the seventeenth to nineteenth centuries. The techniques – especially perspective – needed to realize such a perception in paint are in evidence by the time of the van Eycks. But their crystalline vistas, though integral contributions to the mood of the whole composition, are subsidiary to the human action. It is only in the sixteenth century, in that meeting-place of the north and south, Venice, and above all in the mysterious imagination of Bellini (see pp. 82–83) that man and Nature become equal partners.

With Bruegel, landscape has taken precedence over the people who humanize it, absorbing the tragic or comic concerns of life indifferently into its immensity. In his *The hunters in the snow*, the hunched figures trudging through snow or scattered upon the frozen river are turned into expressive cyphers of winter itself, the brittle stillness, the sharp clarity and stark contrasts of forms in raw air becoming the true subject of the painting. The exaltation of ordinary landscape as "hero" of the picture, and as a distinct and valid branch of art, was the achievement of the great Dutch masters of the seventeenth century who reflected, in their celebration of the material fabric of life, the independence, peace and prosperity of a new-born nation. A spirit of confidence invests their landscapes, ordered according to the demands of an agrarian economy, enclosed fields spreading under a vast summer sky or lying dormant in winter. Unlike Hokusai, Ruisdael, in a painting such as *Wheatfields*, dwells lovingly on detail. Yet for all its particularized appearance, the painting represents in fact a most skilful selection from the unconfined vistas of nature, orchestrated by the light into an overall harmony as grand and solemn as Hokusai's.

Landscape

The ability of an artist to grasp landscape, to order it into coherent and meaningful form, depends on man's ability to control his environment. The vision of Nature not raw and hostile but benign, tamed to serve human needs, is celebrated in many English conversation pieces of the eighteenth century – scenes of landed gentry who sit or stroll through countryside shaped by the hand of man, as ordered and harmonious as their own lives. Posed amid the evident prosperity of their own fields, Gainsborough's *Mr and Mrs Andrews* look out at us with unshakable confidence.

Gainsborough's picture derives from study of factual Dutch landscapes, but equally influential at the time were the Arcadian visions of the seventeenth-century French classicist Claude Lorraine who, with Poussin, gave landscape painting a dimension of poetry and a new artistic status. His mythical scenes, set in the idealized countryside around Rome, established a method of composing the elements of nature into a whole, suffused with a mellow, unifying light, which became a formula for many imitators who lacked his incomparable mastery of real effects in nature. Ideal landscape gave way to a greater realism with the rise of topographical or "view" painting – more or less comparable with a picture postcard – encouraged by travellers on the Grand Tour during the eighteenth century.

In the nineteenth century, it was the more awesome aspects of Nature, its power to transform landscape beyond the control of man, which seized the imagination of Romantic artists. Turner's extreme response was to lash himself to the mast of a ship in a gale, the better to observe its effects, and to spend hours at night recording the conflagration of the Houses of Parliament; here landscape virtually disappears into the volatile elements of fire, air and water. Yet Turner's visions were perhaps another aspect of the urge to control Nature – its fury tamed in a canvas.

Constable, with a fresh awareness of the way shifting light constantly fashions anew the physical world, developed a technique, anticipating the spontaneous directness of the Impressionists, which could capture in flecks of paint the very vibrancy of air and suggest the Wordsworthian vision of "the passions of man ... incorporated with the beautiful and permanent forms of Nature". The Realist Courbet was no less susceptible to such intimations of immortality, and his seascape is an eloquent salute to those timeless symbols of the infinite, the ocean and the horizon – symbols that still strike the onlooker with their profound simplicity.

Modern man's experience of the landscape is radically altered not only by flight but also by the spread of technology across the countryside, shrinking the world and creating new juxtapositions of form within it. Mondrian's distillation of a seascape to abstract, formal values acknowledges this as much as Hopper's inclusion of roads, railways and lighthouses in his matter-of-fact portraits of America's eastern seaboard – evidence of a continuing impulse to record the exact character of a specific place.

GAINSBOROUGH: *Mr and Mrs Andrews, c.* 1748

CLAUDE: *Egeria mourning over Numa,* 1669

TURNER: *The burning of the Houses of Parliament,* 1834

CONSTABLE (left): *Fording the river, showery weather*, detail, 1831

MONDRIAN (below): *The sea*, 1914

HOPPER (above): *Highland light*, 1930

COURBET (left): *Seaside at Palavas*, 1854

Animals

In 1940, boys in the French countryside of the Dordogne, at Lascaux, stumbled into a modest aperture in the earth that proved to open out into a series of caves. The limestone region of the Dordogne is very subject to internal erosion, and caves were no novelty, nor for that matter was evidence of prehistoric man – Les Eyzies, where years before Cro-Magnon man had been discovered, is near by. The calibre of the new find was, however, astounding, rivalled only by the famous Spanish cave of Altamira.

Across the rough, eroded walls and ceilings of the Lascaux caves rampage bulls, stags, bison, horses. They are drawn always in profile, painted direct on to the unprepared rock; sometimes, with a twist of body, an elementary effect of perspective is achieved. Moss or hair probably served as brush for the drawn outlines, but quite large areas are stained by a technique close to that of a modern spray-gun: colour blown on through a hollow bone. The pigments were mineral, the medium just water that soaked into the porous limestone. Anatomically, the delineation of the animals may not be literally precise, but in vitality and grandeur they have rarely been surpassed in the whole subsequent history of human art. Some are vast – more than four metres (13ft) long. What motives inspired their creation, what need they answered and what functions they performed, can only be a matter of speculation. Their intensity suggests a religious or magic relevance; sympathetic magic perhaps entered in – the notion that an image can provide power over the thing it represents; and these animals were mostly man's prey, his food and clothing. They express also, however, the irrepressible fascination of man – himself an animal – with the sheer vitality, the strength, speed and dangerous ferocity of animals, the exultation and at times the fear of their challenge to him – and also, surely, a profound sympathy in the blood with their beauty.

Man himself appears at Lascaux as a mere brittle symbol, vulnerable. The time range of the paintings is extraordinary: they are generally dated within some five thousand years round about 15000 BC, and all through that period men returned to add to them, sometimes superimposing but also sometimes respecting the existence of earlier images and not obliterating them.

The animals seem almost to float as in a dream across the depth of the rock and of time itself, unrelated to any landscape, silent yet suggesting the thunder of stampede. Or rather, they seemed. After 1945 Lascaux was opened up. Crowds thronged to see under modern lighting these marvels as the artists could never have seen them, working as they did in the faint flicker of oil-brand through the centuries, through the millennia, until for some reason the caves were abandoned and sealed in preserving darkness for 15,000 years or more. In a mere decade of exposure to light and the atmospheric pollution of mass curiosity the paintings deteriorated dangerously. Lascaux is now sealed off again, visited only by inspecting experts; its marvels seen by the ordinary viewer only second-hand, in film or, as here, in reproduction.

LASCAUX, FRANCE:
"The Hall of Bulls",
in use *c.* 15000 BC?

Animals

FRANCE (below): *To my sole desire*, detail from *The Lady of the Unicorn*, c. 1480–90

EGYPT: Bronze *Cat*, after 30 BC

CRETE:
Bull's-head *rhyton*, c. 1500 BC

PICASSO:
Vollard Suite no. 85,
*Drinking Minotaur and
sculptor with two models*, 1933

CANOVA (below):
*Theseus and the Minotaur,
c.* 1781–82

REMBRANDT (below): *Three elephants, c.* 1637

DURER (below): *The young hare,* 1502

One of the most idyllic images of the relationship between man and animals is provided by a justly famous ivory panel of the fifth century: the subject is from Genesis, showing Adam at ease in the fork of a tree naming the animals, from the eagle and lion down to the little sprawl of a lizard and even the dreaded serpent. Placid, highly formalized, it expresses a matter-of-fact vision of an amicable Paradise. More than 1,500 years later, Courbet's exultant painting celebrates the critical moment of a very different relationship, but one evidently unquenched since Lascaux: the electric vitality of its composition – the curve of the whiplash, the agonized straining of the stag's head – seems a visual equivalent of the triumphant paean of the huntsman's horn ringing in the cold air.

Man's ambivalent attitude towards animals, veering from pastoral care to the aggressiveness of the hunter, responds to the variety of roles animals play in human life. In art, however, it is their symbolic role that has most consistently provided painters and sculptors with rich subject matter. Akin to man, yet separated from him in the dumb, incommunicable mystery of their own lives, animals have always been endowed in art, literature and folklore with moral as well as physical attributes – admired, disliked or feared – and often, too, with god-like powers. Their identification with certain qualities, real or imagined, has profoundly influenced the way in which they are represented. In ancient Egypt, where the cat was sacred, images of this animal are remarkable not so much for their naturalism as for their aura of aloof power. Whilst cats are comparatively rare in art, the bull recurs again and again with divine or semi-divine attributes, its strength and potency identified with the life force itself, and frequently finding expression in sacrificial objects, as in the elaborate bull's-head vessel (*rhyton*) from Crete.

Artists have also given form and shape to many imaginary beasts – the dragons that romp and swirl through the art of China, for example, or, in the West, the enigmatic unicorn, originally perhaps derived from descriptions of the rhinoceros but taking on in medieval tapestries an elegant beauty as symbol of the courtly synthesis of spiritual and erotic love. Medieval art swarms with animals of all kinds – on the carved misericords under choir seats, in the lettering and margins of illuminated manuscripts and in the carving of architectural bosses and capitals – some representations semi-abstract, some fantastic, some naturalistic.

Animal mythology persists. The legendary Minotaur, a sculptural theme for Canova in the nineteenth century, reappears with characteristic gusto in the etchings of Picasso. Yet from early on, too, there is a strong tradition of objective observation, whether it be Rembrandt conveying with a few chalk-strokes the weight and presence of the exotic elephant, or Dürer tracing the quivering vitality of the hare in the minutest detail. Though Dürer's hare is probably the single best-seller of all animal portraits, the creature which has delighted artists more than any other, as we see on the next two pages, is the horse.

Animals

Artists have always found two contrary qualities in the horse – untamed elemental strength and speed, and the beauty of such power harnessed by man. Even when the horse as a working animal seems obsolete, the combination of horse and rider remains a formidable image of authority and power: thus the Romans portrayed the Emperor Marcus Aurelius, a precedent for Verrocchio to immortalize the military leader Colleoni in the emphatic arrogance of command. Baroque painters – notably Rubens – and Romantics such as Delacroix likewise fused both man and horse into a single compulsive rhythm of energy, as physically indissoluble as the centaurs of Greek myth.

Gods in horse shape may be rare (too useful, perhaps, as vehicles for other gods), but the mythical Greek winged horse, Pegasus, became the symbol of poetic genius. An intriguing parallel in China is the miraculous bronze of a horse rising from the wings of a flying swallow, modelled by an unknown sculptor in the early Han period, about AD 100. Leonardo, who improvised again and again on the theme of the horse alone, expresses in the dynamism of his line a similar sense of boundless energy, almost the force of the imagination itself. Humbler and quieter versions of the horse are among the many realistic pottery animals from the Tang tombs, and in the West, too, many artists have concentrated more upon the horse's solidity, stamina and strength; the patient endurance of the ordinary work-horse has never been portrayed more searchingly than in the studies of a saddle-horse – somewhat tired, nostrils slit, but ears and eyes showing willingness – drawn by Pisanello in the mid-fifteenth century.

The breeding of thoroughbred strains in eighteenth-century Britain inspired that painter of genius, Stubbs, who married the faithful likeness of such aristocratic beasts into a formal rhythm as satisfying as a Greek frieze. Géricault, who used form rather to express the impatient spirit, and whose empathy with animal vitality permeates his work, captured a horse galvanized by a thunderstorm as if the lightning had entered its very bloodstream. Later, Degas was fascinated by vitality of the racetrack, the shapes constantly created and recreated by nervous animal energy responding to the sensitive strength of a jockey's hands and feet. His intense observation and his awareness of the compressed forms of horses in motion paralleled (and perhaps responded to) the work of the photographer Eadweard Muybridge who demonstrated in 1878 that traditional depictions of the horse at full gallop with legs extended fore and aft were quite inaccurate.

Even through the increasingly formal preoccupations of the twentieth century the theme of rider and mount has sustained its fascination, reworked obsessively by the Italian sculptor Marini, whose most deceptively simple images contain harsh tensions, and translated by the Cubist Duchamp-Villon into a metaphor of brute mechanical power. We have yet to see those modern work-horses, the automobile and airplane, replace horse and rider as symbols of energy, grace and control in the imaginations of artists.

VERROCCHIO: *Bartolommeo Colleoni*, 1481–90

WUWEI, EASTERN CHINA: "*Flying Horse*", 2nd century AD

LEONARDO: *Study of a rearing horse*, c. 1498–90

STUBBS (right): *Mares and foals*, 1762

PISANELLO: *Horses, c.* 1433–38

GERICAULT (left):
*A horse frightened by
lightning, c.* 1820

MARINI (right):
Little rider, 1946

DEGAS (below): *A carriage at the races*, 1877–80

DUCHAMP-VILLON (right):
The horse, 1914

MUYBRIDGE (below):
Sally Gardner running, 1878

Still Life

Van Gogh's still life is not a large painting – only 63 centimetres (about 2ft) wide – but it is packed with meaning. The component items are arranged, not casually, but almost regimented, on the most important element of the painting: the drawing-board, its far edge precisely parallel with the top edge of the picture, the grain of the wood emphasized by the thrust of the brush on the thick paint. The subject matter is otherwise much as can be found at almost any time in the long history of still-life painting: pot, plate, bottle, candle, book, vegetables. This time, though, the items are positive characters, and the occasion of their being painted is crucial for the artist.

Van Gogh painted this in January 1889 – one of the first pictures he finished after his calamitous breakdown the month before, when he became finally alienated from his colleague Gauguin, who was staying with him in Arles, and ended up by depositing a severed piece of his own ear in a brothel. Dr Felix Rey, who treated van Gogh, encouraged him to paint as a therapeutic activity, and during the period between the first attack and his near-inevitable relapse in February, 1889, van Gogh appears to have been attempting to reaffirm both his style and his sanity. To his brother and his enduring pillar of strength, Theo, he wrote: "I'm so eager to work that it amazes me". He desperately reworked the famous painting of his chair, and painted a pair of portraits of Dr Rey and of Madame Roulin, together with two important self-portraits of his bandaged head which illustrated a direct confrontation with his sickness as well as his artistic aspirations. His inability to separate his art from his illness is evident in a letter to Theo: " ... let me go on with my work; if it is that of a madman, well, so much the worse".

Still life with drawing-board becomes in this context an exercise in equilibrium. A virtual recipe or prescription for health, it details ingredients: food, drink, book and candle, and van Gogh's inseparable solace, pipe and tobacco. The letter asserts his identity from outside, the envelope legibly addressed to him and, no doubt, from Theo in Paris. The book is not any book, not even a novel by Zola, but titled as F.V. Raspail's *Manuel Annuaire de la Santé*, a treatise on health and hygiene. The vegetable heads shown may be garlic not onion; garlic is recommended by Raspail.

All these are set out on the drawing-board, the latter the arena on which, as on an easel, the painter has to resolve his disorientation. Formally, the picture's composition is strung taut on the thrust and counterpoise of almost exaggerated diagonals and plunging perspective; its tension is almost perilous, just held in check by the two strong assertive uprights of bottle and candle. The candle is lit, the flame alive. In van Gogh's hands the still life becomes a vibrant expression of his own personality, a testimony of faith and of hope. He may use traditional subject matter and devices (many earlier Dutch still lifes are signed thus on a *trompe-l'oeil* letter) but the total effect, and the whole significance of his picture, is entirely different. The still life becomes humanized, almost a psychological self-portrait.

VAN GOGH: *Self-portrait*, 1889

VAN GOGH: *Still life with drawing-board*, 1889

Still Life

ROME: *Mosaic basket of flowers*, 2nd century AD

ZHAO JI: *Birds and flowers*, detail, 12th century

VAN EYCK: *St Jerome*, detail, 1442

CARAVAGGIO: *A basket of fruit*, 1596

VAN BEYEREN: *Still life with a wine ewer*, after 1655

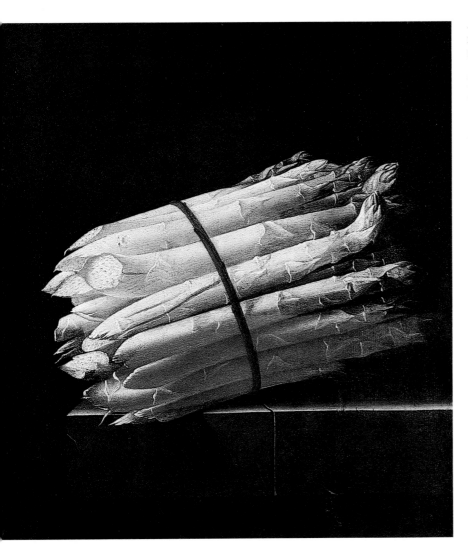

COORTE: *A bundle of asparagus*, 1703

BAUGIN: *Still life with a chequer-board*, c. 1630

As we have just seen, a painting of still life may be more complex than it seems. The artist's state of mind is seldom as relevant to our understanding of a picture as it is in van Gogh's work, however; still lifes are more often painted – and intended to be enjoyed – purely as demonstration pieces which show off the artist's skill. Their history goes back to the legend of the Greek painter Zeuxis in the fifth century BC painting a bunch of grapes with such deceptive illusionism that birds tried to peck them. No early Greek still lifes survive, but examples recur in later antiquity, in wall-paintings, as at Pompeii, and in mosaics rendering fruit, vegetables and other staples of daily life in more or less naturalistic detail. In China, too, there is a long tradition of bird- and flower-paintings which capture with the greatest delicacy the subtle and evanescent beauty of fruit or petal.

The still life is, in large part, a salute to life, a celebration, and the persistence of the tradition may rely largely on the strength of man's re-luctance to admit that, like life itself, the material pleasures of food and drink, the solid preciousness of silver and gold, of jewels and rich fabric are as transitory as flowers. Artists of the early Re-naissance who, after the passage of centuries, began to take up again the theme of still life, were concerned to add a spiritual significance to their arrangements of objects. The items they chose often had some special, symbolic connotation (a lily for purity) and symbols of mortality, con-ventionally a skull, appeared among food or flow-ers as warnings of the passage of time, stern correctives to the vanity of life (*vanitas*). Yet we can see in the Eyckian depiction of St Jerome in his study that the books, hour-glass, writing instru-ments, glass vase, are described with the same loving scrutiny as the saint himself (and more convincingly than his lion).

It needed only for the artist to focus on the still-life elements alone, and indeed this began to happen during the fifteenth century. At the end of the following century the new naturalism of Ca-ravaggio produced still lifes of startling virtuosity. A painting such as *A basket of fruit* does not depend on the narrative or symbolic significance of the objects displayed but bears out Caravaggio's own belief that the inanimate world was a worthy challenge to the artist and that it took as much skill to paint a good picture of fruit or flowers as of figures or faces.

The golden age of northern still life came famously in seventeenth-century Holland, whose citizens delighted in decorating their homes with technically flawless reflections of their own pos-sessions. Artists such as van Beyeren, in his staggering accumulation of fruit, meat, fish, glass and silver on a banqueting table, or Coorte, who could deceive the eye with a simple bunch of asparagus, brought an astonishing illusionism to the genre. Yet profounder messages were often still concealed in even the most precise depictions of objects. The French painter Baugin's *Still life with chequer-board* is in fact an allegory of the five senses – sight, sound, taste, smell and touch – the transitory given a superb, formal permanence.

Still Life

From the seventeenth to the nineteenth century, Western critics and historians argued about the relative merits of the various branches of painting, from "history" painting at the top to, almost invariably, still life at the bottom. If history painting challenged the human imagination to its noblest achievements, still life was held to call on the imagination not at all, to be mere copying, servile imitation of superficial appearance – the basic prose of the inventory compared with the lofty poetry of the epic. Yet quite clearly many of the greatest artists have devoted exactly the same concentration of imaginative vision to still life as to any other subject. Rembrandt's still lifes are rare, but include masterpieces as extraordinary as his studies of the carcass of a *Flayed ox*, in which his characteristic drama of light and shade, of troubled and expressive movement of texture and colour, invests the butchered animal with an almost tragic quality.

Other painters of the period specialized entirely in still lifes, and included a few whose work has a contemplative poetry of form and colour that lifts it far above mere imitation. The eighteenth-century French artist Chardin showed what magical transformations could be effected in still lifes which are no longer cluttered inventories of luxuries but solemn, harmonious arrangements of everyday objects. Chardin's colour is rich yet muted, the texture of his paint revealing in the humblest ingredients nourishment for the spirit.

By the end of the nineteenth century, the Impressionists had shown that literally exact depiction of nature – live or still – was not necessarily the most effective way to capture a subject. Some of the most painstakingly exact still lifes of all were (and still are) of flowers – sometimes focused on an individual plant, essential illustrations to botanical and herbal studies. Yet it was Odilon Redon, Symbolist precursor of the Surrealists, whose flowers went beyond objective accuracy to penetrate the mystery of their ephemeral loveliness. His remarkable pastels can produce an electric, almost supernatural vibration.

Cézanne found in still life an ideal vehicle for pictorial research – for his patient reconciliation of the visible world with the flat surface of the canvas, revealing in his apples, his tilted table-top, a monumental solidity. The reality sought here does not seek to deny the reality of the paint and has nothing to do with sleight-of-hand illusionism; compare his table-cloth with the hanging sheet in Raphaelle Peale's *trompe-l'oeil*. The Cubists, following Cézanne, found in still life a captive for dissection and reconstruction, and then, beginning to turn full circle, used actual elements – packets, newspaper cuttings, as in Gris' *Breakfast* – as deliberate contrast between pictorial representation of reality and reality itself. This relationship has fascinated many twentieth-century artists, obsessed with the nature of perception and with the meaning (or validity) of art. Jasper Johns, transmuting the throwaway metal of beer-cans into the durable bronze of sculpture, seems concerned to make us think hard about the nature of the gap between the actual and the represented.

REMBRANDT: *The flayed ox*, 1655

CHARDIN: *The white table-cloth, c.* 1737

REDON: *Wild flowers*, after 1912

CEZANNE: *Still life with apples and oranges*, 1895-1900

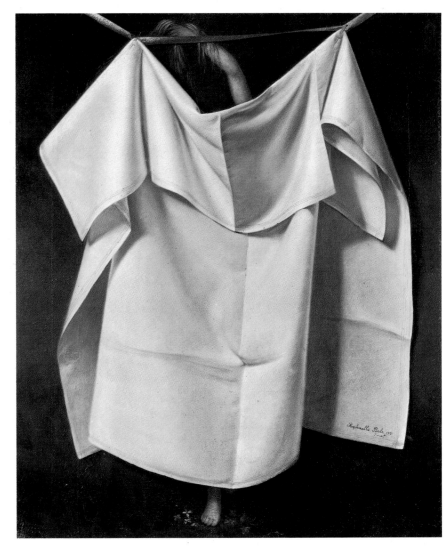

GRIS: *Breakfast*, 1914

RAPHAELLE PEALE: *After the bath*, 1823

JOHNS: *Painted bronze II: ale-cans*, 1964

Images of Divinity

Rembrandt worked on this great etching in 1653, that is, when his genius was moving towards its last phase, as his vision became more sombre but also ever more profound. Then, later still, probably a few years before his death in 1666, he worked the plate again, but he did not just "refresh" it where it was worn from heavy printing; he revised it so that its character in this state is quite different.

This etching is one of the grandest, most sublime of all his works, no less so than his greatest paintings. It is, to start with, one of the largest etchings – 38.7 × 45 centimetres ($15\frac{1}{4}$ × 18in). It responds to the account of the Crucifixion in the Gospel of St Luke: "And it was about the sixth hour, and there was a darkness over all the earth until the ninth hour. And the sun was darkened, and the veil of the temple was rent in the midst"; but it is as if, Christ having cried in a loud voice: "Father, into thy hands I commend my spirit", and died, the cloud has parted and light has cascaded from the heavens upon his body. About him, to left and right, the two crucified robbers are almost submerged in darkness, and at the foot of the Cross, from a disturbed medley of half-seen, half-felt figures, only the Roman centurion on his horse and a second mounted soldier with drawn sword emerge clearly defined. A commotion in the twilight on the left is a third horse, rearing in terror.

These last three elements, the horses and their riders, are entirely redrawn from their earlier state. The centurion must be he who, when he saw what was done, glorified God, saying: "Certainly, this was a righteous man". The figure is ambivalent, however, a profile antique yet familiar, and in fact borrowed from a medal by Pisanello of Gianfrancesco Gonzaga. This anachronistic, almost bizarre borrowing lends a further strangeness, a loneliness, a mystery to this already mysterious and emotionally supercharged setting.

Some prefer the clearer, more defined version, as in the second state of the etching, where the detail is controlled and gathered into the whole like the climax of a great Baroque organ fugue. This revised version, nevertheless, is a vision of tragedy in which the penetration of the natural order by the supernatural is rendered by the drama of light and shade with an intensity unparalleled in any other comparable work. In its inspiration, one may be reminded not of Bach's stately formal majesty but of the elemental pity and terror of Shakespeare's *King Lear*.

REMBRANDT: *The three crosses*, second state, 1653

REMBRANDT: *The three crosses*, fourth state, *c*. 1662

PISANELLO: *Gianfrancesco Gonzaga*, *c*. 1439

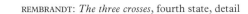

REMBRANDT: *The three crosses*, fourth state, detail

Images of Divinity

ENGLAND: Crucifix, 10th/11th century   GERMANY: Abbess Mathilde's Cross, 974-982   GERMANY: Plague Cross and detail, 1304

GRUNEWALD (below):
Isenheim altarpiece, 1515

RAPHAEL: *"The Mond Crucifixion"*, 1502-03

GAUGUIN: *"The Yellow Christ"*, 1889

EL GRECO (left): *Crucifixion with a landscape*, 1600-10

The image of Rembrandt's *Three crosses* is one of the most moving treatments of Christianity's central motif, the crucifixion of Christ and the Cross itself. As the focus of the Christian mystery and symbol of the faith, the subject has inspired recurrent interpretations, varying in style and approach according to the preoccupations of their artists' own times.

Early depictions of the Crucifixion tend to the schematic. Concentrated upon one of the most shameful forms of execution, reserved for slaves, criminals and agitators without civil rights, the theme must have been hard for many converts to accept when Christianity became the official religion of the Roman Empire, an Establishment creed. In early medieval art, the physical suffering of Christ tends not to be stressed. In some ivories, his body becomes essentially a second statement of the Cross itself, the horizontal of the arms crossing the vertical of the body, the face impassive, registering no pain or emotion. On processional Crosses such as Abbess Mathilde's at Essen, the body of Christ is a jewel, central but minute in the gold and enamel splendour of the crucifix; it disappears altogether on other Crosses which, whether unadorned and starkly geometric or richly elaborated, as in the great "carpet" pages of Celtic manuscripts, are used everywhere as the trademark of the faith.

In the Middle Ages, as interest in the physical world increased and Church doctrine emphasized the cult of Christ's body, the Passion came to be more realistically depicted, especially in the Gothic vision of northern Europe. The horrendous figure of the Plague Cross at Cologne, of 1304, responds to the anguish of the plagues already familiar in Europe and soon to devastate the continent. But the supreme example of the dolorous Crucifixion came later, in the famous Isenheim altarpiece by Grünewald of around 1515, where distortions of form and colour place almost intolerable stress upon Christ's agony. Although these methods were later to be revived by Expressionist artists, alternatives were at the same time being proposed in Renaissance Italy.

The composition of Raphael's early *Crucifixion* is classically serene, based on a scheme of intersecting circles, and radiating a serene, almost glad acceptance; salvation is assured. His solution, characteristic of the High Renaissance, states an ideal far removed from the reality of the Cross, emphasizing the spiritual in terms of physical perfection. A century later, in El Greco's version, Christ's bodily pain as he hangs upon the Cross seems almost transubstantiated into spiritual fire, a flame of ecstasy aspiring upwards, the reverse of the appalling collapse in Grünewald.

The theme endures. In Gauguin's *Yellow Christ* of 1889, the formal concerns of his revolutionary Symbolism are applied to the depiction of Breton peasants at their traditional devotions. A provincial Crucifixion of uncertain date from the little local chapel at Trémalo is here transposed through his highly personal style of flattened colour and decorative patterning into an image of a faith at once simple and profound.

Images of Divinity

Man has always tended to forge gods in his own image; prehistoric awe for the source of life itself is expressed in powerful female figurines whose ripe convexities surely relate them to fertility rites. The benevolence conveyed by such images, squat and faceless though many are, is by no means shared by similar deities in other cultures; the grim Aztec goddess of life and death compels a reverence for inexplicable and terrible forces.

It must often be due to our ignorance of the functions served by some of these images that we can now find delight and wonder in them. An African god of war and metal, rakishly hatted and spindly-legged, may enchant the Western eye as an apparently childlike construction but the sinister aspects of its scale (over life-size), iron body and jerky movement may be more in keeping with its probable religious function. In contrast, the ample curves of Jambhala, an oriental divinity of prosperity, express the comfort and good fortune for which he is invoked. Plump as the cushion he sits on, he bears more than a chance resemblance to the classical god of good cheer, Bacchus.

The complexities of Eastern religious philosophies have created a multiplicity of images baffling to the European eye. Their profusion in Hinduism expresses the infinite forms taken by the single controlling force of the universe, Brahman; in his destructive aspect he is personified as Shiva, graceful and dynamic, a many-armed figure encircled by the flames of cosmic energy symbolizing the continuous cycle of life and death.

Buddhism concentrates the attention of believers upon the dominant image of Gautama Buddha, the teacher who taught detachment and compassion as the means of release from materiality – most often portrayed as seated in meditation, the contours of his face, body and robes evoking absolute serenity. Such a limited range invited stylization, yet among the Buddhas of China, Japan and South-East Asia are some of the most beautiful images of spiritual peace in all sacred art.

For the Greeks and Romans, divinity found its expression in beings who were immortal but dwelt in bodies that were simply larger and perfect versions of the human form. Christian art, too, after the Renaissance, applied the classical canon of spiritual beauty expressed as human physical perfection to Christ and his saints, but most seductively of all to the Virgin Mary, in whom the prehistoric Venuses find their ultimate graceful transposition. Mary, too, signifies fecundity, but also inextinguishable tenderness and love.

While the Christian doctrine of the Incarnation made it possible to depict the unfathomable nature of God in the human person of Christ, the related faiths of Islam and Judaism, without such sanction, regarded pictures of the deity as presumptuous and idolatrous. The continuous arabesques of Islamic decoration express rather the continuity of ideal spiritual existence; Allah's name emblemized in St Sophia, Istanbul, remains as richly associative and symbolic to the faithful as was the Cross to the Christians who built the church in the sixth century.

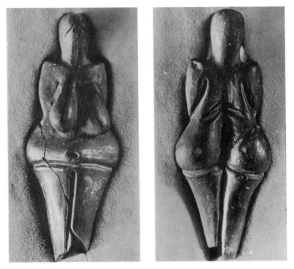

CZECHOSLOVAKIA: *"The Venus of Věstonice"*, c. 14000–13500 BC

MEXICO (below): *Aztec goddess of life and death*, undated

JAVA (below): *Seated Jambhala*, undated

INDIA (below): *Shiva as Nataraja*, undated

DAHOMEY (above): *Gu, god of war*, undated

JAPAN: *"The Kamakura Buddha"*, 1252

RAPHAEL (below): *"The Alba Madonna"*, c. 1511

GREECE (below): *Head of Aphrodite*, 2nd century BC

TURKEY: *Name of Allah*, undated

Allegory, Myth and Fantasy

Allegory is the narrative description of a subject under the guise of another suggestively similar – a technique of ambiguity no less widespread in the visual arts than it is in literature. Artists in every culture have been able to convey layers of rich meaning by depicting figures of mythology or moral or religious allegory, often identified by conventional symbols (attributes). The themes acted out could be used for didactic purposes or simply as pegs on which to hang decorations – pliable raw material from which to shape satisfactory aesthetic forms. As the tradition behind such pictures decays, and as their decoding becomes subject for erudite debate, our enjoyment of them is likely to depend mainly on their visual qualities.

Giovanni Bellini's vision called *"The Sacred Allegory"* is one of the most fascinating and haunting of all, yet by no means untypical in that it is no longer capable of precise interpretation. Its attribution to Bellini, rather than to his brilliant pupil, Giorgione, is now generally accepted. Thereafter agreement ceases; it was long believed to have been conceived as an illustration to a fourteenth-century French poem on the pilgrimage of the soul. That may be part of it, but it is probably right to describe it specifically as a meditation on the Divine Incarnation.

The central figure, seated on a cushion, is certainly the Christ-child; he holds an apple, symbolic of the Original Sin from which he redeems mankind. The attendant little naked *putti* (one holding the Tree of Life) are doubtless angels, redeemed souls, but in form borrowed from pagan classical antiquity. There are further pagan echoes in the zone beyond the formal garden where beasts and even a centaur appear, and the waters, which in many mythologies represent immortality, also recall Lethe, the purging of earthly memories. The Virgin Mary, seated beneath a vine (symbolizing the blood of Christ) appears to judge between the crowned figure (Mercy/Peace?) and the woman on the left (Truth/Justice?). The sword is held by Simeon, who foretold the Passion. Next to him is Isaiah, who foretold the Virgin birth. The two figures on the right are Job and St Sebastian, here admitted to the world theologically conceived as in grace – the zone within the marble terrace.

The obscurity of the allegory to all but the most learned specialists (and even they disagree) is baffling, and yet the picture is spellbinding – inexplicable yet immediately acceptable as a reality in the setting of the north Italian landscape. It is the landscape, so tenderly and lyrically observed in the melting yet crystal-clear light, that was first established by the artist; the contemplative and now mysterious figures, each so solitary and yet linked by the web of some silent, blissful, communion, were then disposed on the marble terrace, the pattern of which is discernible through them in places. The whole has the irrational but compulsive logic of dream, structured on a beautiful counterplay of symmetry and asymmetry, and an underlying geometrically exact use of perspective. It has the intensity of a vision, of a divine order both informing and transcending nature.

BELLINI: *"The Sacred Allegory"*, c. 1490   Mercy/Peace?   Simeon

Isaiah   The Christ-child

Job   St Sebastian

Allegory, Myth and Fantasy

RAIMONDI: *The Judgment of Paris, c.* 1516

RUBENS (below): *The Judgment of Paris, c.* 1632–35

EWORTH (below):
Queen Elizabeth confounding the three goddesses, 1569

BLAKE: *The Judgment of Paris,* 1817

RAIMONDI: *The Judgment of Paris*, detail

MANET (below):
"Le Déjeuner sur l'Herbe", 1863

Many of the most persistent myths in Western culture evidently originated long before the first records of them in art and literature, surviving, no doubt, because they answered some profound need of the human imagination. Potent myths have endured even when the events they explained were forgotten, passing into the shared cultural heritage to be reinterpreted by subsequent ages.

One myth of perennial appeal is the story of the youth chosen by Jupiter to judge who was the fairest of three goddesses and to award her an apple. Paris' choice of Venus, which led to the seduction of Helen, the Trojan War and, indirectly, to the founding of Rome, was understandably popular in Greek and Roman art, but its continuing fascination surely depends on more than its symbolic or historical value.

Many versions exist in art, in part because of the opportunity afforded to paint nudes but also doubtless because the Judgment of Paris is about the irresistible appeal of beauty to the senses. Certainly, from the time of the Renaissance, artists have alluded to each other's versions of the myth, each rendering becoming richer by association with those that preceded it.

Marcantonio Raimondi's engraving is itself based on a lost design by Raphael, and includes divinities not directly concerned in the original story, perhaps water-nymphs and river-gods. In the sky ride Apollo in his chariot and Diana with the crescent moon in her hair, but the main centre of interest is the heroic treatment of the nude, the goddesses scarcely less muscular than the ideal male figure of Paris. Eroticism, entirely absent from this engraving, is the dominant strain in Rubens' version, which unashamedly invites male viewers to identify with Paris in contemplation of sensuously painted flesh.

In an ingenious adaptation of the story, a painter at the court of Elizabeth I allowed the Queen (decorously clad) to award herself the apple, suggesting that in Elizabeth Nature had surpassed the collective perfections of the routed goddesses. The Neoclassical revival of the eighteenth century brought renewed interest in the theme, though Blake's scorn for classical precedents is apparent in the leaping energy of his figures. His contemporary, Rowlandson, transformed the mood from an heroic to a ribald one: Paris becomes an old lecher, Hermes a procuress and the goddesses whores. Later, in one of the most controversial pictures of the nineteenth century, Manet omitted the central characters entirely and based his group on the reclining rivergods of Marcantonio's engraving. Whatever his private reasons for this quotation, the painting was a strong statement of artistic independence, setting free the academic studio nude in scandalous modern picnic with two clothed men. Picasso, in turn, exploited Manet's solution, claiming art equally with nature as raw material for the alchemy of his imagination. Here, with the accretions of the past almost evaporated, Picasso presents himself as a modern Paris, forced to choose the greatest beauty from the endless beauties of nature – an allegory of the creative process itself.

PICASSO: *"Le Déjeuner sur l'Herbe"*, 1962

ROWLANDSON (left): *Englishman in Paris*, 1807

Allegory, Myth and Fantasy

Myths and folklore, whether Greek or biblical, the heroic doings of Persian kings in the *Shahnameh* or the vivid, semi-satirical versions of Samurai legend produced in nineteenth-century Japan by Kuniyoshi, have always provided artists with subjects recognizable and acceptable to their audiences, relevant to contemporary needs yet rich in tradition and echoes of the past. The creation of the work of art may even precede the decision to borrow the myth, as in one of the most famous masterpieces of Giambologna – conceived purely as a formal solution to three figures entwined in vigorous action. As he told his patron, "the subject was chosen to give scope to the knowledge and study of art"; only later was a suitable title added on the plinth: *The rape of the Sabine.*

Two centuries later Tiepolo was still drawing on classical myth for his *Apollo pursuing Daphne*, but, while the trappings of the story are faithfully recorded, with Daphne transformed into a tree before our eyes, the primary intention is erotic, a sunlit celebration of youth and the senses. To an educated audience the classical allusion added both respectability and an extra dimension. Knowledge of the story of Venus and Mars does not help us to interpret Botticelli's painting fully, however. There seems to be another meaning to this strange scene, other than the triumph of love over war.

The situation became more difficult still when the decline of classical education left audiences unmoved by even the clearest classical allusion. For the modern figurative artist who wants to convey more than surface appearances, the problem is to produce images in the absence of any spoken or written story to elucidate their meaning. Yet sometimes an invented mythology, however obscure, may impress us with its suggestive power while more explicable allegories fall flat. William Blake, at the end of the eighteenth century, drew not only upon traditional mythologies but also upon his own, and at his most intense succeeds in convincing us that the vision he records is of another reality. By comparison, the imagery of Ford Madox Brown, a nineteenth-century artist allied in earnestness of purpose with the Pre-Raphaelites, seems curious rather than convincing when he illustrates all kinds of labour in the setting of a suburban London street.

Modern revivals of classical myth have proved largely superficial. While Daumier in the nineteenth century could still parody a commonly accepted idiom for the purpose of social satire, more recent treatments of myth, by Picasso and Matisse, for example, have generally been decorative, if superbly so. It is the fantasies of the Surrealists, notably Magritte, that have most effectively challenged any easy assumption we may have that our feet are safely planted on solid ground; their images, often drawn from personal sources, record with painstaking precision events that we know to be utterly impossible. Less alarming, wholly captivating, are the poetic visions of Douanier Rousseau. Though his, too, were private fantasies rather than public myths, they convince us by their innocent beauty that the fairy story is alive and well.

KUNIYOSHI (left):
Tameijiro dan Shogo grapples with his enemy under water, 1828–29

GIAMBOLOGNA (below):
The rape of the Sabine, 1579–83

TIEPOLO (below): *Apollo pursuing Daphne, c.* 1755–60

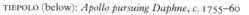

BOTTICELLI (below): *Venus and Mars, c.* 1485

BROWN (right): *Work*, 1852–65

BLAKE (below): *The great red dragon
and the woman clothed with the sun, c.* 1800–10

MAGRITTE (left):
The house of glass, 1939

DAUMIER: *The triumph of Menelaus*, 1842

ROUSSEAU: *The dream*, 1910

The Inward Eye

At first sight, you might think perhaps, not much in it – a vast canvas, more than three-and-a-half metres (12ft) wide, covered with colour areas in maroon and dusty black. At the centre, two maroon rectangles of the same height but differing widths are set vertically, the edges soft, wavering, fuzzy. On closer inspection most of the canvas seems stained rather than painted, with only traces of the brush dragging black into the maroon. Everything is a bit hazy, the colour suffused, permeated with a gentle glowing. The precise colour of any one area is very difficult to define; there seem to be veils of colour behind colour, shifting like cloud in almost still air over the sun. The pale maroon darkens at the edges of the rectangles and again at the edges of the paintings. Nebulous, sombrely glowing, the colour gives the impression that the paint is generating its own light, as in the embers of a fire.

Rothko moved toward this, his late style, away from somewhat Surrealistic biomorphic imagery, through a long series of attempts to reduce his subject matter to the essential, in his own words: "toward clarity, toward the elimination of all obstacles between the painter and the idea, and between the idea and the observer. As examples of such obstacles I give (among others) memory, history or geometry, which are swamps of generalization ..." An American contemporary of Rothko's, and one who taught with him for a time, Robert Motherwell, observed that "the function of the artist is to make the spiritual so that it is there to be possessed".

Rothko came to work on a majestic scale – and the large scale is essential to his work. His huge paintings can create their most profound effect when a number hang together within an enclosed space, as in the Tate Gallery, London, or the chapel of St Thomas's Hospital in Houston, Texas. Then they produce a total environment in which the observer is enveloped, an impression different but comparable to that produced by the orchestration of space in great Baroque churches, or, in Gothic churches, by the magical suffusion of colour from sunlit, stained-glass windows. The chapel in Houston, with its great panels of glowing and shifting dusky red, invites the participant to silent and concentrated meditation. Some have even found, in contemplation of Rothko's work, the transcendental sensation of freedom from terrestial gravity which is the aim of many techniques of oriental mysticism.

This is remote from the traditional visions of Heaven recorded by most Western artists in figurative terms – or those of Hell either, for that matter. As some of the works on the following pages show, the artist's inward eye can define the most precise images as well as the most ineffable, giving them an hallucinatory clarity on the canvas. Rothko's own impulse was to reject definition, to strive for the universal rather than the particular, and there is an inevitable ambivalence in his paintings. The only valid subject matter, he wrote, was that "which is tragic and timeless. That is why we profess kinship with primitive and archaic art". Rothko in the end took his own life.

ROTHKO: *Black on maroon*, 1958

The Inward Eye

BOSCH (right):
The Garden of Earthly Delights,
detail, *c.* 1505-10

VAN DER WEYDEN (below):
The Last Judgment, detail, *c.* 1450?

MICHELANGELO: *The Last Judgment*, detail, 1534-41

GOYA: *The Colossus*, 1808-12

DALI: *3 young Surrealist women holding in their arms the skins of an orchestra*, detail, 1936

CHIRICO (below): *The enigma of the hour*, 1912

BACON (left):
Study after Velazquez, 1953

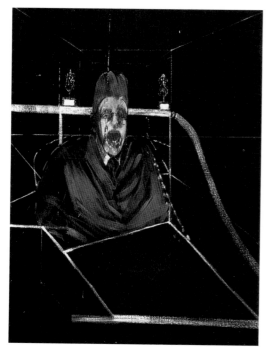

The feeling that the universe is divided into three zones persists, in spite of the explanations of modern astronomy and an almost universal scepticism of the biblical account of the Creation. Though we know the earth is not flat, nevertheless Heaven is still somewhere "up there" and Hell, though we may choose to ignore it, "down there".

Painters in a long tradition seem to have envisaged the torments of Hell with particular vividness. On the day of reckoning, a favourite subject for Christian artists, the lost souls are often shown spilling naked in a cascade down to their doom. The emphasis, though, differs remarkably; whereas despair is conveyed poignantly in the gaunt Gothic victims of a Netherlandish artist such as Rogier van der Weyden, Michelangelo's version calls attention, even at the Last Judgment, to the splendours of the human body rather than to spiritual damnation.

More effective in disrupting complacency are those visions of a Hell in which the artist's fantasy breeds distorted mutations of the natural world. To modern eyes, attuned to the irrational visions of the Surrealists, some of the paintings of Bruegel and Bosch strike home with a force in no way diminished by the obscurity of their imagery. The hybrid inhabitants of Bosch's Hell are horribly credible, detailing with ruthless clarity our profoundest apprehensions.

The twentieth-century concept of Hell as a state of mind rather than a zone of endless physical torment was prefigured during the Romantic age, above all in the nightmare visions of Goya. Images such as his *Colossus*, a vast figure silhouetted against a night sky as if brooding upon the destruction of all life, are characteristic of the mood of many etchings of his old age, and of the famous "Black Paintings" with which he decorated his house. The relevance of Goya's most extreme visions remained unrecognized until later in the nineteenth century, when some of the Symbolists explored the imagery of psychological states of mind and of the occult. The Surrealists were to exploit the Unconscious even more intensively and effectively; in Salvador Dali's imagination the world melts and sets in new, meaningless, yet sinister shape. Before him, Chirico in the baleful light of his deserted townscapes provided a modern urban nightmare of individual isolation and menace.

Less contrived than some of these images are Expressionist visions in which Hell resides within the human body, its contours distorted by the escaping screams of the damned. One of Munch's most famous prints is precisely that – a cry welling out, the solid world melting in its despair as if into lava. If some of the Expressionists seem to anticipate the holocausts of Nazi Germany, it is perhaps Francis Bacon who conveys most ferociously post-War man's realization of his potential for evil. Bacon's famous series of *Screaming Popes* takes a portrait by Velazquez of a man of great power in the splendour of life, of spiritual office – a picture notable for its humane understanding – and explodes it into the shuddering portrait of a soul in Hell on earth.

The Inward Eye

Heaven, no less than Hell, can be a state of mind, though in the nature of life perhaps less frequent. It is also less susceptible to visual expression: an eternity of rapture is difficult to imagine, much less to depict, and there is no heavenly counterpart so convincingly explicit as Goya's images of evil. Bernini's famous *St Theresa* captures the facial expression of ecstasy as almost no other image has succeeded in doing, but it is often claimed that the expression is one of physical rather than spiritual bliss. Likewise the marvellous vision of El Greco, *The Fifth Seal of the Apocalypse*, is ambivalent; its tremendous theme is the end of the world, but amidst the flaring colour and sinuous movement which, if any, are the damned, and which the saved, is arguable. Both the Bernini and the El Greco aspire upwards, and perhaps the most splendid Christian celebrations of Heaven do not attempt description of Paradise achieved, but of the ascent to it – the great Baroque vistas, in ceiling or dome, of Christ or the Madonna soaring into the empyrean from the attendant floating angels.

BERNINI: *St Theresa*, 1646-52

When literally envisioned Heaven often tends to be depicted in terms of the Garden of Eden, the Paradise (from the Persian "enclosed garden"), the Golden Age which must in the end return. In that first great monument of the northern Renaissance, the van Eycks' Ghent altarpiece, the Lamb of God is set on an altar before the source of the River of Life, the glory of God radiating over the landscape and the adoring crowds. Light is in most cultures associated with visions of beatitude, as is music also – the harmony of the spheres, the heavenly melodies of those elected to praise and serve God – a concept expressed most seductively by Fra Angelico's angels, whose lyrical, vernal colours seem felicity itself.

Later artists saw in idealized nature an allegory of eternal bliss, even without angelic hosts; such were Claude's idylls, bathed in serene golden light, and Constable's quick apprehensions of joy in the shifting weather (see p. 63). The most intense visions of the immanence of infinity in human life were provided by the German Romantic Friedrich, who combined sea, sky and isolated figures to produce a mood of contemplative awe.

Some artists have perceived the ethereal in the everyday, none more so than William Blake and, more recently, Stanley Spencer, who saw intrepidly literal visions of salvation even in the mass graves of a Flanders battlefield. The more general impulse of twentieth-century mystical art has been to abandon the human sphere in favour of a more abstract ideal – a balance of shapes, lines and colours visually analogous to musical harmony. The paintings of Mondrian were quite consciously spiritually motivated, providing in a sense a defined counterpart to Rothko's hazy, shifting shapes. Mondrian's clear, hard, geometric precision posits a clear order of things, immutable as the laws of the universe – the austere consolation of an order unaffected by mortal weaknesses and the miseries of the human condition. Though offering little hope to the individual, that is perhaps the only notion of Heaven available to the late twentieth century.

EL GRECO: *The Fifth Seal of the Apocalypse*, 1608-14

JAN AND HUBERT VAN EYCK: The Ghent altarpiece, finished 1432

FRA ANGELICO: The Linaiuoli triptych, details, 1433

FRIEDRICH: *Moonrise over the sea*, 1822

SPENCER (left):
*The resurrection
of the soldiers*,
detail, 1928-29

MONDRIAN:
*Composition in
red, yellow and
blue*, 1921

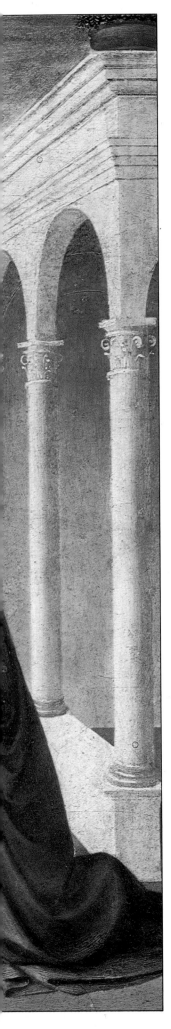

THE LANGUAGE OF PAINTING

"Organized perception is what art is all about"
— LICHTENSTEIN

(left) FRA ANGELICO: *The Annunciation*, c.1451-55; (above) DAUMIER: *The connoisseurs*, detail, c.1860-63

Introduction

How much sense does it make to speak of painting as a language? At least this much: painting, like language itself, is a means by which feelings and thoughts can be transmitted, and there is a real sense in which we can speak of paintings being read by those who have the necessary familiarity with the tradition and conventions being used.

The preceding pages have dealt with the content of pictures, with the culturally determined meanings of the images they contain. Here our concern is with the factors in painting that are common to all pictures, whether figurative or abstract, whether Western or from any other part of the world; factors to which we would continue to respond even if we had no notion what the picture was supposed to represent.

Certain basic associations of colour, line or shape are not specific to time, place or subject matter and many qualities in a painting may remind us of things in the outside world. Smooth, undulant lines, for instance, tend to evoke water; jagged ones suggest crags or lightning. Again, all humans lie down to sleep and are awake when they stand up. Thus verticality and horizontality have opposite associations, and diagonal lines tend to suggest imbalance, movement or dynamism. Circles or ovals call up associations with eyes or breasts or, in other contexts, with the sun, the moon or the totality of the universe. A painting with bright, contrasted colours and angular shapes will set up a mood and suggest meanings vastly different from one having soft colours and gentle curves. The interaction of colours, shapes and lines also creates purely optical sensations, to which everyone can respond.

Paintings may also show distinctive or characteristic features which indicate that they are the product of a particular time or place, or mind or hand – qualities summed up by the word "style". Style (which will be considered in more detail later) is essentially choice of means, whether on the part of an individual or an epoch – conscious or subconscious choice of a particular way of using a number of elements, such as colour, texture, form or shape, each of which ranges between extremes.

Colour is often the most compelling of these elements, but in a definable sense may be secondary to form. The proof is that a black-and-white photograph of a painting that has sublime colour may still convey many excellences of the original, while a mere chart, no matter how accurate, of the colour used, would, when detached from the forms, be largely meaningless even if very agreeable. Therefore this section deals first with all those properties in painting to which a black-and-white photograph would do some justice – what might be called structural properties.

In representational painting the formal means can help to bring out the subject matter, but in abstract painting these means are themselves the subject matter. Just as a composer uses the raw materials of musical sound to generate meaning independent of representation (though association and evocation are often very much part of the listener's experience), so the abstract painter affects us by arrangements of "pure" form, colour,

TONAL ANALYSIS
In all Old Master paintings from the High Renaissance until Neoclassicism, the distribution of light and shade is largely independent of, or contrapuntal to, the outlines of the solids, which therefore weave into and out of clear definition. In *Bacchus and Ariadne* light and shade imperceptibly merge, but in this simplified "map" only five degrees of tone are used, emphasizing the continual interplay of light and dark passages, which contributes so much to the painting's vitality, and simultaneously bringing out the subtle balance of its overall tonal structure – Titian's unity in variety.

PROPORTIONAL ANALYSIS
There is documentary proof that Titian was interested in the use of geometry and numbers for the systematic division of pictorial space. In his time mathematics was part of the training of painters as well as of architects. Here Titian has divided width and height into nine units and placed the main divisions at 4:9 and 6:9 each way. As will be explained later, this can be considered the spatial equivalent of the musical harmony of the double fifth. The bold geometric nature of the composition is further indicated by the diagonals which have been added to the basic grid pattern.

MOVEMENT ANALYSIS
Bacchus' desire for Ariadne and her startled reaction are expressed by Titian in vigorous, varied movement, the main axes of which are plotted here as white lines. The points indicate the direction in which we would normally follow them, though this is a variable since any axis, like any street, can be travelled two ways. But some of the readings are clear and unequivocal, for example that Bacchus' body moves towards Ariadne along the axis from his left foot to his head, whilst she twists spirally away from her right foot to right hand, checking and resolving the surging motion towards her.

shape or texture, which he might accordingly claim lie at the heart of the matter, since they are common to all painting, forming an underlying universal language.

The purpose of the following pages is to show how and to what extent it is possible to analyse this universal language by taking a painting to pieces and examining its distinguishing properties. In doing so, we should bear in mind that a thing dismantled is no longer itself. The parts of a motor-cycle laid out on the garage floor are not in a true sense a motor-cycle: they will not move us from place to place. A painting, when it moves us, does so not as a set of distinct elements but by virtue of the simultaneous interaction of a host of elements in a highly complex psychological event.

It may be argued that to analyse a work of art is to deprive it of a mystery that is its life. In opposition to this view the music critic Hans Keller asserts that "enjoyment is a function of understanding"; that the more we become aware of what are the affective elements in music the deeper and more total the communication and the more joyous in consequence. This section is written in conformity with Keller's view, and examines one by one the principal factors, elements or agencies that work on us in a painting. By way of sampling this approach, Titian's *Bacchus and Ariadne* is shown here along with three different analyses of it. It is a large and magnificent example of the work of one of Europe's greatest artists in his prime, and though Titian's mastery is so complete as to appear effortless the harmony it displays is the outcome of a very careful structural control which holds the dynamic movement in majestic balance. Knowledge of the formal language a painter has used can lead us to appreciate more clearly his intention as well as his achievement.

TITIAN
Bacchus and Ariadne,
1522–23

Scale and Space

Scale, which may be considered first in our list of pictorial values, is one of the most obvious qualities of a painting but by no means one of the most important. Sheer size can be impressive in itself, but no painting was ever good simply because it was large. Many very large paintings are pompous and empty; conversely, much can be conveyed in a very small area, as in a Vermeer or Hilliard.

The effects of scale on a viewer cannot be illustrated in a book and the main thing to be said about it is that it should suit the context, subject matter and purpose of the painting. The more public the destined role of the work the larger it normally needs to be. In domestic or non-public art a picture tends to seem big if it is two metres ($6\frac{1}{2}$ ft) or greater in its larger dimension and small if less than about 45 centimetres (18 in). At about 15 centimetres (6 in) it seems miniature. These, roughly, are the limits (judged very much in terms of human stature) within which a painter makes decisions about the size of a picture. Some mid-twentieth-century painters – Jackson Pollock was among the first – have used very big formats with the deliberate intention of preventing anyone at a normal viewing distance from taking the canvas all in one glance. The viewer is thus enveloped by the picture; being "in" almost more than looking at it – a drastically changed relationship.

With space we come to a category quite fundamental in the visual arts, whether two- or three-dimensional. The space of a painting is to begin with a blank, flat plane having two dimensions only. Normally, the plane is rectangular – a sheet of paper, a panel, a canvas. But if we make a mark of any kind on this plane – even a non-representational one such as a dash, a circle or a dab of colour – at once the surface is seen as having two generic elements. There is a "thing" and there is the space in which it seems to exist.

Perception psychologists use the word "figure" to denote what we perceive as thing and the word "ground" to denote the areas we read as surrounding air or void. They tell us that (largely for purposes of survival) we are programmed to perceive in figure-ground terms, and, as the diagrams here show, we instinctively read even the simplest visual images in this way. In situations where there are insufficient clues to indicate what is figure and what ground, our readings alternate, sometimes rapidly to give a sensation of flicker, as in Op Art.

The figure-ground interrelation is unambiguous and stable in nearly all figurative and much abstract painting. By symbolic extension, ground comes to stand for the entire set of circumstances in which a thing finds itself: and figure, therefore, tends to become the hero of the story, the creature in the predicament – indeed ourselves, to the extent that we identify with it. This is why the figure-ground, or spatial, relationship in a picture often betrays at deepest level the attitudes and outlook of the painter or the culture he represents. Lucid, orderly space, neither cluttered nor desolately blank, suggests a serene, balanced, optimistic personality or culture, whereas space that is confused, congested or

BLAKE (above)
Glad day, c. 1794
A mood of joy or optimism is irresistibly suggested in the relationship between the figure, dominating but not congesting the pictorial space, and the ground its energy seems to irradiate.

BECKMANN (above)
The trapeze, 1923
Here, figure does not so much dominate ground as seem to cram it with all the discomfort of urban life. Everywhere there is a compressed exasperation.

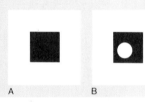

Our figure-ground readings often alternate: is (A) a black patch or square hole? (B) a white circle on black or square-plus-circle on white? (C) a white hook on black or black on white?

A   B

MUNCH (right)
Puberty, 1895
In opposition to Blake, Munch expresses a mood of anxiety and oppression by using ground (which stands for circumstance, life itself) to overbear and dominate figure. The girl intuitively foresees all the complexities and suffering ahead of her, and she cannot face them.

MALEVICH (left)
Composition, c. 1917
This is up-ness in abstract
form, offering release from
the implications of gravity.
A figurative example might
have been a soaring angel
or the resurrected Christ.

COROT (above)
A view near Volterra, 1838
The receding path winding
into the distance and the
rider moving away from us
conjure up all the pleasures

of travel. Moods of release,
opportunity, departure,
curiosity to know what lies
round the next corner, are
characteristic associations
of the "away" vector.

 In (D) the banisters that
look solid if we start at the
left become voids if read
from the right. Ambiguity is
three-dimensional in (E);
only the second image tells
us which square is in front.

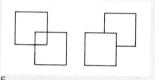

Height, width and depth
were the impersonal vectors
Descartes used to analyse
three-dimensional space,
but in pictorial space they
are charged with highly
differentiated meanings.

depopulated suggests anxiety, disturbance or neu-
rosis, whether individual or collective.

Mondrian observed, and we have all experienced, that vertical lines or shapes unrelieved by
horizontals, and vice versa, create a mood of
melancholy and oppression, while a balance between them is visually satisfying. The six major
directions in which figures can move or be aligned
in space – up, down, left, right, towards, away –
also have their own associations and moods. Up,
for instance, obviously evokes Heaven, exaltation,
aspiration, flight. Down, clearly, tends to the
opposite. Towards could be anything from a
threat to a welcome overture. In either case there is
a sense of intrusion or involvement, while away is
typically the direction of adventure and the unknown. Left and right are the comings and goings
we more or less detachedly observe around us:
though even these terms are not completely neutral or interchangeable: European paintings tend
to be read, like the written word, from left to right,
whereas in Chinese art the opposite holds true. In
paintings of the Annunciation, for example, the
angel almost always moved from the left towards
the Virgin on the right, although this can probably
be explained in terms of tradition and symbolism
as well as of fundamental pictorial psychology.

RUBENS (above)
The fall of the damned,
detail, *c.* 1614/18
Down, in the moral sense,
is the steep path to Hell
and damnation – a fall from
grace. But in principle
it could also symbolize
humility, earthliness or, in
other contexts, relaxation,
repose or weariness. It is,
at all events, a surrender
to gravitational force.

DELACROIX (above)
Liberty leading the people,
1830
The protagonists of this
superbly rhetorical picture
come unequivocally towards
us. With our personal space
thus invaded, we must
either turn and run (as
bourgeois reactionaries) or
join in (identifying with
the people's aspirations
for bread and freedom).

Types of Pictorial Space

There are many different ways in which space can be organized in paintings, but it may be helpful to classify them, however crudely, into three major modes. Not surprisingly, for reasons we have already discussed, methods of treating pictorial space tend to reflect the several ways in which reality is experienced by different artists.

The simplest kind of space is exemplified in the art of tribal cultures or in medieval heraldry, where the things represented are archetypal or conventional images rather than individualized representations of particular objects. The pictorial space in paintings of this kind – we might call it "totemic/magical/heraldic" space – is in essence two-dimensional. It cannot be quite strictly so, since "figure" (an heraldic lion for instance) must necessarily appear to be in front of "ground" (a field azure). But there is no illusory depth, much less perspective. There is little or no overlapping of shapes, and objects are presented in their most typical and informative aspect – frontal or side elevation or some combination of both. All shapes have definite boundaries completely filled with flat, clear, non-naturalistic colours: colours, that is, chosen for their symbolic significance and not transcribed from nature.

This kind of space shades off into a somewhat more complex kind that we might call "spiritual" space, for example that of Byzantine mosaics or icons. Here we find a greater degree of naturalism in the rendering of poses and drapery. Likewise there is more depth: objects overlap, and there is some modulation of colour from light to dark: they are no longer flat. The background, however, is unmodulated blazing gold, and does not represent any actual physical space; it is the space of hearing rather than sight – of attention to the word. In such paintings, the artist is concerned less with showing things as they might look in the everyday world than with making a visual list of things that belong together in the concept we are invited to meditate upon. To use Professor Ernst Gombrich's term, these are "what" paintings – mainly about what belongs with what in a certain hierarchy of ideas.

"Naturalistic or optical" space presents the "how" view: how things look or happen from a single point of view – more or less as we perceive them in everyday life. Apart from some fore-shadowings in Roman art, this kind of space does not occur in European painting until Gothic times. Giotto and Duccio grasped it, but did not as yet make it systematic. Early Renaissance painters perfected it as the science of perspective and it remained the norm until Cézanne modified it and the Cubists virtually attempted to abolish it. It is often, and for good reason, referred to as "Renaissance" space.

In the early Renaissance, space was organized

TINTORETTO (right)
Bacchus and Ariadne, 1578
Tintoretto's swooping and
spiralling figures, their
complex poses made to seem
effortlessly attained, are
typically Mannerist in the
way in which they move so
freely in depth as well as
across the picture surface.

AUSTRIAN SCHOOL (below)
*The Trinity with Christ
crucified*, 15th century
The space in this painting,
and in much other medieval
art, has a certain minimal
depth, but it is consecrated
space charged with spiritual
energies, with relationships
of scale quite different
from those of everyday life.

HARUNOBU (above)
*The evening bell of the
clock*, c. 1766
The space here owes its
character to diagonality. The
parallels do not converge
as in "correct" perspective,
and the two graceful ladies
seem almost to float, at one
with their surroundings.

TURNER (right)
Norham Castle: sunrise,
c. 1835–40
It is most unlikely that the
painter of the Tlingit bear
could have understood this
painting. With our cultural
background, however, we are
able to read these luminous
filmy washes and to feel the
depth they so subtly convey.

in layers parallel to the picture plane, normally in
three distinct areas identifiable as foreground,
middle distance and background, but during the
sixteenth century this calm, lucidly articulated
arrangement was increasingly abandoned in
favour of slewed, oblique structurings in which the
solids are dynamically diagonal to the picture
plane and the viewer's line of vision. This is the
space characteristic – though with different degrees of logicality – of the Mannerist and Baroque
periods. It is highly illusionistic when compared
with Byzantine space, and invites us to take off into
heady, if always ultimately controlled, convo-

lutions in an apparently deep pictorial space.

A quieter kind of slewed or oblique space is
frequently found in Japanese art, and often the
effect is to make us feel that we have accidently
happened upon an everyday domestic occurrence.
It is the very opposite of the monumental, and sets
up a mood of delicate casualness.

A painter has at his command, besides over-
lappings and diagonals, still further resources for
the attainment of depth in pictorial space, another
of which is called "atmospheric" or "aerial"
perspective. This exploits the fact that, because of
the density of the atmosphere, objects look paler
and more bluish in colour the farther away they are
from the spectator. Leonardo, who invented the
term aerial perspective, was one of the first to
explore its possibilities, although the phenomenon
had been discussed by Ptolemy as early as the
second century AD. The intensely blue distances
found in the work of some of Leonardo's immediate followers often look artificial, but later
painters, especially in northern Europe, where the
atmosphere is generally hazier and the effects of
light more varied, became much more subtle in
their observation and depiction of the effects of
aerial perspective. In some of Turner's most
daring late works the atmosphere itself is almost
the subject of the painting and the sole means of
creating pictorial space.

Projection

All painters who seek to represent objects in three-dimensional space are confronted at the outset by a paradox. Unlike sculptors, they have at their disposal only a two-dimensional surface, so they must resort to one or another of a set of possible subterfuges that will describe three dimensions while using only two.

These subterfuges can collectively be called projections: "throwing forward", literally, of solids until they meet a plane surface and assume a flat shape. The mode of projection with which we are nowadays most familiar, optical perspective, is considered overleaf. It is a recent development in history, not having been systematically formulated until the early Renaissance in Italy, so we should, before coming to it, look at projection as it was practised before the Renaissance, and as it has once more been practised by modern painters who, impressed with the power and grandeur of primitive art, have abandoned Renaissance perspective in search of something more timeless, conceptual and archetypal.

To the right are set out, in diagrammatic form, the main *non-perspectival* types of projection. A simple chair-like object made of cubic blocks is taken as the test case, and placed upon its seat are a sphere and cylinder. It is drawn in seven logical and consistent projections and a final lawless and arbitrary one.

There are two criteria for assessing any of these methods. Firstly, one can consider its value as information: how much does it convey, and how clearly, about the object's shape; what items of information are concealed, distorted or ambiguous? Secondly, there can be an aesthetic appraisal: does a given method produce ugly shapes or awkwardness in "reading" it? This second kind of judgment, however, cannot be made in the artificial context of a diagram, but only in that of a work of art which uses the method in question. And in practice it is unusual to find a painting deploying a single method systematically. The Persian miniature reproduced here is parti-

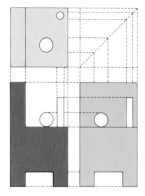

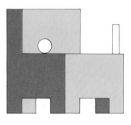

Strict plan, side elevation and front elevation give us accurate information about dimensions (hence their traditional use in architects' drawings) but here only side elevation conveys much about the *look* of the structure represented.

Here side elevation and plan are fitted together. The information has the same level of accuracy as before, but, because the side and top surfaces adjoin, the visual appearance of the structure is more effectively conveyed.

This is another combination of elements from the first group: side elevation combined with elevational views of frontal planes. This is more like the chair we might see, but strictly the sphere and the cylinder should each appear twice.

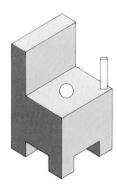

The side elevation is now combined with frontal planes which actively contradict a normal perspective view by diverging. The look is somewhat improbable, but this convention is often used in pre-Renaissance, modern and non-European art for the depiction of depth.

This is the reverse of the preceding system, with some convergence of the frontal planes as they recede. It is very close to orthodox perspective, except that the intervals between the horizontal planes are rather wider than they would be in a strict perspective drawing.

This is an isometric projection where both frontal planes and side elevation are shown at an oblique angle to the horizontal. It is frequently used by architects on account of its exceptionally high level of information and readability in three-dimensional terms.

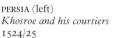

PERSIA (left)
Khosroe and his courtiers
1524/25
The painter of this miniature has suggested depth in a number of different ways. The varied methodologies are held together by a superb sense of texture, pattern and decorative placement to create pictorial unity.

CHAGALL (right)
The birthday, 1915
Chagall here uses, with wonderful freedom and confidence, as many kinds of projection as he chooses, creating a space which accords beautifully with the almost gravity-free choreography of the figures, in poetic disjunction.

cularly rich in inconsistencies. The carpet on four posts which serves as a canopy is tilted obliquely to indicate that it projects over the throne, yet it is shown in full plan. The throne itself is partly in reversed perspective and partly in a convention resembling isometric. The floor tiles and the carpet on which the throne rests are in strict plan whilst the figures are shown in elevation. The Chagall painting also displays a wide variety of projection systems, and in Braque's painting we see several views of the violin from differing angles freely combined in one image. The Egyptian mural is comparatively restrained in that only two kinds of projection are used – strict elevation (trees, fish, people) and strict plan (the pond). In the Chinese example the idea of parallel lines being shown as parallels is applied throughout, but not with overall consistency, for there is no logical pattern in the differing angles of the lines of floor tiles and roofs.

What can be said in general about all the types of projections so far mentioned is that they give primacy not to what the artist optically perceives of the object represented but to what he may know of it – a knowledge gained not simply by standing in one place and looking at it, but by walking round it, touching it, measuring it, hearing it described, fully experiencing it.

The representation in art of this multi-sensory and multi-active kind of knowing tended to diminish after artists in Florence in the early fifteenth century began to observe and represent the world in a scientific way. Since the beginning of the twentieth century, however, artists have progressively resuscitated older modes, stimulated by revolutions in modern physics and cosmology, especially relativity and quantum theory, which have upset earlier certitudes about the nature of the universe. The first signs are observable in Post-Impressionism, especially in Cézanne. These insights were seized upon and developed by the Cubists, establishing new freedoms for themselves and for others such as Chagall.

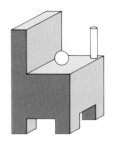

Here the side elevation is combined with an oblique presentation of the frontal planes. This recalls perspective, but the edges of these planes are parallel, not convergent, and thus in a sense give a truer image than linear perspective.

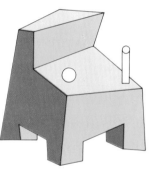

Whereas all the preceding projections adhered to a consistent policy, this one deliberately flouts all logic, but is still readable as a chair-like object. Distortions of this kind are common in the work of Picasso and other moderns as in the Braque opposite.

BRAQUE
Pitcher and violin, 1910
Braque's violin is a particularly clear example of the multiple viewpoints used by the Cubists to express the idea of an object rather than simulate its appearance. The scroll of the head is seen in side elevation, the far pegs in plan, the neck in three-quarter view, the near shoulder or *bout* in frontal elevation – inconsistently with the amount of side planes visible – and so on. Thus might a fly see it if buzzing round it this way and that, up and down – a restless dynamic image, but rich in compositional value as well as in the amount of information it conveys about the third dimension without suggesting recession.

THEBES (left)
Garden with pond
XVIIIth dynasty, c. 1400 BC
Two kinds of projection, plan and elevation, are here used in what today might be considered mutual contradiction. Clearly it is a presentation not of how things look, but rather of what they essentially are.

CHINA (right)
From *The Mustard Seed Garden Manual of Painting; Winding veranda and porches of a palace*, c. 1679
A high viewpoint and what we might call "parallel perspective" were among the traditional conventions of Chinese painting in scenes involving buildings.

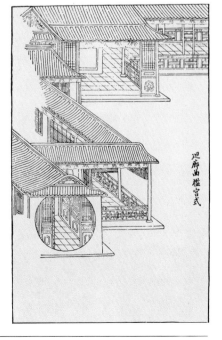

Perspective

The term perspective is sometimes used in a broad sense to encompass projection systems in general, but here we are concerned with it in the narrow sense of what is sometimes called optical perspective. This quasi-mathematical system, invented in Florence in the early fifteenth century, uses as its basis the fact that parallel lines appear to converge and objects appear to become smaller the farther they are from the viewer. This "lie" does not trouble us in the least; we have been mentally adjusted to it all our lives, and it is impossible to imagine vision working at all if, for example, a horse three fields away appeared the same size as one we were standing next to. The perspective system of representing three-dimensional objects on a two-dimensional surface so as to give a naturalistic effect of spatial recession became one of the cornerstones of European painting for nearly five centuries.

Parallel lines that appear to converge, for example the margins of a straight highway when we look along its central axis, will eventually recede to meet at the level of our eyes. This is known as the horizon line, and the points at which any receding parallel lines appear to meet on it are called vanishing points. A form such as the block-chair we saw on the preceding page will, unless seen completely flat on, have one vanishing point to our left and a second to our right. Greek knowledge of vanishing-point perspective and foreshortening formed a basis for medieval artists who, during the fourteenth century, began trying to construct a realistic picture space with consistent recession from foreground to background. The placing and correct relative sizes of figures, especially in the middle distance, were a constant problem until Brunelleschi and Alberti formulated geometric rules for the convergence of parallels and the proportional reduction of objects.

Though "correct" perspective based on these strict rules can give a highly convincing illusion of three-dimensional space with the picture seeming like a window through which one looks, in certain

THE CONE OF VISION
Distant objects appear smaller than near ones, as light rays travel towards the eye in narrowing cones of vision – an effect shown by the image sizes on the glass screen upon which the artist is tracing. He is using a device described by Dürer to draw accurately by sighting a mark through a peep-hole attached to a line which ensures that his viewpoint remains consistent.

CHIRICO
Sinister Muses, 1917
This is the equivocal deep space of a dream, made disturbing not only by the imagery but by the lack of consistency in perspective convergence, despite the emphasis on it. As shown in the diagram, the vanishing points indicated by the box in the foreground, the shadowy *palazzo* on the right and the receding lines on the pavement are not mutually reconcilable.

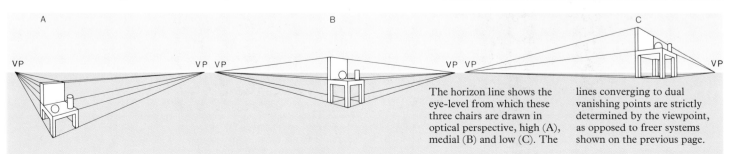

The horizon line shows the eye-level from which these three chairs are drawn in optical perspective, high (A), medial (B) and low (C). The lines converging to dual vanishing points are strictly determined by the viewpoint, as opposed to freer systems shown on the previous page.

RAPHAEL
"The School of Athens",
1509–11
Too obtrusive a perspective
effect can punch such a
hole in the surface of the
picture that unless some
counter-measures are taken
to restore our sense of its
real flatness we are left

with a certain queasiness.
When the group of figures
is removed from Raphael's
painting, the illusion of
depth becomes disturbingly
tunnel-like. Conversely, the
removal of the architectural
features deprives the figures
of much of their solidity
and depth. Raphael disposed

them in a row parallel to
the picture plane to main-
tain an appropriate balance
with the architecture, and
it is only when these two
elements of the painting
are combined that the
composition comes together
to create a sense of serene
and monumental grandeur.

respects it is misleading, not least in that it is
monocular. It assumes a viewer who has one eye
only, held in a fixed stare straight ahead. This is
what the artist in the illustration above is doing in
order to plot his model accurately on the in-
terposed transparent screen. He has rigged up a
peep-hole almost like a gun-sight and has to shut
one eye to look through it.

Anybody could similarly trace the view through
a window by outlining it on the pane without
changing position. But this, of course, is highly
unnatural: we are endowed with binocular, hence
stereoscopic vision; our eyes are continually and
rapidly scanning our surroundings; and we move
our heads frequently. Thus optical perspective
from a fixed viewpoint can, unless carefully managed, seem quite out of accord with our experience. It is because the camera behaves like a
single fixed human eye that amateurs are so often
disappointed by prints of their earliest snapshot –
an impressive building, perhaps, shrunk to the size
of a pea in an acreage of boring foreground. Yet the
camera has faithfully recorded what was in the
viewfinder. The fault lay in the photographer's
unawareness that seeing is at least as much a
function of movement and selective attention as of
optical laws or geometric plots.

In fact, few painters use perspective in a rigidly
systematic way. In Raphael's *"The School of
Athens"*, for example, the architecture is seen from
a central viewpoint and hence has a single central
vanishing point, but each figure is painted as if
seen from directly in front. The sphere which
Ptolemy holds at the right of the painting would
look like an ellipse if it were seen in the same
perspective as the architecture, but such a distortion would look absurd in this context. Most
artists work within a fairly narrow angle of vision,
between about 30° and 60°, so the problems of
marginal distortion are rarely acute.

Devices such as lessening convergence and
spreading out vanishing points into vanishing
areas can also help to soften the harsh effect of
perspective – nowhere more so than in architectural scenes with large buildings close up on one
or both flanks. Only too easily this produces sharp,
stabbing diagonals and thin, mean shapes where
there are doors and windows. At a philosophical
level it could be argued that optical perspective
implies a narrowing of outlook, an over-
simplification of the complex and partly mysterious process by which we see the world, positing
as it does optical experience as the sole source of
visual art and implicitly downgrading other kinds
of knowing, such as the evidence of other senses
and knowledge built up over time.

These drawbacks notwithstanding, perspective
has inspired and made possible – especially in the
early Renaissance, when it was a new and exciting
revelation – some majestic spatial compositions by
painters such as Masaccio, Uccello and Piero della
Francesca. Surrealists who have readopted it, even
though often in breach of the rules, have been able
to accomplish marvels in evoking the nostalgia or
terror of the dream, the wistful strangeness of
spatial recession.

Viewpoint

TINTORETTO (left)
The Ascension, 1583-87
In traditional versions the apostles are arranged evenly at a distance from the painter's central standpoint. Tintoretto, however, with innovative audacity, moves one apostle to the front at the extreme left, putting us immediately in touch with his feelings and making us adopt the same oblique, surprised viewpoint.

VERTICAL AXIS

PAINTER'S VIEWPOINT	HIGH	LOW	MEDIAL
ASSOCIATIONS	Superiority	Humility	Equality: candour: straightforwardness
ADVANTAGES	Inclusiveness: high degree of information	Impressive looming of vertical features	Closeness to normal experience
DRAWBACKS	Danger of excessive remoteness: "Olympian" detachment	Reduction of information through masking of distant objects by nearer ones.	Less information spatially than high viewpoint

RUBENS (above)
The Madonna adored by saints, 1607
The low, close-up, central viewpoint of this full-bloodedly rhetorical work puts the viewer just where the Catholic authorities wanted him – overawed and compliant, towered over by

civil and ecclesiastical powers that stand firmly between him and the grace of the Heavenly Powers. The contrast could hardly be greater with the De Hoogh alongside, a picture that comes from democratic non-aristocratic Holland, egalitarian in its outlook.

DE HOOGH (above)
The courtyard of a house in Delft, 1658
This sets us on the level of the people portrayed. Neither confronting them abruptly nor catching them sidelong, we meet them at a respectful distance, and as equals, in pleasantly domesticity.

In any figurative picture that uses naturalistic space, the viewpoint of the painter is of great significance. He can place himself in greater or lesser degree above his subject, looking down on it so that the horizon, actual or implied, will occur high up on the picture plane. Or he can be below his subject, looking up at it, in which case the horizon on which all parallel lines converge will be near the lower edge. Or again he can be approximately level with what is going on, locating the horizon somewhere near midpoint. Like a film cameraman placing his equipment, he may also move to left or right of his subject, approach it or move back, and focus interest at varying points on the several axes plotted in the table above.

Such placements are usually carefully calculated, and can have a strong influence on the effect of the picture. For instance, a high viewpoint puts the painter (and therefore the viewer) in a superior or commanding position, with a "God's-eye" view. It also encourages analytical clarity, since it facilitates visual separation of elements, as when we look down upon a city from a cathedral tower. By the same argument, a low horizon, or "worm's-eye" view, puts us in a stance of humility before something grand and awesome, as when we view a cathedral from street level or a mountain range from the plains. But if the horizon is midway or thereabouts, we are on even terms with reality.

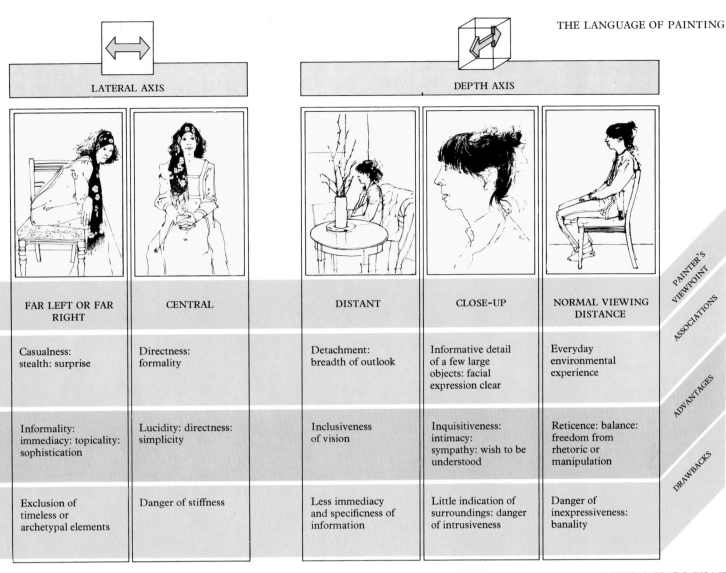

	LATERAL AXIS		DEPTH AXIS			
PAINTER'S VIEWPOINT	FAR LEFT OR FAR RIGHT	CENTRAL	DISTANT	CLOSE-UP	NORMAL VIEWING DISTANCE	
ASSOCIATIONS	Casualness: stealth: surprise	Directness: formality	Detachment: breadth of outlook	Informative detail of a few large objects: facial expression clear	Everyday environmental experience	
ADVANTAGES	Informality: immediacy: topicality: sophistication	Lucidity: directness: simplicity	Inclusiveness of vision	Inquisitiveness: intimacy: sympathy: wish to be understood	Reticence: balance: freedom from rhetoric or manipulation	
DRAWBACKS	Exclusion of timeless or archetypal elements	Danger of stiffness	Less immediacy and specificness of information	Little indication of surroundings: danger of intrusiveness	Danger of inexpressiveness: banality	

PIETER BRUEGEL THE ELDER (below) *Netherlandish proverbs*, 1559
The high viewpoint adopted by Bruegel in most of his large paintings enables him to reveal an amazing wealth of characterization and explicit detail, all the more evident here as he stands well to the right and so sees a receding as well as a frontal side of each structure. No painter has a more all-embracing vision of contemporary social life, yet his spatial remoteness from his subject is in no way cold but rather alive with affection and humour.

DUBUFFET (right)
Business prospers, 1961
In feigning the innocent eye of a child, Dubuffet has abandoned all specific viewpoint. Depicting each figure, vehicle, building or sign in plan, lateral or frontal aspect, he is every-where in the city at once.

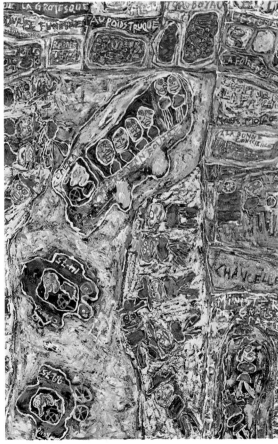

Volume, Mass and Gravity

In discussing the space of painting, we have considered so far mainly the stage upon which pictorial events are enacted. Here attention is turned to the actors themselves, and the props they move amongst; to the items classifiable as "figure" as opposed to "ground".

Much depends on whether these items – human figures, buildings, landscape features, utensils or whatever – are conceived as more or less flat shapes merely indicative or reminiscent of the third dimension or, on the other hand, are fully described and modelled-up solids. For when we reflect on the history of painting we are brought up against the realization that only the Western European tradition, and that only since Giotto, has resolutely grappled with the problem of rendering solids on a two-dimensional surface and giving them full realization in terms of volume, mass and gravity.

These three terms are necessary to the discussion of Western paintings to a degree they scarcely are outside it. The series of diagrams on the right explains the distinction between volume and mass and makes it clear why mass is closely correlated with gravity: quite simply, if you infill a volume you have a mass and it is going to weigh more. Lines and shapes on a flat surface may themselves indicate volume and weight, but the principal means of suggesting mass in a painting is by the use of tonal shading in relation to a fixed light source (see p. 116). That Western painting has made artistically valid, not to say profound and poetic, use of fully described and massive solids should perhaps be reckoned as one of its greatest achievements: and clearly the phenomena of volume, mass and gravity would not have been used at all in art (important though they have always been in physics and mechanics) if they were not capable of carrying a meaning, did not have a range of expressive possibilities.

Nor are these meanings abstruse or far to seek;

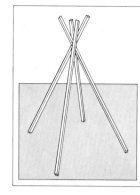

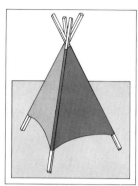

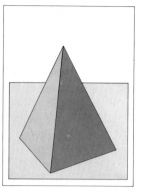

The four splayed sticks define a space which, unlike the space within a hoop, say, has a three-dimensional volume but one that contains only air.

If the sticks are covered with fabric to make a kind of tepee, the volume becomes actual rather than spatial or conceptual, but it is a volume without mass.

The same pyramidal volume acquires mass when it is filled in with solid matter. Conversely, one who makes a canoe out of a log makes a volume out of a mass.

VELAZQUEZ
The water-carrier of Seville, c. 1619
This is the poetry of containment: water fills both clay jars and the delicate conical glass; thirst, no doubt, fills the boy's spherical head. Each form, indeed the entire picture space, is conceived in terms of volume, brought out by shape, line and the fall of light and shade. In the diagram, line is used to analyse the structure of the most volumetric forms, and the lighting scheme is shifted from the left to the front to make tonally clearer the strong three-dimensionality Velazquez has so subtly indicated (compare diagram on p. 116).

WATTEAU (left)
Love in the French theatre,
c. 1719
The actors, their centres
of gravity high, their
bodies tapering to points,
seem to rise weightlessly,
poised in a floating dance.

MILLET (below)
The gleaners, 1857
The downward pull of the
earth is stressed by the
widening of forms as they
bow towards the ground, the
stumpy hands, the darkening
of tone near the lower edge.

they are very much what we would expect. Physical weight or weighed-down-ness stand metaphorically for those same conditions experienced at psychological, philosophical or metaphysical levels. We have already noted some of the associations of the down direction on an up/down axis. Mass and weight have been used by painters to signify such qualities as immovable stability in mountains, buildings or even solid citizens and also – especially in the great seventeenth-century portrayals of life among poor folk by Rembrandt, Velazquez, Zurbaran, de La Tour and the Le Nains – the sense of closeness to the earth and of being relentlessly pulled down into it by toil, deprivation and weary melancholy. In the eighteenth century, Chardin, though his *dramatis personae* are mostly contented bourgeois, gives them (and their kitchen-ware) full gravitational reality. Watteau, by contrast, endows his aristocratic dalliers with a Mozartian light-footedness bordering at times on levitation. Later, in the peasants of Jean-François Millet, the feeling of mass and weight is inescapable.

On the other hand it has been a major enterprise of twentieth-century art to negate gravity, to break up mass and to propose quite other and much less corporeal philosophies of the material world. Cubism, pre-eminently, allows mass and space, figure and ground, to interpenetrate freely and demands that we apprehend volume in terms of shifting, impalpable planes or edges rather than of enwrapment by a continuous surface. Constructivism (see vol. 3 p. 162) goes still further, giving us, in effect, a void with a shape to it. In Constructivist sculpture and architecture the shape tends to be complex and full of open-plan interpenetrations of volumes. In many abstract paintings, the spaces are equally free and interpenetrating, but susceptible to many interpretations. Thus disarmed, the mind is left free to play with multiple possibilities and sensations.

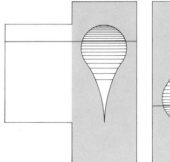

By simple reversal, the shape that seems to rise and float like a hot-air balloon falls like a teardrop when its centre of gravity (blue line) is shifted from high to low. Hatching enhances the effect, as the eye follows the direction of any visual gradients.

HARTUNG (below)
Composition, 1936
Without clues to location in depth, we know only that the lines must be in front of the patches of colour. The shapes simply float, ignoring gravity, and mass is banished. Dematerialization is wellnigh complete.

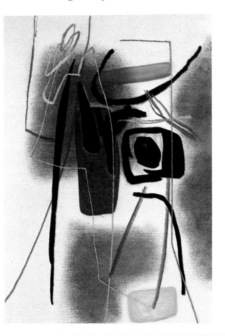

PICASSO (above)
Daniel Henry Kahnweiler,
1910
Some of the clues here are unequivocal – features of Kahnweiler's face, clothes, folded hands, the shape of a bowl and vase. They serve to indicate that the picture is not abstract but renders the spatial experience of the sitter's presence in the reconstituted form of a rising and receding stack of planes penetrated by air.

Line, Shape, Contour, Articulation

In the history of painting there is a significant dichotomy between artists who express themselves through line and those whose basic vision and pictorial construction is in terms of areas. The art historian and theorist Heinrich Wölfflin applied to these ways of seeing and creating the terms "linear" and "painterly": Botticelli well exemplifies the first type, Velazquez the second. Many other great European painters, most notably Rembrandt and Titian, also very clearly belong to the painterly category, especially in their mature work, but line undoubtedly has a kind of basic and primal quality, a descriptive power and magical intrigue which gives it unchallengeable importance in all visual art.

Line is intimately associated with motion, for in following lines with our eyes we tend to endow them with movement. We also judge lines in relation to the force of gravity, perceiving some to be in a state of equilibrium and others – diagonals for instance – to be dynamic. Even the simplest line or arrangement of lines, then, carries with it the suggestion of meaning and depending on the delicacy or force of the painter's brush may suggest anything from dawdling indolence to harsh, stabbing violence.

When a line turns and meets up with itself it generates shape, whether a frankly two-dimensional area like, say, the diamond on a playing-card, or the flat projection of a solid object, for example the man in the road sign warning us that works are in progress. "Contour" refers to the boundary of any such shape, or the outer limits of a three-dimensional shape as seen from any given angle. Broadly speaking we might say that all painting, however mass-based in conception, must arrive at a contour that satisfies our sense of shape. Mass, though often a powerful element in painting, is not a necessary one, being absent or understated in most pre-Renaissance, modern, and non-European art. The exquisite Roman fresco *Maiden gathering flowers* is a case in point. The girl has, it is true, a measure of weight and mass, but if she were reduced to contour alone, much of her enchantment would survive. Some forms of painting, for example certain types of Greek vases or Regency silhouettes, rely for their effect entirely on contour; its expressive power is superbly illustrated here by Modigliani's nude, whose swelling roundness is conveyed with a minimum of modelling.

By "articulation" we mean the manner in which contiguous shapes or forms join. This can vary a great deal from painter to painter. Buffet shows us a hard, brittle world where it seems some shock might cause everything to crack and fall, whilst Michelangelo joins form to form so toughly that nothing could shake them asunder. In a word, the dichotomy is between the inorganic on the one hand – or in our times the mechanical – and the organic and growing on the other. Hence the choice a painter makes in respect of these two extremes when he sets about joining forms is often, as with other kinds of option, ultimately philosophic, telling us something about his view of the world and relationship with it.

BOTTICELLI (near right)
Venus and Mars, detail,
c. 1485
VELAZQUEZ (far right)
Portrait of a man, detail,
c. 1640
Botticelli creates his forms with clear, precise lines, using only very slight shading to help indicate the roundness of the face. In the supremely painterly approach of Velazquez there are no outlines, and the forms merge imperceptibly with each other; the strong contour of the nose is suggested purely through the subtle modulations of tone Velazquez achieves with his unerring brushwork.

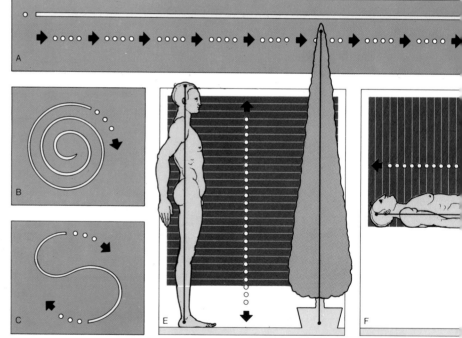

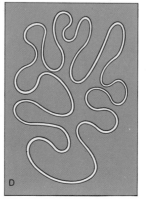

LINE AND MOTION
A line has traditionally been thought of as a trace left by a moving point (A) and we tend to follow lines with our eyes in one direction or another, and even mentally to continue them beyond the point at which they end (B, C); but if the movement of the line becomes too complex we tend to lose interest and cease to follow it (D). This sense of motion which is generated by line is intimately connected with the force of gravity, for there is a vast difference in association (and hence symbolic or expressive quality) between verticals, horizontals and diagonals. Verticality (E) is associated with alertness, daytime, potential activity, dominion; horizontality (F) with repose, night, sleep, submission. We associate diagonals (G) with imbalance, movement and energy, as in the dynamic art of the Baroque.

MICHELANGELO (below left)
The Sistine Chapel ceiling:
The creation of Adam, 1511
BUFFET (below right)
Artist and model, 1948
Michelangelo's tremendous
figure of Adam and Buffet's
stick-insect-like image of
himself represent opposite
extremes of articulation.
The fluent, cohesive rhythm
of Adam's body suggests his
wakening power, the resilient
knitting together of youthful
muscles, sinews and tendons.
Buffet presents himself
to us as a pathetic hinge-
jointed marionette, hardly
more substantial than the
easel at which he stands.
The confidence of the one
image, the anxiety of the
other, relate directly to
their differing articulation.

In nature forms rarely meet
at sharp angles: a gradual
merging of contours is
characteristic, as when a
tree spreads out into its
root formation. A roman
letter with its serifs, as
distinct from a modern block
letter, imitates this kind
of organic articulation.

MODIGLIANI (below)
Reclining nude, c. 1919
There is enough modelling
only to prevent the taut
outline from creating a
sense of flatness. Yet the
figure's flowing articulation
suggests the solidity and
suppleness of the forms.

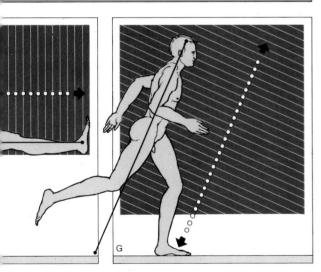

STABIAE, ITALY (left)
Maiden gathering flowers,
1st century AD
This mural, found near
Pompeii and one of the most
precious survivals of
ancient painting, is a
triumph of linear design.
The contour of the figure,
sometimes called *Flora* or
Spring, embodies graceful
contrasts between curves
of the arm and shoulder and
the rippling silhouette of
the drapery, creating a
mobile and expressive effect.

Visual Dynamics

On the preceding page we noted that diagonal lines, and in consequence diagonally oriented shapes, have a dynamic and kinetic quality due to their imbalance in relation to the force of gravity. But the seemingly energized nature of some shapes has other causes as well, and these may conveniently be called the visual dynamics of shape.

For the time being, shape is considered only in terms of flat areas – as a two-dimensional way of looking; the dynamics of form in deep space will be considered later. But, whatever the illusionary deep-space structure in a picture, its component forms must, except in a relief, arrive on the painted surface as flat entities, and must function aesthetically as such.

How then do flat areas or shapes behave? To understand this we must revert to what was said earlier about the basic dualism of figure and ground. All painting, looked at from this point of view, becomes a sort of dialectic or argument between these two elements – and the metaphor of arguments is not inappropriate, as there does seem to be a kind of mutual aggression between them. More often than not a shape (figure), if we look at it prolongedly, appears to want to expand relative to the surrounding space (ground): whilst ground, reciprocally, seems to counter-attack figure at its weakest points.

In the diagrams at the top of the page, the outward, positive, penetrative thrusts of figure into ground – the visual equivalent of what are called *Yang* forces in Chinese philosophy – are plotted in light blue; the countervailing inward *Yin* pressures (are they a sort of embrace?) are in grey. A figure leaves longer exposed flanks, and has progressively greater vulnerability towards its centre the further it extends itself in a spearhead

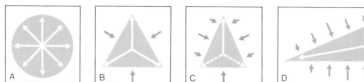

SHAPE DYNAMICS

The circle (A) is the only shape that is uniformly convex, hence uniformly positive in relation to ground; it expands in all directions equally. The equilateral triangle (B) stabs into space at each of its corners, with some degree of negative pressure along the sides. The more acute corner at the top of the scalene triangle (C) generates a greater thrust there than at the other two corners. A long spear-like isosceles triangle (D) increases the thrust at its most acute corner. There is correspondingly greater negative

pressure on the long sides. The corners of the square (E), which are marginally blunter than those of the triangles, have slightly less outward thrust, and a more stable balance of positive and negative forces. A heavier negative build-up occurs along the extended sides of a long rectangle (F), which begins to lose outer thrust at the corners and to develop some thrust along its central axis. The final, narrow rectangle (G) acquires a strong axial thrust and still more marked lateral vulnerability. It is this effect which is countered by slight swelling in the column shown at the right.

attack on the space that we perceive as ground.

This is not mere fancy, but rather a psychological constant built into our perceptual apparatus. Columns in classical architecture were designed with a slight swelling towards the centre, a procedure called *entasis*, to counteract the impression of concavity and hence instability which perfectly straight-sided columns would create. The Corinthian column from a Roman temple in North Africa (above right) is an example. Such an optical corrective would be impossibly costly nowadays: hence the tendency of some contemporary tower blocks to seem slightly waisted when they are viewed from certain angles.

In painting, the behaviour of shapes does not depend exclusively on their contours, promontories and axial thrusts, but also on relationships of tone and colour. The general rule is that a shape's expansiveness will be increased if the local colour is light or warm relative to its ground, and diminished when these relationships are reversed. In both paintings illustrated here, certain areas stand out brilliantly from their darker or cooler backgrounds and tend to look less static than the surrounding shapes.

Visual dynamics in positive and negative terms are not difficult to recognize when shapes are painted flatly, without modelling, as in Arp's *Configuration*. In order to reveal the two-dimensional dynamics of the forms in non-abstract painting, however, it is often necessary to try to think away the impression of three-dimensionality and depth which the artist has created by tonality. In Titian's "*Noli Me Tangere*", for example, it is only when the figures of Christ and Mary Magdalen are artificially flattened in the diagram that we become aware how much the theme of the painting is inherent in the shapes created by their expressive outlines.

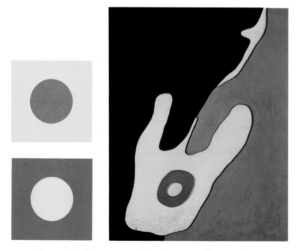

ARP (above right)
Configuration: Navel, shirt and head, 1926
The liveliness of this painted plywood relief is created largely by the dynamics of the contrasted blue and yellow shapes which interpenetrate deeply, as land and sea penetrate each other in promontories and estuaries. There are some spatial ambiguities – black seems to overlap at

the top, yellow at the bottom – but overall the tonally light and warm yellow areas seem the most expansionary. The effect of colour on shape dynamics is made clearer in the two adjoining diagrams. Whereas the yellow ground seems to curb the naturally expansive shape of the blue circle, making it retreat or shrink, if the colours are reversed the circle seems to swell.

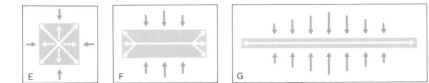

TITIAN (left)
"Noli Me Tangere", *c.* 1512
Christ appears to Mary
Magdalen on the morning
of his resurrection, and
as she reaches out towards
him, gently withdraws with
the words "Touch me not".
The visual dynamics of
the underlying shapes of
the two figures are shown
in the accompanying diagram,
the long arrows indicating
the main axes of thrust.
Christ's mantle is shown
in a different tone from
his body because we can
consider the shape he
generates either with or
without it. The interplay of
thrust and counter-thrust
is varied, but the essential
nature of the confrontation
is an attack by the compact
lower shape on the more
vulnerable upright shape,
which seems to give and
move towards the left. A
drama is enacted even
without colour and detail.

Movement

VASARELY (above)
Lomblin, 1951–56
Vasarély's title gives
nothing away, and according
to one reading the picture
is static, with the inden-
tations in the two black
shapes defining an invisible
white square. Yet the more

immediate impression is
of a balloon-like form
rising from a space it has
vacated on the ground –
the upward movement being
suggested irresistibly by
the two little "fins" and
the high centre of gravity
of the floating shape.

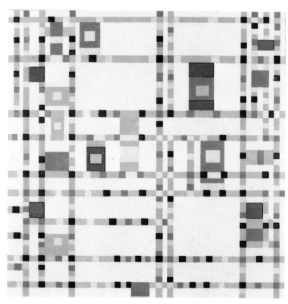

MONDRIAN
Broadway Boogie-Woogie,
1942–43
Mondrian was delighted by
the ordered animation of
New York. Here we might be
looking down on a grid of
streets, the small squares
representing the stop-go
of the traffic while the

larger rectangles are the
major buildings, monuments
or squares. Only verticals
or horizontals (the most
static of directions) are
used, but the restless
dance of our visual per-
ception from one coloured
patch to another gives a
sense of energy and motion.

The word movement, when used in the context of
painting, can have a variety of meanings, few of
them literal, because the contents of a painting do
not move in reality; any appearance of movement
must necessarily be illusory – a psychological or
perceptual event rather than a physical one. On
the other hand, looking at a painting can be – and is
often designed to be – a highly active event as our
attention is led from one area to another.

We have already looked at three kinds of perceptual events that imply some sort of movement:
the tendency of our eyes to track along and even
extend lines; the off-balance dynamism of diagonals; and the apparent directional thrusts of
shapes such as sharp-pointed triangles. These
perceptual forces were grouped together under the
heading of visual dynamics, and dynamics of this
kind are normally used by painters whenever they
wish to convey impressions of motion and change.
A glance at the pictures on this page will show a
wealth of such activity.

Apart from the vitality generated by the thrusts
and counter-thrusts of shapes or lines, the main
kinds of pictorial treatment which in one way or
another convey or evoke movement are five, beginning with the most obvious kind, depicted movement – the representation of things arrested in
mid-action in such a way that we can tell they are
in motion. Someone is shown leaping, running,
dancing or making some momentary gesture; a
cloud drifts by, a wave breaks, foliage is stirred up
by the breeze. Such arrested movement may be
represented two-dimensionally, and in pre-
Renaissance painting, on Greek vases for instance,
normally was. But by the time Tintoretto painted
his *Bacchus and Ariadne*, depicted movement
enjoyed the full freedom of deep space.

Implied or suggested movement of a slightly
different kind occurs when a set of elements, in
themselves abstract, is so arranged as to suggest

SEMI-ABSTRACT MOVEMENT
Though each of the seven
different configurations
grouped in the diagram
below has representational
associations, all evoke
movement in a way that is
mainly abstract. Both (A)
and (B) are explosive, but
one is brittle, the other
viscous. The shape of (D)
suggests the splash of a
liquid into which something
has been dropped, and the
movement is upward rather
than outward. The other
four configurations all
show movement created by
visual gradients, (E) being
a gradient to the right from

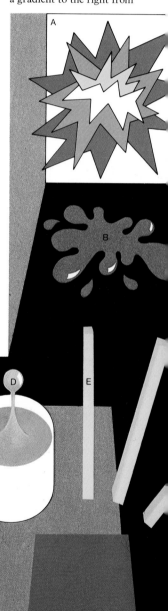

the vertical bar (and, by implication, also a stroboscopic illustration of something falling down). In (C) the radii of a set of concentric circles increase gradually, conveying slow movement outwards, as when ripples spread from a stone dropped in a pond. In (F) the size of the blocks and the intervals between them increase so that the eye is carried upwards and to the right. The visual gradient in (G) is from light to dark, or vice versa; in either case, the sequence impels us to move upwards or downwards progressively.

some kind of energized or kinetic event. For instance, the painting by Vasarély shown here is strictly speaking abstract, but can readily be interpreted as a hot-air balloon rising.

In stroboscopic movement the same action is shown at successive stages in a single image. There are hints of this in traditional painting – for instance in Goya's *Stilt-walkers*, where the leading walker is in a posture which the one following him will adopt a second or two later – but as a major resource it did not come into its own until it was vigorously exploited by the Futurists, influenced no doubt by the stop-frame photographs of walking figures by Eadweard Muybridge and by early cinematography. None of the Futurists, however, made more subtle and poetic use of it than did Duchamp in his *Nude descending a staircase*.

A fourth kind of movement is created by visual gradients – the increase or decrease of size, brightness, tilt, elongation, hue or any other measurable quality in regular sequence through pictorial space. We can scarcely avoid "reading" a sequence like those in the bottom diagram progressively, and feeling carried along as we do so.

A final category, induced eye-movement, depends on the fact that our eyes, as noted earlier, are intensely active and mobile organs, engaged in incessant scanning of our visual field. Moreover, there is a tendency on the part of the eye – or rather, of the perceptual system within which it works – to make myriad cross-comparisons hither and thither throughout the field between items which are in some way similar. Like is constantly associated with like, and the eye is forever jumping gaps in search of similitudes and analogies. The more it is persuaded to do so, the livelier the sense of movement we experience. It is this which animates Mondrian's *Broadway Boogie-Woogie*, for instance, in spite of its otherwise static configuration of lines and shapes.

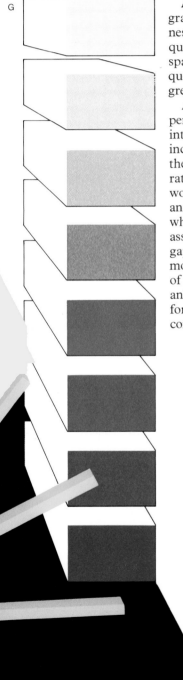

G

TINTORETTO (above)
Bacchus and Ariadne, 1578
The hurtling movement up from the right plotted in the diagram threatens to break out of the frame at top left, but Tintoretto,

with the merest of swoops, brings the momentum back to the middle through the arms and shoulders of the flying figure. Energy thus controlled gives an enhanced sense of its potential.

DUCHAMP (left)
Nude descending a staircase no. 2, 1912
This is stroboscopic movement, but not of a literal kind; it conveys the idea or feeling of descent. There are strong analogies with the machinery of the age – cylinders, pistons and connecting rods. That all is in motion is evident at a glance. Yet the diagonals lean together at the top in a manner that holds them within the picture space.

GOYA (above)
The stilt-walkers, c. 1788
Goya, himself an athletic man, had an unrivalled sense of the physical poise of dancers, bullfighters, acrobats and stuntmen such as these stilt-walkers. They are stylish and confident yet wary of their balance. The tilted axes move our eyes diagonally into the picture space but are then ingeniously held back on the far side by the angle of the building support.

Illumination and Tonality

A picture's quality of light is amongst the most telling characteristics of a painter or a school of painting. For instance, the typical light of the Florentine early Renaissance is a cool, vernal, bright, all-revealing radiance; of Venetian painting a warm afterglow; of seventeenth-century Dutch landscape the clear but cloud-filtered midday light of the Lowlands.

At one level these characteristics reflect differences of climatic experience, but there are symbolic and indeed philosophical or religious issues at stake also. Obviously enough, light has in every age and place stood for that which is divine, holy, beneficent; and dark, for the unknown, for death, for evil, for spiritual anguish – "the dark night of the soul". Thus the dark-light dualism is as primeval and profound as any we could name, and the emphasis given to it by artists can tell us much about their individual temperaments.

At this point, with acknowledgments to Marshall McLuhan, the interesting distinction should be made between "light through" and "light on". Light through, in its more literal sense, is exemplified by a stained-glass window viewed from a church interior with the light coming from the sky outside. Nothing could better accord with the medieval Christian world-view, which held that the visible universe was a manifestation of the Divine will, hence man-made things both stood between us and celestial illumination (literally and

symbolically), and were also to varying degrees transparent (by the operation of Divine grace).

A similar but lesser quality of radiance is characteristic of most paintings until the Renaissance, when Leonardo and others introduced strong contrasts of light and shadow (chiaroscuro). Conceptually, it is true of nearly all painting before, and outside of, the High Renaissance and its aftermath, that the light comes towards us off the painting: we receive it rather than observing its effects within the painting. Conversely, "light on" implies luminosity coming from a specific source rather than an omnipresent metaphysical one. This in turn accords well with the new scientific world-view gaining ground throughout the Reformation and triumphant in the epoch of Descartes and Leeuwenhoek. By the seventeenth century, especially in the work of *tenebrist* painters, pictorial space is typically dark in tone, and objects are picked out by strong, often single-source light that strikes their top or side but leaves much of them unlit and causes them to cast deep shadows – the cast shadow, let us note, being virtually unknown outside the Western tradition.

The epoch of chiaroscuro gave birth to some of the greatest European painters – to Caravaggio, to Velazquez, Rembrandt and many others. A poetry of single-source illumination was brought into being, and with it a poetry of tonality exploiting the different expressive effects of slight or em-

The dualism of light and darkness is summed up by the *Yin-Yang* symbol: each area contains the seed of its own opposite and each grows out of the other in unity and interdependence, as night succeeds day.

CHARTRES (above)
"*Our Lady of the Beautiful Glass*", mid-12th century. In the stained-glass image of Mary, "light through" has both metaphysical and literal meanings: as the vessel chosen to manifest the Divine on earth, she is someone through whom celestial light shines with especial brilliance.

VELAZQUEZ (below)
*The water-carrier of Seville, c.*1619
It is a sense of the almost sacramental beauty of everyday, normally unregarded, experience that moves us. A shaft of strong daylight finds its way into a dark market-place, turning some facets of the solids into bright islands while almost losing the contours on the shadow side. The strength of the light and shadow structure is shown by the diagram, which simplifies the painting to only four tones without destroying it.

REMBRANDT (right)
A scholar, c. 1630
What streams through this
tall window is not so much
the Divine light that shines
through the Virgin Mary as
the fading (but returning)
light of day. The analogy
of the thinker wresting the
light of truth from a vast,
dark universe is tempting,
yet the artist may simply be
investigating the effects
of light through bottle glass.

CHARDIN (right)
Still life with a marmite,
c. 1762
In this beautiful instance
of "light on", the subtle
management of illumination
and design produces not a
photographically banal
account of light and shade,
cast shadows and highlights,
but a quiet, lyric poem in
praise of the daily miracle
of natural light falling on
a group of familiar objects.

phatic tonal contrasts, of subjects hidden in shadow or theatrically spotlit. Gradations of tone as
surfaces turned away from the light became a
principal means of suggesting three-dimensional
form and volume. In addition to modelling forms
rather than simply delineating shapes, painters
used tone to indicate the spatial dimensions of
their pictures and to create rhythmic patterns of
light and dark, often running counter to the colour
pattern. In order to achieve the subtlest, most
poetic tonal rendering of the fall of light, intense
colour must be restricted or avoided: it competes
with and destroys the delicate play of tone. To a
great extent, therefore, a painter is obliged to make
the choice between full eloquence of tone, of "light
on", and the brilliance of colour so suggestive of
"light through". Only small areas, if any at all, of
strong colour are found in Velazquez, Vermeer,
Constable, Corot or Ingres.

At least in its silvery-grey seventeenth-century
sense, tonality began to evaporate with the onset of
Impressionism; and in Cézanne, Gauguin and van
Gogh, along with many of their contemporaries,
there seems to be a reversion in whole or part to
"light through"; a reversion which becomes still
more marked in the work of Klee and some other
abstract artists. With some exceptions – Super-
realism, for example, – it is in photography rather
than in painting that the nuances of "light on" are
now explored.

MONET (left)
Beach at Ste-Adresse, 1867
The luminosity that almost
warms our faces is arguably
a secular version of "light
through", since the sunlight
comes towards us directly,
filtered only by high cloud.
The few, fairly small solids
that obstruct the wash of
light suggest its strength
by their emphatic darkness.

KLEE (above)
Painting on black back-
ground, 1940
As with much of Klee's
work we have the impression
that light is coming through
the objects rather than
falling on them. There is
no lit or darkened side on
any shape and no cast
shadow. The black back-
ground enhances this effect.

Texture and Surface

Our response to texture in paintings depends in large part on the closeness of the link between our visual and tactile senses. The roughness of bark or the smoothness of glass are apprehended not only by looking but by many experiences of touching their surfaces, and it is the force of this tactile memory which, in painting, can make depicted textures seem almost as convincing as real ones. The distinction between the two needs to be understood. Even when the surface of the picture itself is almost smooth, a realistic and minute rendering of uneven surfaces may be achieved either by linear drawing – of wrinkles in a face or grain in wood, for instance – or, still more illusionistically, by using changes of tonality in a very meticulous way to indicate irregularities in a surface. This technique of depicting texture depends on the painting having a source of directional light which reveals more and more irregularities as surfaces turn away from it.

Jan van Eyck's "*The Arnolfini Marriage*" (see p. 36) is a supreme example of literal and exact textural representation: wood, metal, glass, cloth, fur, hair, lace are lovingly described in terms of their tactile and surface qualities as revealed by the light from a window. In the wake of this achievement came the great tribe of genre, still-life and flower-painters in the seventeenth-century Netherlands. *Trompe-l'oeil* painters of the eight-

CONSTABLE (below, with detail, below right)
The leaping horse, 1825
Constable expressed in a letter his involvement with natural textures and processes of time and wear: "Willows, old rotten banks, slimy post and brickwork, I love such things ... As long as I do paint I shall never cease to paint such places ... Painting is but another word for feeling. I associate my careless boyhood to all that lies on the banks of the Stour. They made me a painter."

eenth century followed suit and so, in their own fashion, did the Pre-Raphaelites. The Superrealist school is the latest expression of a perennial human fascination both with mimetic skills and with the *frisson* of minute observation, exemplified here by Ralph Goings' trailer with its careful painting of reflections and of details as small as the rivet heads in the metal.

In this tradition, the quality of the paint surface itself tends to be smooth and anonymous, since fluid pigment and very fine brushes are the only means by which Eyckian or Pre-Raphaelite renderings are possible. Relatively smooth surfaces may also be found in some abstract paintings in which texture is predominant, as in much of Tobey's work, where the markings are too small and close to be read as distinct shapes yet not so

GOINGS (left)
Airstream trailer, 1970
The textural verisimilitude that may be achieved by a subtle and methodical handling of tone and cast shadow is seen in Goings' rendering of the polished aluminium sides of the trailer. Wavering shadow along the underside of the body explains every slight dent in the metal, and the hard shadow of the two canisters, the flare of light on the front, make the heat of the surface almost tangible. The painting retains the textual sharp-focus of the photograph on which it was based.

TOBEY (right)
Barth rhythmus, 1961
This is pure, abstract texture, the myriad hooks, squiggles and threaded trails of paint energizing a luminous surface which seems as impenetrable as quartz yet has depth upon depth of faceted colour.

regularly spaced out that they form a pattern. It is quite otherwise with an Action Painter such as Jackson Pollock, whose pigment positively shouts out its own life-history – what kind of stuff it is and how it got there. Here we are confronted by the real texture of a worked substance – by the tangible qualities of impasto layers, glistening blobs or looping skeins, furrows, scorings or churnings of pigment. Pollock's intention is less to create textural interest for its own sake than to make explicit, by his handling of paint, the story of his own actions and state of mind.

Such evidence of the artist's hand is by no means the monopoly of Abstract Expressionism, however: it has been a powerful auxiliary in much figurative painting, as is clear from a study of the pictures here by Constable, van Gogh and Céz-

INGRES (below)
The spring, 1856
Clearly, the teased-up paint surface of Constable's landscape, perfectly suited to expressing the rough processes of nature in the Suffolk countryside, would be wholly inappropriate for the subject here. Discreet perfection of drawing, subtle tonality and creamy pigment all work together to convey a voluptuous and fluent serenity. Such contrasts of texture in painting are as delightful as textural variety in food.

anne. The quality of the paint surface – the real texture – in each case corroborates or may be even richer than the texture depicted. By his handling of paint each of these artists also makes eloquent the effect of time on the material world: wear and tear, erosion, crumbling, cracking, rotting away. For whereas smoothness speaks of newness, growth and resiliency, or of the durable hardness of machine-made products, uneven surfaces tend to be associated with wear, ageing, mortality – a tragic emotion but not wholly so, since decay implies regeneration. Most of us have felt some measure of agreeable nostalgia in contemplating the ravages of time: why else do we seek out weathered walls, sea-wrack, ruined temples and all those light-fracturing irregularities that the eighteenth century referred to as "picturesque"?

There is a second and more technical collusion between texture and time: quite simply, uneven textures of any kind – and patterns also – slow down our scrutiny of a picture. Their opposites, smooth surfaces and sinuous curves, those delectable attributes of youth which Ingres sets before us in *The spring*, allow our glance to slip readily from feature to feature. In contrast, Cézanne, by the manifold touches of his brush, obliges us to experience with him the heave and turn of the masses formed over slow geological time and analysed by him with such patience.

CEZANNE (left)
Mont Ste-Victoire from Bibémus Quarry, detail, 1898
Brush-strokes reminiscent of the marks left by a stonemason's claw chisel reveal the artist's slow assemblage of his pictorial architecture, his relish in the grand simplicities of mass – and something, too, of the quarryman's cleaving interventions in Nature.

VAN GOGH (above)
Chair and pipe, 1888-89
Thick, emphatic brush-marks tell of the rough workmanship of this chair and its long, sturdy service, the generations of scuffing and scrubbing undergone by the tiled floor, and the working man's consolation from the feel of his pipe. In both subject and handling, this is the poetry of use.

Edge Qualities

EDGE AND COLOUR
Quality of edge can have a marked effect on tonality. The two squares above are objectively identical in tint, but because the one on the right-hand side has a hard edge it makes a sharper contrast with the white background than its neighbour, and consequently we read it as being darker.

JAMMU, INDIA (above)
*Mian Brij Raj Dev with attendants, c.*1765
Although this painting does not wholly exclude volume and depth, it relies for its effects almost entirely on the clarity and unwavering grace of its contours.

MANTEGNA (right)
*The Agony in the Garden, c.*1460
Mantegna's world is flintily hard-edged, even the clouds having explicitly defined limits. But the number of small clear steps around the forms moderates the effect.

Painters today are often classified according to the way they manage the contours or limits of their colour areas: certain abstract artists, for example, are said to belong to a "hard-edge school". It would be entirely correct to infer from this that the treatment of edge is very important aesthetically, that is in terms of its effects, and also philosophically, in terms of the preferences and values one or the other treatment reveals. In discussing line and contour (see p. 110) we noted Wölfflin's distinction between the linear and the painterly, and a similar kind of polarity can be distinguished between hard/continuous and soft/broken edge quality. Hard-edge corresponds broadly with the linear approach (a line, after all, implies continuity) and soft-edge with the painterly.

What is at issue here? Very largely it is a matter of the painting's function. Totemic or heraldic works, those that function almost as signs, will invariably need hard edges for the sake of ready

ROTHKO
Red, white and brown, 1957
If Rothko had given hard edges to the shapes he uses we might find this merely a handsome abstract painting. Its compelling quality comes from subtle manipulations of fading edges, and the glowing vastness they make us feel.

RENOIR (below)
Bather drying her leg, 1910
Renoir's edges, especially
when they enfold the
human figure, are the very
essence of softness. The
paint is fluidly touched
on to the canvas with a
soft brush, suggesting the
gentleness of a lover's
caresses – the poetry of
touch rather than sight.

LEGER (above)
The mechanic, 1920
Léger gives us man re-created
in the image of a machine;
his limbs, like piston-rods,
shaped for work. This is
the hard-edge art born of
industrial civilization.

LEONARDO (right)
The Virgin of the rocks,
detail, c. 1505
Leonardo was a pioneer in
the modelling of forms in
light and shade. Here the
forms emerge from the deep
shadows of a rock grotto,
the contours dissolving in
a play of lost and found.

REMBRANDT
Self-portrait, detail, 1660
Rembrandt's edges vary here
from thin, sharp, clearly
formed accents, where light
strikes his cap, eyelid and
collar, to contours so deeply
sunk in shadow that they
are almost blended with
their neighbouring areas.

decipherability. In more recent history hard edges
have corresponded with an intellectual, structural,
architectonic approach, as against a sensory or
intuitive one. Hard-edge art is strongly visual: it is
the outcome of clear illumination and accurate
focus. Soft-edge, by contrast, is tactile and caress-
ing, conveying the roundedness of things and the
way curved surfaces fade gently off at their contours. It marks, too, a response to the effulgence,
the glow of objects in light, and how the impact of
light seems to fracture and modify the sharpness of
their silhouettes; or how, as can be seen here in the
heads by Leonardo and Rembrandt, envelopment
in deep shadows causes a local "lostness" of
contour and elision of shapes.

Generalizing still further, we could say that
hard edges are usually chosen whenever separation of parts, categorization and intellectual
analysis are the aim; whereas if an artist is
concerned primarily with unity, integration and

fluency, then softness or brokenness will typically
be preferred. As intellectual clarity is at the heart
of classicism, classic art inclines strongly to the
hard side. The pursuit by Romantic artists of unity
and totality has often – though by no means always
– propelled them towards a soft-edge treatment.

To some extent, indeed, we have here an
antithesis between the rational or commonsensical
and the imaginative or visionary. While it is
probably true that supreme mystical experience is
accompanied by great clarity and that linearity is
characteristic of many visionary painters, notably
Blake, nevertheless imagination is often freed by
images which are suggestive rather than specific.
Hence, perhaps, the soft edges of the rectangular
forms in Mark Rothko's paintings, typical as they
are of what the critic Robert Melville has called
"the abstract sublime", in radical contrast to the
literal quality of many American hard-edge paintings of the 1960s, with their clean severity.

Pattern

As soon as leisure and skills have been available, people everywhere have wanted to decorate surfaces – those of their bodies, clothes, utensils, carpets, walls, weapons – with ornamental patterns of frequently breathtaking beauty and ingenuity. Elaboration and artistry by no means always correlate; there are many instances of patterns becoming too intricate and garrulous for an educated taste, and conversely, of simple but subtle ones (on much Song dynasty pottery) which are of the highest quality.

In painting, patterns can be formed by any repetitive sequence of lines, shapes, tonal accents, colours or even brush-marks. Figure/ground ambiguity can occur in abstract patterns, a chessboard being a simple example; are the white squares on a black ground, or vice versa? Most patterns in figurative art are unambiguous, however, and painters have traditionally delighted in them: one thinks, for example, of the costumes in Japanese prints; the textile and architectural decoration in Persian and Indian miniatures; the damask hangings of Crivelli or Veronese; the spots on Titian's leopards; the wall-papers and cretonnes of Vuillard and Matisse; the bold decorative passages in Picasso and Braque from Synthetic Cubism onwards.

What lies at the root of this seemingly unconquerable urge, and what does pattern do in painting? It has already been suggested that pattern, like texture, serves to slow down our eye as it traverses the picture surface, much as repeated ridges on a road would slow down a car. But whereas natural texture is often an index of wear and tear through time, a patterned surface, by contrast, whether it is the work of nature or of human hands, speaks of a sense of constructive purpose or design and often, too, of exuberance, vitality, relish, the determination to enjoy and to enrich life.

In the early twentieth century, pattern in the sense of surface ornamentation for its own sake fell into disrepute among some critics of art, architecture and design – largely in reaction against the indiscriminate application of decorative motifs, plundered from every culture, to every available surface in the homes of the newly affluent classes in the late nineteenth century. Following the precepts of Adolf Loos in architecture and the Bauhaus in industrial design, there emerged a positively puritanical disdain for any surface treatment that had no "functional" purpose. But the

BRAQUE (left)
Still life on a red tablecloth, 1936
Addicted both to texture and to pattern, Braque has woven at least six motifs, in repetitions sufficiently regular to qualify as pattern, into one of the handsomest of all Synthetic Cubist still lifes. He can create a monumental grandeur from elements as banal as the Christmas tree motif on a piece of oil-cloth, which can be discerned when the picture is held upside down.

HOKUSAI (left)
Carp leaping in a pool, late 18th century
Without any loss of truthfulness to nature, the maker of this woodcut manages to confer upon his representations of the ripples, the water-weed, the fins and the scales value also as pattern. Nature and stylization (the concentric rings depicting water), the momentary and the deliberately organized, are miraculously at one.

HILLIARD (right)
Young man in a garden, c. 1588
The bold pattern on the doublet of the dreaming youth lends piquancy to the smoothness of his white hose, and the entwining leaves and flowers among which he is posed are so delicately formalized that they, too, fall within the definition of pattern, even though their repetitions are not strictly regular. As with Hokusai's stylized carp, natural appearances have been vividly rendered and at the same time fully exploited for their pattern potential – their value as sensuous ornamentation.

SPENCER (right)
Swan-upping, 1914–15,
finished 1919
Spencer celebrates a unity
between the natural patterns
of the cedar, the vine and
the wavelets, and man-made
patterns in the roof tiles,
the bridge parapet, the
cushions, the timbers of
punts and landing stage.
These are played off against
each other but together
enhance the plain areas
of the foreground and the
metal plates on the bridge.

MATISSE (top left)
Odalisque, 1922
The Middle Eastern theme
reflects Matisse's lasting
fascination with Islamic
traditions of rich and
variegated pattern. Apart
from its decorative value,
pattern often enabled him
to suggest form by linear
changes of direction rather
than by modelling in tone
and losing the purity and
brilliance of his colour.
In the small copy shown
below Matisse's picture, the
patterning has been replaced
by colours that approximate
the effect of the combined
hues; the bed which seemed
to rise so solidly becomes
flat and formless. At the
same time the liveliness
of the picture is depleted.

WARHOL (right)
Marilyn Monroe, 1962
Here is repetition far more
blatant than can be found
in Braque or Spencer, its
few variations suggesting
rather the accidents of
screen-printing than any
deliberate intent. It is
precisely the monotony of
mass-produced glamour that
is being – not celebrated,
for that would imply some
delight – but methodically
rehearsed in the paradoxical
context of highbrow art.
Obviously enough, pattern
is one inescapable result,
but it is questionable
whether Warhol seeks to
please us by it, as do the
other artists represented.

demand for austerity and economy of means did
not reduce the allurement of symmetrical pattern,
as Mondrian's abstract work shows. To this day
we have Minimal painters such as Frank Stella,
who is decorative before he is anything else, and
modular or "serial" art in which painters and
sculptors are concerned above all with regularity
and repetition, and on achieving an almost mathematical objectivity within a closed system.

Pattern is not "merely" decorative; as well as
being a primeval human pleasure, not lacking in
deeper implications, it can be used to convey
symbolic meaning, as in the stylized patterns of
much Islamic and Eastern art, and can also serve a
range of formal uses. It may provide a sense of
continuous visual harmony and order or, when
combined with unpatterned areas, satisfy our wish
for visual variety. How delectable it is to savour, in
simultaneous contrast, the slipperiness of butter
with the crunchiness of toast. The pleasure derived from looking, for instance, at the contrast
between the plain and patterned areas in the
pictures by Matisse, Hilliard and Braque shown
here is not dissimilar; an effect of mutual enhance-
ment is taking place, and we can see, in the altered
version of the Matisse, what a loss is suffered when
pattern is eliminated.

If we concentrate on a patterned area in a
painting – say the striped counterpane on which
Matisse's odalisque reclines, or the deep buttoning
of the cushions in Stanley Spencer's riverside
scene – we may become aware also that we are
being offered an enriching double experience – a
sensation of surface regularity together with a
realization that its departures from regularity (the
curvature of the stripes in the Matisse) signify
changed orientation in space; we have two readings for the price of one.

The Dimensions of Colour

Colour has become, for many twentieth-century abstract artists, the most essential attribute of painting, a means not simply of enriching a design but of creating space, volume and movement and of expressing and even inducing emotional states. The main dimensions of colour are hue (the spectrum name), intensity or saturation (degree of purity), tone (degree of lightness or darkness) and temperature (relative warmth or coolness). A vast number of variables comes into play when colours are used together in the restricted space of a picture, however. As everyone knows who has tried to paint, each addition or extension of colour alters the total equation in ways very hard to predict, so that any good painting is a prodigy of only partly conscious calculation.

Three colours – red, yellow and blue – are primary in the painter's spectrum. These form the basis of all others, countless pure chromatic hues being made by mixing any two primaries in varying proportions. When these hues in turn are shaded by the addition of black or grey, tinted by the addition of white, or overlaid by other colours in semi-transparent glazes, the permutations of hue become infinite. Their mutual behaviour – how they consort together – may depend on another variable, the relative sizes of colour areas. "A metre of green is more green than a centimetre of it", said Gauguin; conversely, a small accent of red in a field of green can have an impact out of all proportion to its size. By conjuring with the relationships between adjacent hues, artists can make colours that objectively are muted appear

THE COLOUR WHEEL
Colours differ from each other not only in hue (red from orange) but also in tonal value, their lightness or darkness. The tonal range charted by the grey segments on the wheel shows that yellow is inherently much brighter than violet and that bluish hues are darker in general. Each hue could be made tonally lighter or darker by tinting or shading to produce, say, a dark yellow and a light violet. But the chromatic purity or intensity would then diminish. Between each of the three primary hues (yellow, red and blue) are shown three intermediate colours. Complementaries lie opposite each other on the wheel and form strong contrasts of hue – red with green or blue with orange – while those that are close to each other harmonize. Hues also have a perceived "temperature"; we feel that reddish-yellow colours are warm, the blue-greens cool.

MATISSE (below)
The red studio, 1911
Matisse's commitment to strong, pure colour without light and shade is daringly expressed in a picture which seems deliberately to challenge the convention that colour used as a background must necessarily be neutral in tone and hue. The huge field of warm, rusty red dominates all, advancing to flatten a space which is nevertheless indicated unmistakably by the delicate linear sketching and the angles at which frames lean against the walls. The painting is also an inventory of his own work disposed about the studio, the picture on the right showing the direct, flat, contrasting colours of his early Fauve period.

pure and glowing. "Give me mud", wrote Delacroix, "and I will make the skin of Venus out of it if you will allow me to surround it as I please."

Because of the elusiveness, subtlety and complexity of colour, systems of mapping or calibrating it, as on the colour wheel shown here, can do no more than establish basic terms and indicate some of the main options open to painters. A picture with colours from opposite sides of the wheel (complementaries) juxtaposed at full chromatic strength will tend towards powerful, perhaps disturbing effects as each colour competes for attention. Optical vibrancy is reduced when colour contrasts are slight, inducing, perhaps, a more contemplative mood. Subtly differentiated chords can be struck within these extremes, however, and the strongest contrasts can be controlled by the mediating effect of neutral areas.

Similarly, while the red-yellow side of the wheel suggests the warmth of fire, and the blue-greens the coolness of ice, such psychological perceptions of "temperature" are highly relative. Just as hues degraded towards grey can be made to seem pure, so cool colours may sometimes look warm against others. The spatial aspects of colour are no less subtle. Fields of pure, unvarying hues jostling each other tend to flatten a painting and have been exploited most vigorously by modern colourists who have discarded illusionistic depth. Yet even without modelling in light and shade, the differing tonal values and relative temperatures of colours can be used to give convincing effects of depth and volume, the light, warm colours tending to advance, the dark, cool ones to recede, an effect used by Cézanne to create an extraordinary three-dimensional solidity. Matisse and the Fauves went even further in discarding conventional tonality and expressing form simply by combining line with rich, forceful colours.

POUSSIN (above)
Lamentation over the dead Christ, c. 1655
The wide range of colours strikes a plangent chord which is nevertheless made harmonious by greys, near-whites and other mediating neutral areas. An emphatic light-and-shade structure crossing the colour areas also helps to offset the intensity of colour contrast.

BONNARD
Self-portrait, 1940
Unlike Poussin, Bonnard reduces light and shade to a minimum and chooses a fairly narrow range of hues to suggest the pervasive yellow of reflected sunlight. The head is less three-dimensional than Cézanne's but the picture is suffused with warmth.

PUVIS DE CHAVANNES
The poor fisherman, 1881
The melancholy power of this picture depends not on strong contrasts, as in the Poussin, but on muted, near-monochrome tints, subtly modulated and in balance with the linear design. When colour is used in this restrained manner, even a small increase in intensity – the purple of the distant headland – registers in full.

CEZANNE
Self-portrait, c. 1880
Brush-strokes of mutating colour make both a web of harmonic changes across the surface and an analysis of volume and space. Light hues used for the advancing planes are further projected by the complementary action of the darker, cool colours – and opposites in the spectrum wheel – chosen for the receding surfaces.

Ways of Using Colour

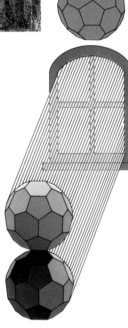

NOVGOROD SCHOOL
The Archangel Michael,
early 14th century
In the tradition of icon
painting stemming from
Byzantium, verisimilitude
must be kept at bay, since
the object is to present
sacred figures as living in
a transcendent world rather
than the everyday one. The
icon painter intended to hold
the eye of the faithful by
strong and simple beauties
of shape and colour, not to
render symbolic red wings,
for instance, as they might
look in a given light. This is
different from atmospheric
colour, shown in the lower
part of the diagram, where
red and green are modified
by both light and proximity.

In a simple way we have already charted the basic
colour and tone keys that are at the painter's
disposal. The question remains why a painter or
school of painting may habitually prefer one rather
than another and what social, personal or aesthetic
intentions are revealed by these choices. The main
typical ways of using colour are discussed below.
But first another distinction must be made, this
time between local and atmospheric colour.

In a local-coloured picture a red garment is
more or less fully red from edge to edge: and the
same would apply to a green tree or a gold throne.
Atmospheric colouring, on the other hand,
acknowledges that although a red garment is
predominantly red it may have, broken into its red
hue, tints and reflections of other colours from the
environment, modulating it here and there towards purple, say, or brown or grey. Obviously
enough, local colouring generally corresponds
with concept (what a thing is thought of as being)
and atmospheric colouring with observation (how
it may really look at a given moment). To appreciate the difference, we have only to glance from
the Archangel Michael on this page to Seurat's
seascape and back.

Local colour in a painting tends to be flat, of one
hue and tonality throughout. St Michael's wings
and the gold background are quite flat, for instance, though his green tunic has slight modulations and highlights. Atmospheric colour is by
definition modulated: it must necessarily change
from one tint to another across small distances (the
shadow side of Seurat's jetty) and may have
declensions of tone as well.

With these antitheses in mind we may now
distinguish several significantly different ways of
using colour, beginning with its heraldic or symbolic use in paintings produced within well-
established stylistic conventions. Such paintings

TIEPOLO
*The marriage of Frederick
and Beatrice,* 1753
A great master of swagger,
Tiepolo courts verisimilitude
– the blue of Beatrice's
train is modulated to render
its surface quality – but his
clear, local colours are
deployed with decorative
intent, to create a lively,
stylish, worldly atmosphere.

TISSOT (below)
The ball on shipboard, 1874
Balanced to a nicety, with
asymmetrical neutral areas
played against clear, local
colours (little modified by
the light), the composition
conveys the passing moment
with snapshot-like realism.

SEURAT (left)
*Fishing fleet at Port-en-
Bessin,* detail, 1888
Seurat uses the vibrancy
of pointillism, dots of
separate colour interacting
in juxtaposition, to define
and celebrate everything
that, in Auden's words,
"the leaping light for your
delight discovers". He is
acutely aware of a need to
render the essential and
typical in terms of the
optical and the transient.
At the same time his use
of atmospheric colour has
a structural intention; he
locates carefully selected
and simplified solids with
extreme precision to realize
a volume of deep space.

PIERO DELLA FRANCESCA
(right) *The baptism of
Christ, c.* 1440–50
The calm equilibrium, the
grave, exalted atmosphere,
are achieved with a limpid
chord of colours, a hybrid
between Byzantine formality
and subtle naturalism. The
colours are treated as local
but modulated by a clear,
vernal light from the right.

FRIEDRICH (right)
*Man and woman gazing at
the moon*, detail, *c.* 1830–35
Friedrich's choice of a
sombre, near monochrome
scheme of greenish browns
and salmon pinks enfolds us
irresistibly in an elegiac
mood of dusk and moonrise.

have an assigned function, often a ritual one,
involving colours with known symbolic connotations (the Madonna's blue robe in Western
painting or Krishna's blue skin in Indian art).
Colour tends to be local, edges hard.

Decorative colour, on the other hand, is intended to provide an agreeable background to
daily living or to draw attention to the person who
has commissioned the work. It could be himself, in
the case of an African tribesman painting his hut,
or a prince, as in the Tiepolo shown here. Colours
tend to be chosen for their restful, pleasing or
stylish properties, and to be local rather than
atmospheric, very often painted rather flatly.

Realistic colour is chosen when the painter is
making a documentary record of contemporary
life, normally in an easel picture, as in the genre
paintings of nineteenth-century salons and aca-
demies. Colours tend to be literal and descriptive:
often local rather than atmospheric (see the Tissot
on this page).

In Impressionism and Divisionism, "realistic"
colour is reinterpreted; the painter's preoccupation is with the visible world as manifested by
light in atmosphere. Small touches of relatively
pure and often complementary colours are juxtaposed, almost mixing in the viewer's eye, thus
creating vibrancy: yellow and blue touches combine as optical green, for instance, as in Seurat's
seascape. Colours are based on the pure hues of the
spectrum: black and greys are eliminated, except
greys made by juxtaposed hues cancelling each
other out. A significant extension of this principle
is the use of colour for analytical-structural purposes: the painter selects and modulates colours to
help create pictorial space and light in the manner
of Seurat or to bring out aspects of volume and
mass as Cézanne did by using light, warm colours
on advancing planes, cool dark ones to suggest
recession (see preceding page).

Symbolist colour moves sharply away from
realism; the painter's overriding aim is to express
his feelings about the theme of the painting, and
colour thus becomes a powerful symbol of emotions, thoughts, aspirations, recollections, moods.
Whistler's *Nocturnes* and Picasso's "Blue" period
paintings are typical. A single mood-colour often
dominates, as in the Friedrich shown here. Expressionism, a more extreme manifestation of Symbolism, has very much the same intentions but
shows still more marked departures from realism
and often much more saturated colour (see, for
instance, the Chagall on p. 102).

Finally, the abstract painter, being under no
constraint to render appearances, concentrates on
choosing colours that will create movement, space
or structural form, or "sing together" the pictorial
tune he has in mind, as in the Mondrian on p. 114.
It is important to emphasize that these usages are
not always mutually exclusive: Tissot, for instance, is firmly realistic but also very decorative;
Piero's *Baptism* embodies aspects of heraldic,
decorative and symbolist colour and perhaps a
foretaste of Impressionism. Yet the recognition of
a dominant colour mode can tell us much about an
artist and the meaning of his work.

Pictorial Organization

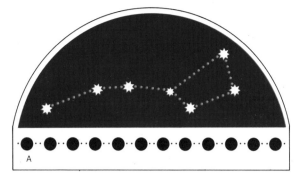

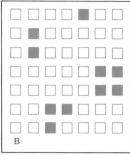

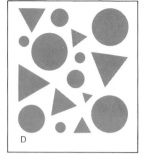

Why, in some pictures, does the arrangement of the shapes and of the intervals between them give us particular pleasure even when we are looking only at a black-and-white reproduction? To the extent that this question – the question of composition, design, organization – can be answered at all, it is best tackled case by case. But there are a few significant generalizations that can be made, and which apply in some measure to all pictorial art, whether figurative or abstract.

There is, to begin with, the phenomenon which Gestalt psychologists call visual grouping. If in any visual field there are various items, separate in space from one another, which nevertheless have some marked characteristic in common, then our vision will jump to and fro between them in such a way that they are perceived as a sort of network or constellation. Perhaps the best-known example of this is the constellation Ursa Major in the night sky – a set of seven stars which happen to be brighter than any others in their celestial neighbourhood: hence our perceptual grouping of them into a unified shape, which our ancestors described as a plough.

Most instances of grouping in pictorial art are much more complex than this. Some resemblances are too far-fetched and faint to influence our reading of the painting, others are weakened by contradictions and cross-groupings. For instance, the visual groupings in a picture scattered with circles and squares all painted pink or blue are clear enough if all the squares are blue and all the circles pink. But if both circles and squares are coloured some pink, others blue, then our groupings by shape will run counter to our grouping by colour. Such cross-groupings are intriguing, and in paintings very common.

The principle, however, is simple; it is that of similarity. Like is associated with like, whatever the kind of likeness may be. In pictures with many human figures there is a tendency for us to group the heads together – often the hands as well; or diagonal limbs with other diagonal limbs. Painters

VISUAL GROUPING
Identical circles in a straight line are readily grouped as a sequence, but we also discern order in random arrangements, so that the constellation Ursa Major is read coherently as a "plough" shape (A).

Grouping by tone, the eye reads the black squares together in (B) and is attracted by these clusters rather than the numerous white squares. Size alone determines which squares we group in (C), but in (D) the situation is complex:

we alternately group the triangles or circles, or combine shapes according to size. The final three examples are simpler, and show grouping by colour (E), orientation, sloping against upright (F) and edge quality alone, hard against soft (G).

VASARELY
Betelgeuse-1, 1957
Vasarely is here exploiting *Gestalt* grouping theory to lead us on an animated dance through a space that was divided, in the first instance, by a regular grid of squares. This has been wittily destabilized, and there are as many

visual paths through the composition as there are points of entry into it. Perception is dominated in fluctuating pulses first by groups of large, dark close-spaced circles, next by the white intervals, next by the sloping discs or by the linear paths or patterns of tonal blocks.

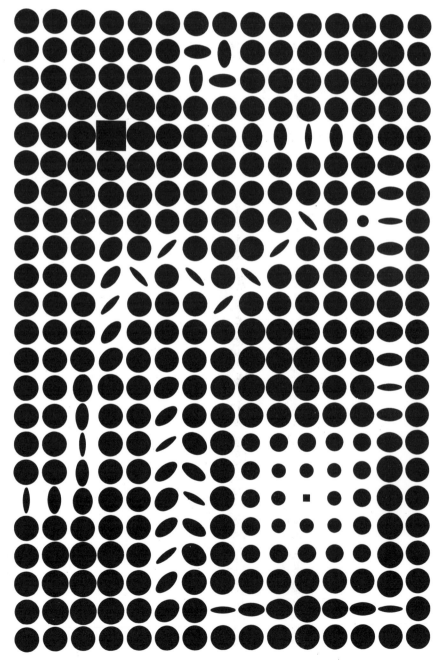

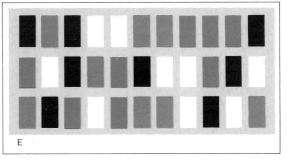

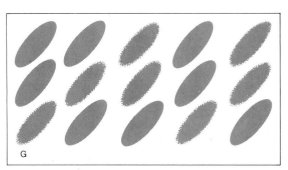

may use these conscious or unconscious groupings to establish a balance and sense of order or to set up a dynamic rhythm.

In abstract terms the categories of similarity are more easily identified. There can be grouping by similarity of size, shape, location (clustering; alignment), orientation, tone (brightness), colour, texture, or edge quality. Diagrammatic examples of each are given here; many of them have been exploited by Vasarely in his *Betelgeuse-1*. Our active insistence on grouping within a field demonstrates that our perceptual apparatus is not at all a passive receptor like the unexposed film in a camera that simply registers light-impulses as they arrive, but that it is, on the contrary, a tireless active searcher for order, coherence and cross-reference within our environment. Indeed, this unremitting search has always been a condition of survival: our ancestors had to distinguish a snake from a pile of leaves, and we inherit their vigilance.

Thus we bring to any visual field both energy

ANALYSIS BY GROUPING
The isolation of only four similarity factors in Titian's *Bacchus and Ariadne*, and their final superimposition, reveals an underlying unity. The rounded shapes of the heads are linked in a zig-zag line across the centre of the picture, carrying the eye from right to left. A second strong shape group is formed by flourishes of limbs and hands. Next, the horizontal and vertical accents show grouping by orientation. When foliage and draperies with similar rippling edges are added the essential design emerges.

and a determination to confer upon its manifold data as much structure and meaning as we can. If we look at the Vasarely we can feel this happening: he is very much aware of *Gestalt* theory and has based his artistic strategy on it. We are reminded, of an earlier example: Mondrian's *Broadway Boogie-Woogie* (see p. 114) in which grouping by size, shape, location and colour are simultaneously operative, generating a sense of stop-go movement. Figurative paintings are more complex and difficult to analyse; but the attempt is made here to bring out just a few of the many interlocking networks of similarity that Titian used to bind together his *Bacchus and Ariadne* – some other analyses of which have already been studied. Whereas the earlier examples examined proportion, movement and tonal grouping, these diagrams aim to bring out the more conspicuous groupings in terms mainly of shape, orientation and edge quality, all of which Titian interweaves to build up the eventual image.

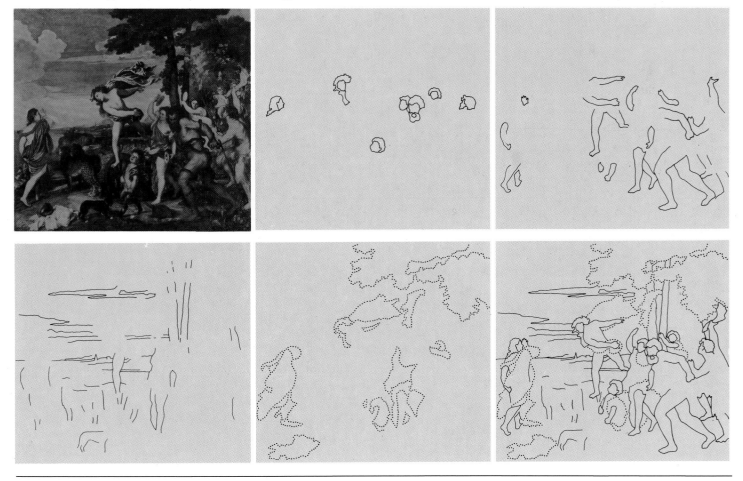

Proportion

Proportion is of major, if not central, importance in any kind of design. No painter would dispute this, though nowadays some would say that it is better left to intuition and the impulse of the moment. But it was not always so: most painters, until towards the end of the eighteenth century, received, as a matter of course, some instruction in geometry, as did architects and craftsmen.

The tradition of mathematical proportion is very ancient: perhaps as old as civilization itself. Methods of the ancient Egyptians were learned by the Greeks and, from this classical source, in turn transmitted through Middle Eastern contacts to the master masons who built the great cathedrals of medieval Europe.

At the root of these ancient practices lay a religious aspiration. Thinking men must have become aware, through such phenomena as the movement of the heavenly bodies, the cycle of the seasons, the relation of cause to effect, that regularity and structure were inherent in the universe. To the extent that these seemingly divine attributes could be embodied in human artefacts, such artefacts could be seen as miniature analogues or rehearsals of divine creation, calling down a sympathetic benison on human affairs.

Regularity, order, imply economy – an adjustment of means to ends; and in painting, nothing so well conduces to such economy as similarity, of which, as we saw overleaf, visual grouping is a special and important case. In proportioning, the similarity factor is subtler, more hidden: it is similarity of relationship which remains constant through changes in magnitude. This can easily be exemplified in numbers: the geometric progression 1, 2, 4, 8 ... has the obvious similarity factor that the ratio 1:2 is maintained throughout. Thus the best proportional method, which is also the oldest, is that which divides a space (normally a rectangle in paintings) into smaller magnitudes which are members of a geometric progression. We seem to respond to this harmonious progression in pictorial designs.

Certain rectangular shapes have unique properties of subdivisibility – a dynamic symmetry. They may all be constructed from the square according to the method shown diagrammatically here (A-E) – the transfer of diagonals of one rectangle to make the long side of the next – and their sovereign advantage is their divisibility into an almost infinite number of smaller rectangles having the same shape (ratio) as themselves. Thus, for instance, the rectangle (E) divides into five of itself and is the format Titian chose for his great *Presentation*; we can see how respectfully he followed its natural "fivefold subdivision". The Golden Section ratio of 1:1.618 – a proportion between two unequal parts of a whole, where the smaller part is to the larger as the larger is to the whole, which may be expressed numerically roughly as 5:8 – is also applied to a rectangular format much used in painting. Golden Section divisions are often used to fix a focal point in the composition at, for example, a five-eighths ratio on either the vertical or horizontal axis.

Towards the end of the fifteenth century in Italy a rival method (which Titian also knew, and used in *Bacchus and Ariadne* – see p. 96) began to supersede, in sophisticated circles, the older method. It was first formulated by the architect and theorist Alberti, who proposed the use of ratios based on the first few whole numbers: 1, 2, 3, and 4, to which later theorists added 5. These, and a few of their simple multiples, would yield all the ratios an architect or painter might need: in our diagram the main basic rectangular shapes that arise (J-O) are shown below the ones they so largely displaced.

Alberti could claim an august precedent. The numbers he advocated were the ones used by the Divine Artificer in the primal creation of the cosmos – according to the account of it given by Timaeus in Plato's dialogue of that name – and Plato in his turn had got it from Pythagoras. The latter, it is said, also first discovered the relationship between numbers and musical harmony: thus a stretched string, which when plucked sounds middle C, will, if stopped exactly halfway with a finger, yield the C above when one of the halves is plucked. Thus the ratio 1:2 in physical space corresponds to the musical consonance of the octave. And, using the same procedure, 2:3 yields the musical fifth and 3:4 the fourth. All this persuaded Pythagoras – and Plato and Alberti centuries later – that the universe must be organized as a kind of vast musical composition – "the harmony of the spheres". This method, of which one advantage is its ready calculability, is theoretically less rich in similarity factors than its predecessor: but many artistic achievements, including the whole of Palladian architecture and much sixteenth- and seventeenth-century painting, have been based on the proportions using small whole numbers.

TITIAN (above)
The Presentation of the Virgin, c. 1534–38
It has been suggested that Titian based his composition on a grid derived from four equidistant verticals, as in rectangle E. Superimposed are firm diagonals such as the line of the steps or the line of sight set up by the figures at the base of the flight, which, in combination with certain horizontals such as that indicated by Saint Anne's pointing finger, create a system of triangles which seem to contain and isolate groups or individuals. The Virgin stands alone, while the participants in the story exist separately from the group of donors on the far left; finally the old woman selling eggs, who, it is thought, represents Judaic law, is set apart below the line on which Mary stands, symbolizing the passing of the Judaic era with the presaged coming of Christ.

KLEE (left)
Individualized measurement of strata, 1930
Klee was an accomplished musician and his paintings often have the effect of musical compositions. In this subtly ordered design, he instinctively balances the horizontal rhythms with less weighty vertical bands and his sonorous and unusual colour groupings resound like chords within a rhythmic and harmonious structure.

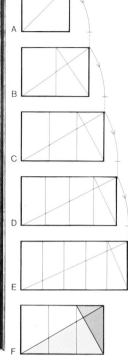

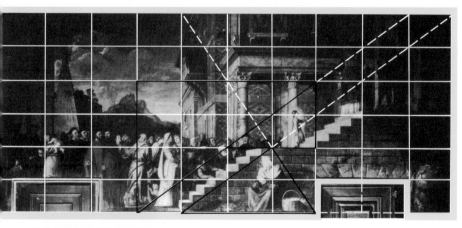

The rectangles B-E are first generated from a square, the long side of the next being equal to the diagonal of the previous rectangle. Each of these may be sub-divided as shown into a number of small rectangles having the same proportions as the larger; similarly the triangles created by their diagonals have con-gruent angles (F). This property of easy comodu-lation reaches a peak in the rectangles formed from the Golden Section ratio, (G, H), supreme in economy and harmony, in that the short side is to the longer as the longer is to the sum of the two; this rectangle may also be created from a square, the long side being derived by pivoting the diagonal of half the square. The remaining rect-angles I-O are those allied to musical intervals: uni-son (1:1), the fifth, the fourth, the octave, the tone (8:9), the double fourth (9:16) and double fifth (4:9).

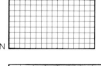

RAEBURN (above)
The Reverend Robert Walker skating, c. 1784
Raeburn's skater is as felicitously poised as he is wittily observed. Our analysis proposes that the placing of the figures is based on a rigorous system of grid intervals combined with a skilful use of arcs having their centres on intersections of the grid and their radii derived from constituent lengths.

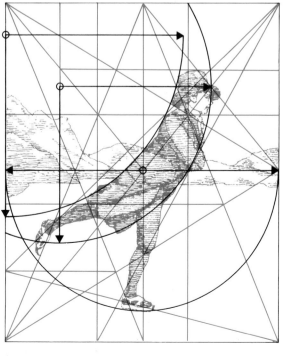

Abstraction

Nobody expects music to be "of" something, said the founders of abstract art; why then should any such demand be made on paintings? In a sense, this whole section of the book has shown that, as the pioneer abstractionists contended, spaces, shapes, lines, tones, patterns or colours can indeed work on us emotionally and, in a sense, intellectually as well, even when we encounter them unattached to any recognizable image – just as do melody, harmony or rhythm in music.

Without the yardstick of truthful representation that marks out a skilful figurative work from a clumsily executed one, we may find it hard to explain why one abstract painting is completely satisfying while another is unconvincing or simply messy. On the other hand it can be claimed that the depiction of objects according to strict rules of perspective was a false and restrictive yardstick in the first place.

This argument, though valid in its own terms, does not close the controversy, since there is obviously loss as well as gain involved in the abandonment of representation. Nor does the infinite freedom of abstraction mean that certain major trends or traditions cannot be distinguished in abstract painting. A bipolarity suggests itself at once between the impulsive and the calculated, the rough and the tidy. While some abstract paintings succeed by intuition, risk, gesture, free handling and the rich, unforeseeable textures and edges that result, others are measured, deliberate, neatly finished and usually hard-edged.

A broad analysis of these two trends must begin with Kandinsky's painterly "writing down" of

KANDINSKY (left)
Study for *Composition no. 7*, 1913
This might be called the landscape of Kandinsky's (evidently turbulent) psyche at the time he painted it, and is typical of his early expressionist style. The strong drive travelling from lower left to upper right leaves whirlpools in its wake. Colours are intense, edges often broken and blurred, yet there is much forethought.

MONDRIAN (above)
Composition, 1921
Subjectivity, caprice and accident are banished from Mondrian's mature art; the whole of reality as he experiences it is reduced and compressed within an austere structure of black bars with infillings of white, grey and the three primary colours of yellow, red and blue. These were the elemental constants.

RAJASTHAN, India (left)
Sri yantra, 18th century
The *yantra's* formal pattern of outer gates and petals, overlapping triangles and central point provides a visual focus for meditative concentration. In both its abstract simplicity and its optical effects there are analogies with American hard-edge abstractionists such as Noland who have sought to conjure away therapeutically the fuss and complication of modern life.

MIRO (below)
Catalonian landscape (The hunter), 1923–24
Though more playful than Kandinsky, Miró was no less interested in what he called "the golden flashes of the mind". Nature is the point of reference for an impulsive abstraction in which appear "Monstrous animals and angelic animals, trees with ears and eyes, a peasant in his Catalan beret holding a shotgun and smoking his pipe".

form and colour equivalents for his feelings, since this was historically the first kind of abstraction and, by virtue of its individualistic gestural character, points straight towards all subsequent kinds of painterly and expressionist activity, most notably that of the New York School in the 1940s. Kandinsky also pioneered a more controlled idiom whereby small, clearly defined but non-specific shapes float in abstract space, an idiom adopted by several painters on the abstract wing of Surrealism, in particular, Miró, though much of his imagery has associations with the natural world.

The more premeditated kind of abstraction may be subdivided into two categories. Suprematism, as developed principally by Malevich (see his Composition on p. 99), reveals a search for pictorial equivalents of psychological states akin to Kandinsky's, but the forms used are more sparing, more geometric and measured, and further from any suggestion of the real world. Malevich aimed, he said, at the "feeling of true being", and his art influenced Kandinsky himself to move towards more geometric forms. Almost simultaneously, Mondrian was developing a geometric abstraction arrived at by analytical reduction of natural forms, as in his celebrated apple-tree sequence (see vol. 3 p. 189). While the eventual "pure plastic art" of Mondrian and his De Stijl colleagues has a meta-

LOHSE (below)
30 vertical systematic shades with red diagonals, 1943–70
Richard Lohse's picture calls to mind the analogy between structured abstract painting and music with its permutations and combinations occurring across a regular matrix or "beat". It can be read in many different ways, some melodic, some chord-like, some syncopated, some on the beat. The use of similarity factors and cross-groupings is complex and fugue-like; the total effect both intellectually satisfying and formally grand.

physical significance, the move away from expressionist tendencies has become clear: the search is for fundamental principles of order, expressing not individual feelings but a universal coherence. This category of abstraction points towards the wholly impersonal art of the recent Minimalists. Like the more spatial and three-dimensional approach of Constructivism, its concern with formal structure makes it a natural ally of architecture.

The second major category of abstraction proceeding from premeditation rather than impulse is more diverse; it is based on experiments in geometry, mathematics, optics and theories of colour, proportion and perception (exemplified here by Lohse). The categories are not mutually exclusive; some optical paintings, for instance, are not simply concerned with visual phenomena in an objective, unemotional way but are intended to induce states of mind, almost in the manner of *yantras*, which, in Tantric art, seek to concentrate cosmic energies. Yet the dichotomy between the impulsive and the tidy is clear enough, and corresponds loosely with that noted earlier between the painterly and the linear, the romantic and the classical. It is possible, therefore, with some exceptions and hybrid forms, to boldly divide twentieth-century abstraction into the two camps of romantic/painterly/expressionist as opposed to classical/linear/hard-edged. Each has its own potentialities, and the recognition in each of a continuing artistic tradition provides some means of guidance through the frequently confusing cross-currents of modern art.

FRANKENTHALER (above)
Madridscape, 1959
Abstract Expressionist techniques as developed in New York from the 1940s, though they owed much to Kandinsky, outdid him in audacity and in unquestioning obedience to impulse. An initial gesture started off a dynamic dialogue between artist and canvas which had to be discontinued before it went dead, and in which drips, slashes, splatters, wipings, were as far as possible dictated by the painter's Unconscious. Here a kind of order emerges: repeated sickle shapes, "eyes", bunched verticals.

Language and Style

The introduction to this chapter put forward the idea that the combined effect of all the decisions a painter makes about pictorial language, the elements of which have now been discussed separately, amounts to what we call "style". Style is the sum of a set of decisions – or rather the flavour of it – and to the extent that these decisions stem directly from personal preference, we may speak of personal style. But style is influenced also by collective factors and there can be strong family resemblances among the output of a given epoch (period style) or a given geographic or cultural zone (national or regional style).

Period style is usually the easier to recognize, for paintings reflect the times in which they were produced as much as architecture or costume or any other aspect of society. For example, the Rococo style satisfied a class of patrons among whom a light, witty eroticism was fashionable, and contrasts sharply with the severe Neoclassicism that succeeded it.

National or regional style is hard to define but also often easy to recognize. French paintings, for example, of whatever period, are usually more elegant than their English counterparts, which tend towards forthrightness, and this is an expression of national temperament which is evident in many other fields. Much more subtle differences than this are apparent to the trained eye; the expert in seventeenth-century Dutch painting, for example, can place paintings produced contemporaneously in towns only a few miles apart.

Personal style represents individual variants on the prevailing conventions of period and country or region. Artists, like everyone else, notice different things and feel differently about what they do notice. Thus under the general umbrella of the Florentine Renaissance we find the sinewy strenuousness of Pollaiuolo coexisting with the delicacy of Botticelli.

The matrix on the right gathers together all the elements of painting which this chapter has considered, in a form which enables stylistic assessments to be made in a methodical way. The two paintings analysed have been chosen deliberately to contrast in as many ways as possible, having almost nothing in common apart from subject matter (the Rubens being, in reality, huge by comparison with the Indian miniature). The opposed qualities listed in the matrix are deliberately disposed so that those on the left tend to characterize non-European, pre-Renaissance (and twentieth-century) painting, while those on the right are more often found in European art of the fifteenth to nineteenth centuries. Not surprisingly, given the very different origins of the two paintings, their stylistic plots are strikingly different.

The same matrix could be used to plot the properties of any other painting. In addition to throwing some light on the infinite subtleties of style, any such analysis must lead to keener scrutiny of paintings, shrewder, more informed comparisons and – it is to be hoped – greater pleasure from looking at art, vindicating Keller's dictum, quoted at the beginning of this chapter, that "enjoyment is a function of understanding."

RUBENS
The Adoration of the Magi, 1624

PUNJAB, INDIA
The Emperor Akhbar being entertained by his foster-brother Azim Khan, 1571

THE STYLE GAME
In the vertical axis of the chart at the right are listed the main elements of style in horizontally opposed pairs, between each of which there is a scale of degrees, with a balance point in the middle to accommodate cases showing neither of the two opposed qualities in question, or else both in equal measure. Sometimes, horizontals and verticals might be equally stressed, in which case the appropriate dot would go in the central column.

INDIAN MINIATURE ● ○ RUBENS

Category	Left pole			Right pole	Category
		max	mid max		
SCALE	large : public			small : domestic	SCALE
SPACE	conceptual			realistic	SPACE
	shallow			deep	
	layered			non-layered	
	flat layering			oblique layering	
	crowded			empty	
	shapes separated			shapes overlapping	
ASPECT	typical : frontal : lateral			accidental : foreshortened	ASPECT
VIEWPOINT	non-specific			single	VIEWPOINT
	high			low	
	centred			laterally displaced	
	distant			close-up	
PROJECTION	conceptual			optical perspective	PROJECTION
VOLUME	flat shape stressed			volume stressed	VOLUME
MASS	unemphatic			heavy	MASS
	balanced			off-balance	
	horizontal axes predominant			vertical axes predominant	
	no or few diagonals			diagonals stressed	
LINES	mainly straight			mainly curved	LINES
	simple curves			complex curves	
	line around contours			no line around contours	
SHAPES	geometric			organic	SHAPES
	simple : long-phrased			complex : short-phrased	
	high definition			low definition	
	decorative			structural	
	abrupt			sinuous	
	frame acknowledged			frame transgressed	
ARTICULATION	angular			ellided	ARTICULATION
PROPORTION	important			non-operative	PROPORTION
ANATOMY	exaggerated			ideal : normal	ANATOMY
MOVEMENT	localized			ubiquitous	MOVEMENT
	gentle			vigorous : violent	
	across only			in depth	
ILLUMINATION	light through			light on	ILLUMINATION
	diffused light			directional light	
	top light			side light	
TONALITY	non-tonal : chromatic			tonality predominant	TONALITY
	conceptual			naturalistic : 'photographic'	
	generally pale			generally dark	
	low contrast			high contrast	
	no atmospheric perspective			full atmospheric perspective	
TEXTURE	little or none			much	TEXTURE
	depicted			actual (paint surface)	
	fine			coarse	
	man-made			natural	
QUALITY OF PAINT	smooth			rough	QUALITY OF PAINT
	thin			thick	
PATTERN	much			little or nil	PATTERN
	geometric			organic	
	refined			bold	
COLOURS	symbolic			naturalistic	COLOURS
	local			atmospheric	
	flat			modulated	
	matt : opaque			glossy : translucent	
	generally brilliant			generally subdued	
	generally cool			generally warm	
	contrasted : complementary			neighbours on colour circle	
HANDLING	handling unobtrusive			handling stressed	HANDLING
	deliberate			impulsive	
	calligraphic			non-calligraphic	

MATERIALS AND METHODS OF PAINTING

"The supreme misfortune is when theory outstrips performance" – LEONARDO

(left) CHARDIN: *The attributes of the arts*, 1766; (above) BRUEGEL: *The painter and the connoisseur, c.*1566-68

Introduction

We have already seen how widely paintings can differ according to the context in which they were created and the artist's individual approach to composition. But their appearance may be influenced equally by the techniques used to make them. Each medium of painting, drawing or printmaking has its own possibilities and limitations, and the purpose of this chapter is to bring out the expressive characteristics of each.

For anyone who has tried to draw or paint, and knows something of the difficulties, it is impossible to watch an image take shape beneath the hand of an adroit artist without a sense of wonder at what seems a kind of alchemy. The analogy is particularly apt for European painting, which for centuries was linked to chemistry and to the craftsmen's guilds of metalworking and dyeing. It was a skill laboriously learned, using materials that were often expensive or difficult to obtain and techniques (sometimes jealously guarded) which determined the character of the painting within fairly strict limits. The development of a wide range of vivid colours in tubes and of other equipment that makes possible rapid, direct painting is comparatively recent in the West, and has influenced the kind of painting produced.

As art terminology is often ambiguous, a few basic definitions will be helpful. The word "medium", for instance, is used sometimes to mean the water, oil, turpentine or synthetic resin added to bring paint to the consistency the artist wants. But in its wider sense it means the different painting methods in general – tempera, encaustic, fresco, oil, acrylic, ink, watercolour, gouache, pastel and also the various drawing and printing methods. The basis of all painting media is powdered pigment – colouring matter, which may be produced chemically or derived from coloured earths and crushed minerals or plants. It is bound together and made adhesive by a "vehicle" – glue, casein, egg, oil, wax or resin – except in fresco, where the pigment, dispersed in water, is bound simply by chemical action with the damp lime-plaster wall on which it is laid. By adding water, oil, turpentine or synthetic resin, artists can further extend the paint, thin it and influence its speed of drying and matt or glossy appearance. The dry media used in drawing may also be coloured, but of these only pastel is considered a painting medium because it can be spread: the others are basically linear methods. Finally, the term "support" refers to the surface on which the image is made – usually wood panel, canvas, paper or wall plaster.

The tools, technique or support employed by an artist can extend the inherent expressive and textural range of a medium, but the characteristic qualities of one medium cannot always be achieved with another. Of the quick-drying water-diluted paints, tempera and gouache favour linear designs with sharply defined images, relatively flat colours and decorative textures; the special fluidity and transparency of watercolour and ink demand swift execution and facilitate imperceptible tone and colour gradation and soft, atmospheric effects; oil-paint allows illusions of volume and

The varying surface effects in this composite image are created by a range of media and supports, each with its own characteristic qualities. Ink on gesso (left) provides a washy underdrawing for the sharply-defined layers of tempera (above) built up with a small brush in neat lines.

Gouache (above) and watercolour (above right) are both suited to quick sketching, but the greater density of gouache can be seen in the unstippled area. Watercolour has a transparent lightness, allowing light to be reflected up through layers of washes from the paper – often left unpainted in the highlights.

The sketching in chalk (left) and pencil (above) is done on the same coarse paper but the more friable chalk gives a denser, grainy line and can more easily be used to create tonal depths by smudging or drawing with a broad surface – so also can charcoal and pastel.

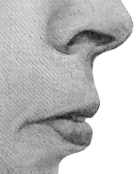

The more tractable medium of oil, which dries slowly, can be used to blend tones and colours in successive layers, beginning with thin underpainting blocking in the hair and establishing the design (above), then with glazes and touches of local colour translating the canvas weave to softer skin, and finally with thicker paint laid on with a palette knife or loaded brush (below).

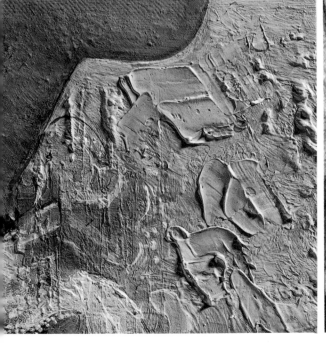

space to be created by subtle fusion of tones; acrylic paint is still more versatile, combining the plasticity of oils with the precision and quick-drying capabilities of tempera and gouache. Texturally, the tiny cross-hatched brush-strokes of tempera or the broad washes of fresco or water-colour create effects quite different from oils, where brush-lines may range from blade-sharp contours made with pointed sable hair to the rougher, whiskery marks of a hog-bristle brush or the heavy slabs created with a painting-knife.

Similarly, a painter's use of tone and colour depends largely on the materials at his disposal. Tempera and fresco colours dry to relatively light tones; only with the development of an oil medium was it possible to achieve the darker and richer shadow depths of a Caravaggio or a Velazquez. Movements such as Impressionism and Fauvism which astounded contemporaries by the way they exploited colour as a means of expression were not technically possible until the researches of nineteenth-century chemists and dyers made available permanent pigments along the full spectrum. Before this, the range of colours expanded only gradually. The brilliancy of some pure colours available now could not be obtained from natural substances; other vivid mineral colours were expensive and sometimes unobtainable, and large canvases of the sixteenth century onwards were painted primarily in cheaper and readily available earth colours, artists relying on the optical effects of overlays or colour contrasts for subtlety or illusionistic intensity of hues.

The nature of some techniques can be only surmised and rash restoration or alteration have meant that many great works cannot be appreciated in the original form. Recent advances in historical research, however, allow a deeper appreciation of the skill of those who painted them and a better understanding of the complex interaction between medium and meaning, technique and expression.

BOTTICELLI (below):
Venus and the Graces bringing presents to a bride, detail, c. 1486
The grandeur and simplicity of Renaissance frescos came from quite a limited range of colours mixed in water and flooded with large brushes on to damp plaster which bound the colour as it dried. Less arduous ways of creating large-scale works superseded this technique.

Tempera and Encaustic

Tempera was known to the Egyptians, Greeks and Romans but was fully developed during the Byzantine period to become the main process used for small-scale painting until the development of oil-paint in the fifteenth century.

Originally, tempera was a term given to all colours "tempered" with a vehicle to make them workable; the early encaustic medium, for example, was pigment tempered with hot, liquid wax. Encaustic colours and brush-marks were fused, and the pigment driven into the wood panel surface, when a heated spatula or a metal plate was passed across the completed painting. The ancient Greeks probably invented encaustic, and it was used most skilfully by Egyptians in mummy portraits of the second century AD. Their smooth finish contrasts with the rough surface of modern wax-emulsion paintings, in which a wax vehicle is used intentionally to retain a texture of brush and spatula marks, as in the *Flag* and *Target* Pop Art works by Jasper Johns.

In traditional casein, or "cheese-painting", techniques, pigments were tempered with liquid milk-precipitate. Casein paints dry quickly to a matt finish, and it is not easy to blend tones and colours, but impasto textures can be made with a spatula or a stiff brush. Modern artists such as Matisse and Motherwell have used these paints, which are now manufactured ready-mixed in tubes. Modern gouache paints (see p. 161) are also often wrongly described as "tempera colours".

The true tempera medium is pigment mixed with the yolk or the white of egg, and thinned in use with water. It is so fast-drying that the technique of painting with it is not unlike drawing. The linear nature of the medium is reflected in the neat, delicate, stylized and unambiguous work

STYLE OF ORCAGNA (above)
The Adoration of the shepherds, c. 1370–71
The angels shown in the retouched detail (right) are taken from this gabled tempera panel, part of a large altarpiece with an elaborate frame, probably fitted before painting began.

UNDERPAINTING
The painting of the three angels began, as on the right-hand figure in this reconstruction, with an underdrawing in warm grey lines (*verdaccio*), which showed as a guide through subsequent paint layers, and with green on the face and hands. Laid over the white gesso to provide a subtle base colour for semi-translucent flesh tints, the green underpainting can sometimes be detected through the faded colours of early paintings. Areas to be gilded were brushed over with red bole (gilder's clay) to provide a fixing surface, or mordant.

ANDREA PISANO (below)
Painting, c. 1431
The intent attitude of the panel painter depicted here suggests the painstaking nature of tempera. He may be using a stylus to incise the outlines of a halo against the gold-leaf background. On the work-stool beside him stand jars of pigment ready for use. Colours were mixed with egg and a little water and lightened by the addition of white, producing smoother paint with more covering power. Small brushes were hand-made by inserting sable hairs tied with waxed string into a quill, which was then mounted in a cane or wooden handle. Since the shape and thickness of the tip helped to determine the character of the brush-stroke, the brushes were individually trimmed to suit the needs of the painter. Preparatory work, including gilding, was often done by work-shop apprentices.

JOHNS
Numbers in colour, detail, 1958–59
The ancient wax medium, encaustic, has been used here in a modern form, on crinkled newspaper stuck to canvas (the print is visible in places). The uneven ground, combined with swashy brush-strokes of quick-setting encaustic colour, demonstrates that familiar images – letters, numbers, flags or maps – may acquire the status of fine art when rendered in such a painterly manner.

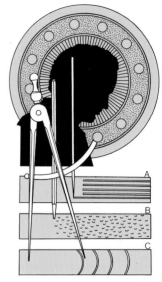

GILDING

The gold-leaf of the haloes was fixed to the red bole in small squares of paper-thin beaten gold which was then burnished with bone, ivory, agate or even the back of a spoon. Smoothed down into a hard lustrous coat by the burnisher, the gold could be incised with a stylus (A) or compass (C), or impressed with a punch (B) or die stamp engraved to the artist's design. Drapery could be embellished with highlights and tiny stencilled patterns by using gold powder in a thin solution of egg, which stuck only where glue was applied to form a mordant and brushed off elsewhere.

typical of medieval and early Renaissance artists.

The luminous quality of many tempera paintings depends on a ground of brilliantly white gesso (gypsum mixed with glue) which carries the paint. Successive layers of gesso were applied to the support – traditionally a well-seasoned wood panel – and the final layer was burnished for an enamel-smooth surface. The design could be drawn free-hand with charcoal directly on to the gesso, but for larger works might be traced on to greased paper and transferred by incising the gesso with a metal stylus or by dabbing carbon through the perforated design. There was relatively little scope for corrections in the course of the work.

Gold-leaf decoration was an important element of panel painting until the middle of the fifteenth century, used for backgrounds as well as haloes and drapery details. Icons and altarpieces were gilded not only to enhance their value but to symbolize divine radiance and to catch the light in churches. Medieval manuscripts on vellum (animal skin) were also enriched with gold-leaf; the tempera was usually bound with white of egg.

Tempera painting involves adding colours over a light ground; after the initial monochrome drawing describing the forms a green (terre-verte) underpainting was laid on in some areas to provide a neutral base for flesh tints. Much of the painting was done in earth colours, which could be successfully applied in one coat. But for the more precious pigments – such as vermilion, ultramarine and malachite – a glowing intensity and characteristic sheen might be achieved by building up as many as ten layers of thin colour. The paint was laid on in swift, successive strokes of the brush. Tempera dries too quickly for brush-strokes to be blended but details such as drapery could be further modelled by a series of fine brush-strokes hatched and interwoven on the surface.

During the Renaissance, tempera was gradually replaced by the more flexible medium of oil. But the traditional tempera technique has been revived by such modern artists as Ben Shahn, Edward Wadsworth and Andrew Wyeth, who have exploited its linear precision and clarity.

SHAHN (right)
Handball, detail, 1939
Many of Shahn's tempera paintings are political or social commentaries. The medium's precision suits his interpretation of bleak city settings, texturally enlivened only by stark patterns of wire netting, brick or crude graffiti. His flat, shadowless forms and reliance on contour have affinities with the work of early tempera painters.

Wall-painting

Wall-painting is one of the oldest and noblest traditions in the history of art. Where tempera demands precise craftsmanship, the sheer scale of most murals, and their public rather than private nature, challenge the artist to create correspondingly powerful works in which the overall breadth of the conception is usually more important than meticulous detail.

The earliest of all paintings were drawn in charcoal on cave walls and coloured with raw earth pigments, taking on the contours of the rock itself. In the ancient civilizations of Egypt, Greece, India and Asia, enormous murals covering the temples, tombs and palaces were conceived as an integral part of the architectural decoration. Some Roman murals in private houses featured *trompe-l'oeil* effects. The Byzantines preferred to enliven the interiors of their churches and monasteries with glittering mosaics, but the older tradition of mural painting was continued, particularly in Italy, leading to great picture cycles in churches of the Gothic period.

Fresco, meaning fresh, was the major Renaissance method of wall-painting. It developed gradually from the technique, chiefly used until the thirteenth century, of painting on walls *a secco* (on dry plaster) in egg or glue tempera. This was a straightforward and reasonably durable process in which the colours were applied to a slightly dampened wall and adhesion was provided by a binder of egg or glue. Wax was sometimes laid over the paint to preserve it from humidity, which might cause flaking, and to give lustre to the characteristically matt colours.

The true fresco method (*buon fresco*) is difficult but rewarding. Pure pigments, mixed only with water, were applied directly to fresh, damp plaster which absorbed and bound them as it dried. The range of colours was limited to those that were lime-resistant, such as the ochres and umbers, chalk and charcoal, and the pinks and greens that occur naturally in clay. These earth colours tend to be subdued, producing the airy and muted harmonies characteristic of most frescos. Vivid mineral colours, particularly the blues, could only be added in tempera over areas painted in earths that were already dry.

The whole work had to be conceived clearly in advance. From preliminary sketches, the main axes of the composition were marked out and the design sketched on a coarse plaster layer (the *arriccio*). This was the first opportunity for both painter and patron to see the work in context and assess the relationship of the design to its architectural setting, often a fundamental compositional aspect of wall-painting.

The thin top coat of plaster on which the painting was done (the *intonaco*) was laid an area at a time according to the artist's estimate of how much he could paint in a day. The day-piece (*giornata*) therefore varied in size according to the amount of detail it covered. The artist might have had to do the final plastering himself to achieve the surface he wanted. When he came to paint, the drawing showing at the boundary of the new day-piece served as a guide in relating the different

MICHELANGELO (above)
Head of Adam, detail from the Sistine ceiling, 1510-12. Michelangelo used a full-size plan, called a *cartoon*, to trace his design on to the plaster with a stylus. The resulting score lines are still visible in the head of Adam. He worked unaided, on high scaffolding with his head thrown back and his brush held up at arm's length. The discomfort and eye strain he suffered were bitterly described in a poem and a caricature of himself as a hunchback.

LEONARDO (above)
The Last Supper, detail, *c.* 1495-98
Damp can ruin murals, particularly if the artist's technique is faulty. Seeking a less piecemeal method than fresco, Leonardo invented a process that was perhaps designed to allow him to work over *The Last Supper* at leisure and as a whole, uniting the tones of the composition. He tried oil on a resin undercoat which failed to dry out. The surface of the painting quickly began to deteriorate.

elements in the composition. Colours were not easily matched with those of an adjacent day-piece, however, which would have dried matt and lighter in tone than newly-applied paint. For their work to stand out in the dim natural light or candlelight of interiors, artists often used a range of pale shades, mixed with white, giving cool, rather high-key colour schemes.

Fresco painters laboured for long hours in tiring, often badly-lit conditions and needed physical stamina as well as skill and decisiveness. Mistakes were not easy to rectify as the brush-strokes were absorbed rapidly into the plaster surface. Retouching could be done *a secco* but major corrections were possible only by hacking off dried plaster and starting again.

The beauty of the method lay in its freedom and scale. The little sable brushes commonly used in tempera were employed only for finishing *a secco*. As fresco paint was made up in quantity and spread like watercolour it was easy to cover large areas quickly, using big brushes in sweeping strokes. This encouraged monumental settings and figure groups, and impressionistic rather than detailed handling of distant scenes. The use of fresco declined after the sixteenth century, partly because of a growing demand for intimacy and naturalism but mainly because oil and canvas provided a more versatile and convenient method of painting, even for large-scale works.

Ⓐ

Ⓑ

Ⓒ

STAGES OF A FRESCO
The reconstruction (left)
shows how Andrea del
Castagno and assistants
may have worked on the
*Crucifixion, Deposition and
Resurrection of Christ*,
c. 1445-50, in the Convent
of St Apollonia, Florence.
He worked up from an underdrawing in red paint, the
sinopia (detail above) to
finished sections such as
the left-hand *Resurrection*,
shown here as it may have
looked when first completed.
The entire *sinopia* was
sketched out on coarse
plaster, the *arriccio* (B),
covering the wall plaster
(C). The original design
was transferred to the
arriccio by using a full-
size paper pattern fastened
to the wall over a blank
sheet, the outlines being
perforated with a tailor's
tracing wheel. With the
pattern removed, charcoal
dust was dabbed (pounced)
through the holes in the
blank sheet to provide the
basis for the underdrawing
in red earth pigment. This
sinopia was covered by
the *intonaco* (A), the thin
section of fresh plaster on
which the artist painted
his day-piece, but Castagno
reused the pattern to map
out the design in charcoal
again (as illustrated here)
before he began to paint.
His method of drawing up
his design on the wall was
exceptionally thorough;
most artists began painting
directly on the *intonaco*.
Assistants had to haul up
large tubs of water to
thin the ready-mixed paint,
keep brushes clean of lime
and wet out the *intonaco* as
the day-piece proceeded.
The scaffold was secured to
the wall by crossbeams.
Castagno's fresco, in the
refectory of the convent,
was discovered in 1890
under a layer of whitewash.

Early Oil Techniques

MASTER OF THE VIEW OF SAINT
GUDULE (immediate right)
A young man, c.1480

Although oil has been supremely important in the history of Western painting, its early development as a vehicle for colour was slow, difficult and tentative. Oil was used from ancient times for tinting and varnishing, and as a medium for colouring Egyptian mummy cloths, Roman shields and medieval processional banners. Among medieval panel painters who employed oil varnishes to preserve their work or give it a surface sheen, there were those who perceived the potential usefulness of a vehicle which would allow colours to be blended and tones to be deepened without recourse to the minute hatched brush-strokes of tempera. Ways of mixing pigment into oil were discussed in treatises on painting from the late thirteenth century, but it was found difficult to control the drying process or to develop an oil vehicle suitable for delicate work. Much experimental work has deteriorated or been lost. Florentine painters of the fourteenth and early fifteenth centuries restricted the use of oil-paint to less detailed parts of the composition where fine work was less crucial.

It was left to northern European artists, notably Hubert and Jan van Eyck, to turn to account the gradual refinement of the oil medium. In their painting technique during the early fifteenth century, they and other early oil practitioners followed closely the careful, considered approach of the tempera masters, laying colour in a thin, transparent glaze of oil and resin over a detailed underdrawing in a water-based paint – a method not unlike the tinting of a black and white photograph. Gesso grounded panels were still used as supports and the smooth white surface of the ground helped to give clarity and brilliance to the subsequent colour layers, which could be further lightened by applying a thin layer of white tempera over the oil glazes.

Early oil-glazed temperas are characterized by glowing colour and incisive draughtsmanship;

The reconstruction (above) of the underdrawing, beside the finished head, is based on the method of Jan van Eyck, whose realistic draughtsmanship set a precedent. The drawing medium was a glue tempera, applied with the tip of the brush. This could be employed directly by following a preliminary design, or used to reinforce a preliminary sketching out in charcoal. Individual styles varied between highly detailed and summary work. Pencil-thin strokes served to outline forms and define shadows. When the drawing was dry, areas of colour could be blocked in, the brush-strokes blending easily, owing to the spreading power of the oleo-resin medium. The final stage, once the colours were established, was to work up highlights and details with dabs of varnish, to make them glow with colour or reflect light.

MILLAIS
Mariana, detail, 1851
In true Pre-Raphaelite tradition, Millais painted with close attention to naturalistic detail. Work such as this fastidious copying of the stained glass at Merton College, Oxford prompted a critic to compare Millais with van Eyck.

MEMLINC
The Nieuwenhove diptych, detail, 1487
The fish-eye mirror, the crest in the window and the slit opening on to a glimpse of the garden indicate the delight with which this Netherlandish artist, an early master of oil-painting, observed and recorded detail.

EDDY
Untitled, detail, 1971
Don Eddy's interest in the literal, impartial quality of found images leads him to copy from his own black and white photographs, which provide an even tighter basis for the picture than could be achieved by a meticulous underdrawing. Here, he uses oil to create a flatly-painted, illusionistic surface, adding colour which is realistic but not necessarily true to the original source.

lines were drawn with the precision and control of a master heraldic sign-writer. Successive colour overlays fused the cross-hatched tempera shading into imperceptible tonal gradations, extending the scope for varying effects of lighting, so that the picture space might seem to be illuminated by diffused light – a flickering candle or supernatural glow – or by harsh, direct light. Subtle modulations of light and shade combined with skilfully simulated cast shadows brought a magical solidity to the volume and weight of things. But since the whole design had been determined by the underdrawing, the completed picture retained much of the compositional character of medieval panels. Figures and background features were usually drawn in meticulous detail and, whatever their spatial position in the picture, defined in sharp focus – then separately identified by colour, with map-like clarity. The systematic technique brought a still grandeur to the formal portraits and to the frozen tableaux of statuesque figures. The sense of emotional restraint was reinforced by the faultless finish of the paint surface, which dried without any evidence of the artist's brush-marks.

Subsequent developments in oil-painting technique established a variety of painting methods and a greater spontaneity of brushwork. Yet many later painters have followed self-imposed technical limitations. Using close-weave canvas and fine brushes, Neoclassicists such as David and Ingres returned to a systematic painting procedure controlled by precise underdrawing. The nineteenth-century Pre-Raphaelite school found inspiration in temperas executed "before the time of Raphael", and employed painstaking oil techniques to seek "truth to nature". More recently, Surrealist painters such as Dali and Magritte, concerned with expressing the persuasive clarity of irrational dream images, have suppressed the expressive brushwork and texture available to the modern artist, using an even application of paint which gives their surfaces an anonymous, illustrative quality. Photo-Realist painters, while pursuing very different aims, have used oil-paint to achieve an intensely objective detail derived directly from photographic sources.

ANTONELLO DA MESSINA
S. Cassiano altarpiece, detail, 1476
Antonello's deft handling of light and colour opened the eyes of other Italian Renaissance painters to the new possibilities of oil-paint. The solidity of the book, the volume of the spheres, the contrasts of textures and the luminosity trapped within the glass are simulated with a skill that owes much to Netherlandish techniques. If Antonello did not himself visit the north, he could certainly have seen Netherlandish work in Naples, where he studied under Colantonio, who worked in the style of van Eyck. This altarpiece, painted in Venice and now surviving only in fragments, may have been executed in an egg/oil emulsion or in oil glazes over tempera. Its subtle modelling and glowing colour decisively influenced Giovanni Bellini and the whole future course of Venetian painting.

Oils on Coloured Grounds

TITIAN
(left) *Bacchus and Ariadne*, detail, 1523
(right) *The death of Actaeon* (unfinished), detail, c. 1559
The treatment of Bacchus, frozen in mid-leap with his cloak curling in sculptured folds, shows the legacy of oil-on-tempera techniques, colour serving mainly to define and enrich a tight, calculated linear design. The potential expressiveness of oil and canvas is more fully realized in one of Titian's later works, where Diana is painted with almost impressionistic freedom and instantaneity. Forms blend fluidly, and the spring and texture of the canvas weave are exploited with vibrant contrasts between glazes and "scrubbed" opaque paint.

From the early fifteenth century painters were using canvas as a support for paintings and this gradually became standard, as international patronage brought demands for large pictures and transport abroad. Whereas even strongly braced panels might warp or split with a change of climate, canvas could be rolled for shipment, and its lightness made it convenient for large-scale works. The suppleness of canvas and its woven surface facilitated a wider range of textures than the smooth, inflexible panels; sharp contours of rocky or metallic forms, for example, could be contrasted with blurred edges of fleecy clouds and soft velvets.

With the development of oil-painting, gesso was found to be unsuitable as priming on canvas, and in Italy the practice evolved of priming the canvas with an oily paste. From the beginning of experiments with oil-painting, some painters had spread a thin layer of colour (*imprimatura*) over the white ground to establish an overall tone for the composition, either before or after the underdrawing was complete. In the late sixteenth century the Venetians developed the use of coloured oil priming for canvas, actually mixing the pigment into the priming layer. Working on a coloured ground prepared by one or other of these techniques was the standard method of oil-painting for more than three hundred years.

With the development of the paper industry from the fifteenth century onwards, paper became cheaper and more freely available, enabling artists to build up a body of reference drawings and to try

ZURBARAN (below)
A painter at the foot of the Cross, detail, c. 1635-40?
The immediacy of oil-paint is well suggested by the loaded brushes held by the artist (possibly Zurbaran himself) and by his palette with its colours arranged neatly to hand in two tiers and in order of decreasing tonality. The brushes seem to carry colours from the lower tier, probably used for glazing and for the final highlights and dark accents that intensified his dramatic chiaroscuro.

out ideas before starting the actual painting. The oil on tempera technique of carefully colouring in a linear underdrawing gave way to less formal preparatory work; richer, more painterly methods of underdrawing in oil-paint were used on the coloured grounds, including a liberal use of white to give body to the form and establish areas of light and shade. This was similar in principle to *grisaille* (literally a painting in tones of grey), where the composition was laid out in wash rather than line and highlights applied with opaque white paint.

The colours chosen for the *imprimatura* or for the priming layer were various and had a significant effect on the final painting. Artists of the Italian school, notably Caravaggio, who wished to establish a rich depth of tones, often worked from a dark red or brown priming. Dutch landscape painters of the seventeenth century continued to use white grounds, laying over them a variety of cool greys and ochres, according to the depth of tone they hoped to achieve in the most luminous details of sky or water. The English school of the eighteenth century favoured warm grounds which had a reddening effect on subsequent colour layers, while the French, admiring the airy qualities of pastel drawing, preferred light tints tending towards bluish tones.

With the tonal basis established by the coloured ground and the underpainting, subtle modulations could be achieved through careful handling of the brush when colour was applied. By lifting or depressing the brush it was possible to achieve a wide range of tonal variation and degrees of colour

RUBENS (below)
Sketch for *The Annunciation*
panel, detail, 1620-21
The technique of *grisaille*,
here used by Rubens in a
preparatory sketch for a
ceiling painting, became
for some northern painters
a convenient means of
underpainting the full work,
allowing the composition
to be worked out swiftly in
monochrome oil. Rubens laid
a streaky brown *imprimatura*
over a white, gessoed panel
to provide the general tone
and indicated volume rapidly
with strokes of loaded white
and thinned grey umber.
Grisaille was often used to
indicate relief before the
advent of chiaroscuro.

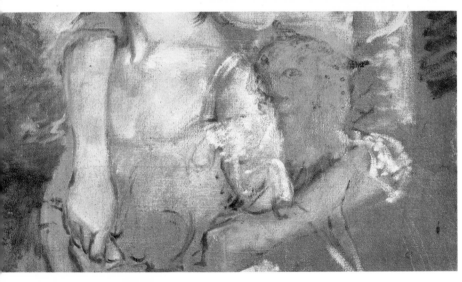

GAINSBOROUGH
*The painter's daughters with
a cat*, unfinished, c. 1759
The use of a coloured
ground to provide a middle
tone can be clearly seen in
unfinished 18th-century
portraits where the standard
procedure was to complete
the sitter's head, leaving
the ground empty or perhaps
with shapes indicated only
sketchily. Gainsborough has
used a red-brown priming,
and sketched in the figures
in iron oxide red, blocked
in with an admixture of
white. His characteristic
rapid, grainy stroke is
shown in the detail, with
some scribbling at the right
in what looks like pastel.
The cat has been partly
obliterated by a patch of
yellow ochre. Gainsborough
might have excluded the cat
in the finished picture and
he would probably have
cooled and greyed the
background to add, by
contrast, translucency and
warmth to the flesh tones.

intensity in one application. Pressing the loaded
brush firmly on the canvas left colour at full
opaque strength, while if it was skimmed lightly
across the tinted canvas weave it would produce
scumbles – broken passages of less intense, semi-
transparent colour, optically influenced by the
ground tint beneath. The colour range could be
increased further by the free application of alternate glazes of warm and cool colour, overlapped to
produce harmonious transitional mixtures or juxtaposed to create optical contrasts. Strong colour
accents and definition of detail could be clarified in
the final stages of painting.

These procedures helped to overcome the limitations of the relatively small range of colours
available to painters until the nineteenth century.
Initially paintings were executed primarily in
earth colours and it was necessary to exploit
properties of complementary contrast to achieve a
real intensity of hue. Earth red could take on an
intensity similar to vermilion when juxtaposed
with *terre verte*, and yellow ochre gained a golden
brilliance against a field of blue.

Even though the development of a full range of
painters' colours was very gradual, the free techniques of oil-painting and scope for improvisation
demanded that the painter had all his available
colours to hand, and a palette became essential
equipment. Powdered pigment was mixed with oil
on the palette with a spatula and, until satisfactory
methods of storing mixed paint were invented,
pigments were ground fresh each day and colours
mixed as required.

Oils: Surface Effects

As oil-painting techniques developed, artists began to exploit the plasticity of the paint itself and to achieve a wide range of surface effects by varying its opacity and thickness. Although oil-paint eventually oxidizes to form a tough skin, its fluidity and slow-drying properties allow changes to be made by scraping, wiping or reworking while the picture is being built up, making possible an improvising spontaneity of style and composition. For some styles of painting it is necessary to let each layer of paint dry before applying subsequent colours, but there are early instances of artists painting swiftly into wet layers (*alla prima*) to achieve the final effect in one operation. Freedom and speed of attack were further encouraged by the development during the late seventeenth century of ready-mixed paints stored in bladders.

The surfaces of paintings worked over in successive layers had a richness and luminosity unknown in earlier mediums. Glazes allowing light to be reflected back from lower layers were played against soft, textural scumbles and impasto areas in which paint was laid on with a thickly loaded brush or with the spatula. Forms could be shown submerged in shadow or suffused with light, compositions made in dramatic tonal patterns of woven light and dark masses.

Painters established individual styles according to their intentions; it was possible for the Dutch still-life painters, for example, to build up carefully detailed, illusionistic works in which a range of textures and surfaces were simulated, while artists such as Velazquez and Hals, both of whom sometimes worked wet-on-wet, developed a characteristically personal use of the brush, where a dextrous shorthand of dots, loops and dashes sufficed to suggest the glitter of metal or the sheen of satin, the droop of a mouth or eyelid and the weight of tumbling hair. Rembrandt's mature works demonstrate most clearly the expressive textural range of oil-paint; pigment is spread with rag and spatula, smeared with thumb and palm or scraped with brush handle, with crusty, pitted mounds of paint forming a sculptured infrastructure for final colour glazes. His method of working is so complex – and varied – as to defy precise analysis, but the effect is one of unparalleled subtlety, depth and richness.

HALS
A member of the Coymans family; and detail, 1645
Hals' assurance enabled him to dispense with laborious underpainting or multiple glazes and to achieve his effects at the surface. Most of this portrait is painted wet-on-wet over a very thin brownish ground. The detail shows the confidence with which shadows and lights are brushed into the grey of the sleeve. Final accents of black and yellow were then dashed on to define the folds and to suggest the texture of the brocade.

CANALETTO
(left) *The harbour of St Mark's towards the west*, unfinished, *c.* 1760-66?
(below) *The harbour of St Mark's from the east*; detail of S. Giorgio Maggiore, 1740
Working from a ruled-up ink-and-wash drawing mapping the view, Canaletto proceeded towards a free handling on the surface of the picture. The unfinished oil shows that a fluid sky colour has been washed over a warm brown *imprimatura*, with hazy clouds and tonal gradations added while the pigment was wet. The lit sides of the buildings have been blocked in with opaque tints, the ground colour retained as shadow. Patches of the ground also appear through the greyer blue of the water. The reflection of a building is dragged vertically in a semi-opaque scumble. The detail of a finished view shows the use of a fine brush to sharpen features, and white highlights flicked in with tiny strokes on the water to give a scalloped pattern suggesting lapping waves.

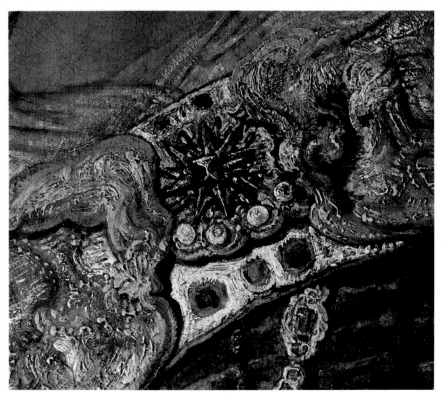

REMBRANDT
Belshazzar's feast; and detail, 1635
Reproached for building up his pictures so heavily, Rembrandt said he was no dyer but a painter. Unlike Hals, he developed his rich effects through a heavy structure of underpainting and glazes, using unusually thick oil, which dried quite quickly, and resin varnishes which preserved the body and texture of the paint. Except in final glazes, he rarely blended different applications of paint. The jewel-encrusted brocade of Belshazzar's cloak is built up over a layer of umber which is allowed to show through in some areas, and at the cloak edge seems to have been scratched with the brush handle or a finger-tip. The surface is covered with thick blobs of yellow paint like golden snail trails. In parts, the paint is visibly raised, giving the surface a real, not illusionary texture and, by catching the light, adding to the overall sparkle.

Oils: Direct Methods

WHISTLER (right)
Symphony in white no. 3,
detail, 1867
The impact of Eastern art
brought important changes
in European attitudes to
design and technique. The
influence of Japanese brush
drawings is evident in the
calligraphic brushwork of
Whistler, who delicately
exploits the plasticity of
oil in his feathery wet-
into-wet brush twists.

During the nineteenth century events conspired to encourage direct methods of painting in which the use of coloured grounds was abandoned and the hand of the artist became more visible and assertive. Scientific research introduced intense, permanent pigments that made it possible for painters to achieve, in an initial application of paint, hues earlier approximated only by the optical effects of overlays and complementary colour contrasts. Portable equipment and the development about 1840 of commercial paints in soft metal tubes increased the mobility of artists and freed them from the strict traditions of studio practice. At the same time, the invention of photography, which threatened to usurp the painter's function as a literal recorder of people, places or events, provided a spur to experimentation and to a redefinition of the artist's role as expressive creator rather than as dutiful illustrator.

Constable and Delacroix, in the energy and spontaneity of their brushwork were among the forerunners of a growing interest in the textural

CEZANNE
(below) *Woodland scene*,
1882–85; (left) detail
Each deliberated brush-mark
contributes to the building
up of volume, structure,
texture, space and light,
yet an overall pattern of
local colour is maintained.
In his mature technique,
Cézanne began by loosely
indicating main contours
and receding planes in
thinned blue. Retaining
patches of white priming as
frontal planes, he then
used overlapping strokes of
colour, modulated in tone
and temperature, to establish
the transitions from shadow
to light in faceted planes.
To sharpen these transitions,
to project forms towards
the viewer and to imply a
changing viewpoint, nervous
wiry contours were drawn,
modified, obliterated and
finally determined throughout
the progress of the picture.
The brush-marks seem almost
to cut into the canvas.

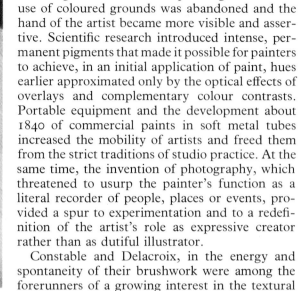

qualities of oil-paint itself, an interest also championed by Whistler, whose paintings emphasized formal, decorative values, his composition and technique reflecting the influence of Japanese prints and brush drawings. Trends towards spontaneity and away from the smooth finish of salon art culminated in the work of the Impressionists, many of whom regarded photography more as a stimulus than a rival. They were excited by the unconventional viewpoints of arbitrary snapshots and by the camera's ability to capture transitory effects of light and weather, which they set out to render with vibrant brushwork.

Plein-air Impressionists such as Pissarro exploited the colour strength of the new pigments by painting in direct, unmodulated strokes on white-primed canvas. Illusions of volume and the simulation of tactile surfaces gave way to sensations of shimmering light suggested by a vivacious handling of juxtaposed colours. Impressionist techniques demanded a rapid, skilled judgment of a landscape's shifting tones and colours as they appeared under momentary lighting conditions. Monet advised: ". . . you must try to forget what objects you have before you – a tree, a house, a field – merely think, here is a little square of blue, here an oblong of pink, here is a streak of yellow, and paint it just as it looks to you".

Cézanne and Seurat attempted to bring a classical order to Impressionist discoveries – Seurat by a scientific analysis of colour, Cézanne by more intuitive methods which evolved slowly and with great effort into a technique of rendering form by using his brush almost as if it were a chisel. The plasticity of oil-paint was employed more passionately by van Gogh, who vividly represented space, volume, texture and light with writhing streaks of unmerged pigment, and by the Expressionists who followed Munch. In the twentieth century this interest in the gestural, emotive and textural possibilities of oil-paint has been carried further, most vehemently in Abstract Expressionism which often became an explosive celebration of the act of applying paint.

PISSARRO
The Oise near Pontoise, 1873
Solid forms are summarily treated and detail kept to a minimum in short, broad strokes of thick paint on the boat and buildings. Glints of light are suggested with dabs, flecks and dots. To retain full intensity of colour and a sense of the immediacy of application, Impressionist paintings were usually left unvarnished.

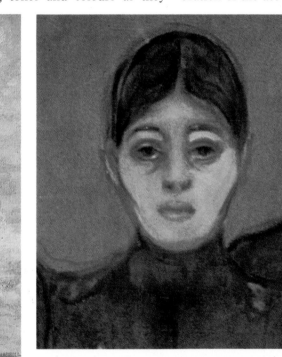

MUNCH (left)
Death in the room, detail, 1892
Technical refinement is subordinated to an anxious mood helped by map-like patterns in which traces of preliminary drawing are incorporated. Lapped by swirling tides of greenish colour, the woman's face is insubstantial, haunted.

JORN (below)
Green ballet, detail, 1960
In the apotheosis of direct painting methods – Abstract Expressionism – colour may be squeezed straight from the tube, splattered or dripped from a can on to raw canvas and spread with knives, trowels or hands. The Danish painter Jorn manipulates oils savagely to create a maelstrom of brilliant colour, looping contours and impasto skids.

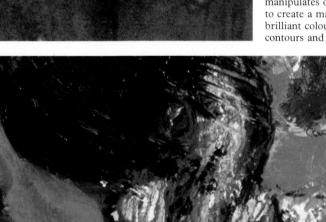

Twentieth-Century Developments

The physical nature of paint, and its collaboration with other materials, together with the texture and shape of the painting's support, have become formal elements in the design of many modern pictures; in some they constitute the very theme of the work. The rejection of the long Western tradition of spatial illusionism in painting – accelerated by the prankish works of Duchamp and other Dadaists early in the twentieth century – went hand in hand with a willingness to experiment with new techniques of handling and combining different media. Braque and Klee both delighted in original picture-making recipes. More recently, Dubuffet, Tàpies and others have expressively mixed pigment with materials ranging from tar and gravel to sand and mud.

The central place of brushwork has itself been questioned by artists such as Ernst, who created forms and textures by scraping a wet painted canvas (*grattage*), by rubbing impressions from textured relief surfaces (*frottage*) or by decalcomania techniques – pressing tacky painted shapes against dry canvas or alternatively pressing materials against wet canvas and then lifting them to produce partly accidental patterns and images. Others have gouged or slit the canvas, or built up projections to introduce an element of real space and cast shadows into an art once considered essentially two-dimensional. Painters have also countered the "window" effect of the framed rectangular canvas by the use of shaped canvases or boards, often unframed, which austerely emphasize their own flatness or suggest spatial extensions beyond the edge of the picture.

The freedom of modern artists to work rapidly and experimentally, often on a large scale, has been increased by technological advances, including the development of acrylic and vinyl paints, the first new painting medium for some 500 years. These are refined forms of industrial paints – pigments bound with synthetic resin, most of which can be thinned with water or given greater plasticity by the addition of various media. They dry quickly to form a waterproof and tough yet flexible skin. The hues are characteristically clear and intense, including a range of fluorescent and metallic colours, and it is claimed that they will not yellow with age as oil-paints tend to do. Acrylic paintings are also easily cleaned and less susceptible than oils or tempera to heat and damp.

Acrylics can be applied to almost any surface in a variety of ways – with a brush, sponge, rag, airbrush or spray-gun (normally used with masking tape or some form of stencil), or flooded directly on to the canvas – and can be used in any form varying from liquid to a thick paste. Their drying speed allows successive coats of paint to be applied almost immediately without smudging or colour change. For colour blending, drying can be retarded with additional resin medium. Surface textures range from thin, vibrant stains of colour to smooth hard-edged areas of opaque paint or heavily brushed impasto. The effect is sometimes indistinguishable from that of oil-paint and the choice of medium in recent styles of painting has been largely a matter of personal preference.

DUCHAMP (right)
Tu m', 1918
The emergence of the canvas as an art object in its own right was heralded by the works of the Dadaists. This mocking summary of traditional illusionistic devices includes deft examples of linear and atmospheric perspective, systems of portraying form and volume in terms of tonal modelling, cast shadows and colour contrast, and a *trompe l'oeil* tear "mended" with a real pin. The pin, together with the pointing hand (added by a professional sign-writer Duchamp hired), seems to challenge the artistic value of technical virtuosity.

TAPIES (right)
Ochre gris, 1958
Primeval earth textures are implied by the parched, pitted ground where a putty of oil-paint, mixed with shredded sponge and marble dust, is spread across the canvas, impressed with pieces of rope and card and gouged in scored tracks.

ERNST (below)
Forest, 1929
Natural shapes and textures (including wood and leaves) are imprinted in black. Over these, Ernst stained counterpoint areas of transparent colour, then used opaque paint to suggest figures and foliage texture.

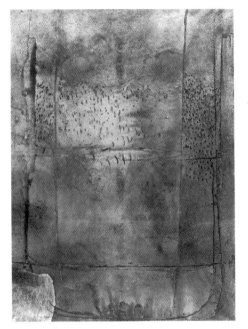

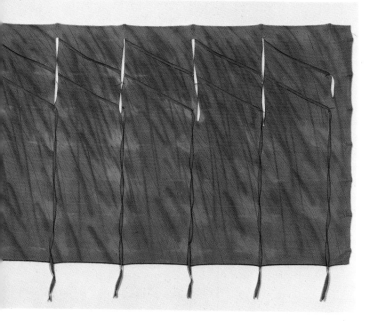

RICHARD SMITH (left)
Sudden country, 1972
Smith's canvas, delicately streaked in fluid acrylic, is loosely tacked and laced with limp fabric ribbons. The soft, threaded colours suggest grass, trees, drifting rain, but illusionism is countered by the slackness of the canvas, hinting at practical uses – kites, sails?

HOYLAND (right)
Drape, 1978
Acrylic is the natural medium of an artist who has said that paint should be put on "the way water flows, and if there is an accident it must be controlled". Over initial colour stains Hoyland uses rollers, spatulas and broad brushes to build contrasting layers of heavy impasto.

FRANK STELLA (left)
Agbatana 3, 1968
Stella wants his canvases to be regarded primarily as coloured objects. His respect for pure shape, his antagonism to illusionism and nuance are emphasized by the severity of the geometric design and by the clear, luminous acrylic and fluorescent polymer colours, mixed by the artist himself.

LOUIS
Theta, 1960
The manual dexterity of the traditional artist is here replaced by the flow of thinned paint down a tilted surface of raw canvas. Louis retains an interest in pictorial depth; his painting engulfs the viewer, its size making it difficult to focus on both banks of acrylic colour at once.

Mixed Media

CARLO CRIVELLI
St Peter, detail of the
Demidoff altarpiece, 1476
Continuing a medieval
tradition of decorative
embellishment, Crivelli's
"assemblage" includes
raised ornament in gesso
(on the cloak border and
bands of the crown), wood
(the keys) and pieces of
red, green and clear glass.

SCHWITTERS (below)
Opened by Customs, c. 1937
"What nectar and ambrosia
were to the Greek gods",
said Arp, "glue was to Kurt
Schwitters". His subtly
beautiful *merz* (rubbish)
collages were composed of
debris from the street – here
overlapping, pasted fragments
of cut and torn stamps,
envelopes, adhesive tape,
newsprint, newsphotos and
paint-scribbled paper.

Collage and assemblage – techniques of building
up a picture wholly or partially from found or
manufactured pieces of material – have enabled
modern painters to cross the boundaries between
one art form and another, and also between reality
and representation. Early mixed-media works
were often made as precious devotional objects,
embellished with gold-leaf, beaten metal or gems.
Sources for the imagery and materials of
twentieth-century assemblages have been more
often the junk-yard, sidewalk and supermarket.
Responding to a flood of new visual stimulation,
artists have shown that an almost limitless range of
ingredients can provide the formal elements of line
or shape, colour or texture. The creative ability to
organize these ingredients into effective images
does not depend on the laboriously acquired
technical skills needed for representational painting, and the ease with which pieces can be tried,
moved, discarded or reassembled makes the contrast with any earlier artistic discipline all the
sharper. Matisse, himself a superb draughtsman,

WESSELMANN (below)
Bathtub collage no. 3, 1963
Posed amid the sanitary
trappings of a partly
real bathroom, the figure,
depersonalized and flatly
painted, seems to throw
doubt on the actuality of
assembled real materials –
the curtain, wall-tiles, mat,
radiator and door with
hanging towel. Though it is
life-size, the assemblage
is only 45 cm (18 in) deep.

HAMILTON (below)
My Marilyn, 1965
In a montage based on
contact prints of Monroe
(some crossed out by her)
Richard Hamilton comments
on the repetitiveness of
mechanically-produced
images by overprinting
hand-drawn marks and
stencilled shapes to show
"art obliterating reality"

MATISSE (above)
Sorrows of the king, 1952
After 1950, confined by
arthritis to a wheelchair,
Matisse created joyous
gouaches découpées – works
composed entirely of shapes
cut from gouache-coloured
paper and pasted on a paper
ground. He called this
"cutting the colour out
alive". These flat collages,
often of mural size, became
progressively more abstract.

RAUSCHENBERG (above)
Reservoir, 1961
A provocative and poetic
scavenger whose works are
almost inventories of city
life, Rauschenberg seems
fascinated by the way in
which the ephemeral may be
transfixed by glue, nails
or paint into art. He set
the upper clock going when
he began this painting, the
lower one when he finished.

put the case for a free choice of means with
characteristic directness when he said: "Composition is the art of arranging in a decorative
manner the various elements at the painter's
disposal for the expression of his feelings".

The materials of a collage are glued in place,
usually remaining virtually flat. An early example
is the traditional Chinese craft of pasting together
intricately cut shapes of transparent coloured
paper. Collage became a major art form in Europe
when Picasso and Braque began to introduce a
greater variety of colour, texture and references to
real objects in their Cubist works by combining
found materials with painted and drawn areas.
Newspaper, muslin, textured card and patterned
papers, cloth and cane gave way to more three-
dimensional objects in the work of the Dadaists.
The materials in some of Kurt Schwitters' magpie
nests included wire, string, nails, cork, rusted
metal, splintered wood and worn rag.

While collage materials are often combined for
their emotive, political or comical connotations
they may also be arranged for purely formal, non-
literary reasons. Sonia Delaunay composed her
Orphist abstracts in geometrical shapes cut from
flatly coloured paper and worked over in chalk and
watercolour. Arp's Dada collages were created
"according to the laws of chance" in arabesque
patterns dropped at random on colour-stained
paper and pasted where they fell. At the end of
their lives Mondrian and Matisse made major
abstract compositions from coloured paper alone.

Montage, a collage technique incorporating
prints or photographs, was exploited by the Surrealists to produce absurd, amusing, disturbing or
lyrical fantasies, and photographs became a major
element in the work of some Pop artists. The
introduction of mirror glass or other reflective
materials into collages is another Surrealist device
taken up by more recent artists, some of whom
have used areas of polished steel or aluminium in
combination with painted or collaged figures. The
visual texture of paintings has been further enlivened by the revival of word imagery in Synthetic Cubist collages, and in the stencilled sign-
writing of Pop artists such as Indiana.

Combine paintings, or assemblages, are an
extended form of collage where a part or all of the
finished object is essentially three-dimensional,
fastened in place. "I am a painter and I nail my
pictures together", said Schwitters. In the combine
paintings of Rauschenberg painting "becomes
an adventure, like walking down the street".
Shattered road signs, buckled metal plates,
burning electric lights, stuffed birds, radios or
ticking clocks may be combined with screen-
printed images of ball games and moon landings,
advertising symbols and famous faces.
Rauschenberg's use of gestural brush-marks to
subdue, isolate or integrate such disparate components preserves a link with the traditional
concept of painting, but the tendency has been for
modern artists to reject limitations of space and
time and progressively to dismantle the barriers
between painting, sculpture, architecture, theatre
and life itself.

Watercolour

Watercolour has a fluency and adaptability which most other art media cannot match, and its exacting simplicity has challenged many artists who have painted chiefly in oils. The basis of the medium is powdered pigment bound with a solution of gum arabic which is thinned with water and laid on paper or card with pointed and square-ended brushes of soft squirrel or sable hair. Its special quality of luminous delicacy arises because light reflects back from the paper through the colour, making the whole vivid and translucent.

Dürer was probably the first to exploit the fluid immediacy of the medium in the atmospheric studies of lakes and mountains he made on his travels through Europe to Italy. But for the next three hundred years it was to be employed mainly for colouring prints and tinting botanical and architectural line-drawings. During the eighteenth century it came to be favoured by travelling topographical artists for its quick-drying properties and light, compact equipment. Paper quality was an important element in the development of the technique by English masters at the end of the eighteenth century, when a range of tough, absorbent paper, hand-made from linen rags, which could stand repeated flooding with water, was available. To prevent its cockling during painting, the paper was pasted to card, or dampened and stretched over a board, or frame.

In order to express the evanescent qualities of colour and light in a landscape and to retain the freshness of the completed watercolour, certainty and swiftness of execution were essential; all stages of the painting were carefully planned and corrections and second thoughts avoided. The picture progressed from light to dark: the taut sheet was sponged with water and the pale sky tints washed over the entire picture surface; next the colour silhouettes of the main landscape features were superimposed. Tints were obtained by diluting the pigment with water, highlights and white forms made by leaving patches of the paper untouched, giving watercolour's characteristic sparkle. Hues could be intensified or deepened in tone by applying successive transparent stains and

TURNER
(above) *Sunset on the Jura*, 1841; (right) *Tintern Abbey*, 1794
Turner's early watercolour is really a tinted drawing, the colour washes clarifying landscape features already outlined in pencil, in the manner of topographical artists of previous eras.
In his later, almost abstract work, he moves beyond even the direct techniques of his contemporaries, resorting to thumbnail and knife-scratches or flecks of opaque white to create effects of suffused atmosphere and dancing highlights. Turner's 36 cakes of watercolour (left) were carefully preserved and recorded, after the artist's death, by his influential champion, the critic Ruskin.

colours were often blended in the same way rather than by mixing them first on a palette. Progressive thinning with water made tonal gradations almost imperceptible, though to blend these wet bands of colour required considerable judgment and skill. Undispersed particles of pigment in the crevices of the rough surfaces of the heavier hand-made papers produced effects of broken colour, and coarse textures, such as bark, brushwood and tufted rock, were suggested by dragging a wide-ended brush of drier pigment across the irregular surface of the paper. Details could be added and focal points in the design sharpened when the paper dried. Leading exponents of this near-Impressionist, "direct" manner were John Robert Cozens, Thomas Girtin, and Richard Parkes Bonington. Though less purist in technique, Turner exploited the full range of the medium in watercolours ranging from studies centimetres across to paintings the size of large oils and meant to hold their own beside them in a gallery.

English watercolours of the nineteenth century often became little more than showy displays of bravura handling, but in America a vigorous tradition of fluidly expressive marine painting developed with the watercolours of Thomas Eakins and Winslow Homer and later of the expatriates James Whistler and John Singer Sargent. More recently, the emotive character of buildings and interiors has been a particular theme in American watercolours – Charles Burchfield's eerie windswept streets painted in sinister drips and spooky squiggles, or Edward Hopper's shadowed rooms and shuttered shopfronts, expressed in neat clear washes. Although gouache has been the preferred medium of most European artists, watercolour has also been brilliantly employed in the twentieth century by Kandinsky, Klee, Dufy, Picasso and Nolde.

The medium is often expressively combined with others – ink, crayon, body-colour and pencil. Cézanne, for instance, used pencil concurrently with wash in the manner of his line and colour-plane oil method, combining an exploration of structure with a sense of transitory effects of light.

EAKINS (above)
John Biglen in a single scull, detail, 1876
A systematic technique of tiny overlaid brush-strokes and streaks of bare paper gives sharp-focus realism, yet the direct handling and accurate tonality sustain the medium's freshness.

NOLDE (below)
Summer flowers, detail, c.1930
Nolde's approach is spontaneous rather than calculated: across dampened paper, he laid flat glowing patterns of colour, gradated and intensified with deeper hues dropped from a full brush.

KLEE (below)
Hamammet motif, detail, 1914
Klee exploits the fissured quality of the paper itself, creating rich contrasts in texture between lightly painted squares and those with more depth of paint.

CEZANNE (left)
The black château, detail, c.1895
Much of the paper is left untouched and pencil used to demarcate the main forms in terms of frontal planes and projecting and interlocking surfaces; this outline is then enlivened by deft, transparent strokes of watercolour, which give the building, despite the light handling, a feeling of depth and carved solidity.

Ink

Ink is a principal medium in Far Eastern painting, which relies on line and tone as the main expressive elements. Oriental artists attempt to capture a sense of cosmic unity through harmonious communion with the spirit of Nature – the Tao; the very act of painting becomes a spiritual exercise in which the controlled handling of the brush demands an apprenticeship as exacting as that required from a ballet-dancer or a pianist. A traditional choreography of brush-movements (learned from standard works of instruction) is practised with extreme dedication, giving basic formulae of prescribed brush-sequences.

Chinese and Japanese painting cover a wide range of subjects: nature and the changing seasons are central to both traditions, though history, genre and portraiture were very popular. There are important differences in design and interpretation: the Chinese style of composition is generally linear, the mood classically disciplined and austere; Japanese artists emphasize silhouette-pattern, the approach is more emotional and subject matter is often dramatic and, at times, humorous. The technique used is basically the same, however. The ink, known as "India" or "Chinese" ink, is made from wood or vegetable soot, mixed with animal glue into a paste which is formed into sticks and tablets and dried. In preparation for use, the hardened ink is rubbed on a rough stone as drops of water are added. By diluting this dense black ink with varying amounts of water, a range of grey tones is prepared. Paintings are executed on absorbent paper made from pulped bamboo, hemp, reed, cotton or mulberry bark, and on silk, sized with a solution of

HAN GAN (right)
Night shining white,
8th century
Brushes of wolf, goat or deer hair, tied in a conical shape and set in a bamboo tube, were the only tool of Chinese painters. Effects range from the needle-point brush-strokes conveying the tension of the horse's harness to the soft shading which defines the muscular forms and accentuates the nervous head and dancing hoofs.

XIA GUI (below)
Landscape, c. 1200-25
An exponent of the "boneless" technique (painting without contours), Xia Gui creates a landscape from flecked, hooked and writhing strokes which seem blown across the surface of the picture.

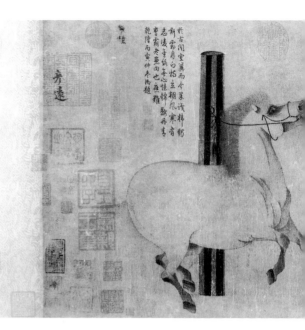

TAN-AN (above)
Heron, detail, *c.* 1570
Eastern brushes respond to the slightest pressure; a lifted brush produced the fine or "bone" line of the heron's bill, a depressed brush the fat, or "flesh" strokes of the feathers.

TOSA MITSUYOSHI (right)
The battle of Uji river,
detail, 16–17th century
Clan struggles are a popular theme of Japanese handscrolls; the narrative essentials were outlined in ink and the scene enriched with gold, silver and colour.

alum and glue. In traditional procedure, the paper or silk is spread across the floor or table, and the brush poised vertically above. The artist never paints confronted with his subject. Instead, after a period of inward contemplation, he sees clearly in his mind what he wants to paint; he is "moved by the spirit" of the subject, and begins to "write" its image with swift, rhythmic movements of the flexible arm and hand. His control is such that his palm never rests on the paper; this would "earth" the spirit of his theme, which is felt to be passing through the brush. A calligraphic panel with a poem or a piece of narrative often accompanies the painting, carefully placed to provide a textural and harmonious element in the design.

In Western art, watercolours or gouaches are often outlined first in ink or completed by pen, but ink has seldom been used as an independent medium. Among the few examples of autonomous works in ink are some of Rembrandt's drawings, the black and white book-illustrations by Aubrey

Beardsley and others, and the line-drawing of van Gogh, Picasso, Matisse, Klee, Henri Michaux and Wols. Many artists, however, have employed ink as a medium for preparatory studies, and some of these bring out the special qualities of the medium so brilliantly, and are such complete statements, that they stand as works of art in their own right.

A range of inks has been used in the West. Medieval manuscript illuminators used a dense black ink extracted from the gallnut which, in time, turned brown. India ink, formerly imported from the East in sticks and bars, began to be made in liquid form in Europe from the fifteenth century. Although India black has been the most popular, brown inks have also been used, alone or in combination with black. Rembrandt, for example, drew in bistre, a yellowish-brown ink made from the soot of burnt wood (see vol. 2 p. 213); Goya and Constable, among others, made brush-drawings in sepia, a cooler brown extracted from cuttlefish. Chinese white, applied with a fine-pointed brush, has also been used, generally on tinted paper and in conjunction with black and brown ink, to produce illusionistic effects of space and sculptural volume.

Pens, the conventional Western tools for ink, have an ancient ancestry. The reed is the oldest form, and artists such as Rembrandt and van Gogh superbly exploited its characteristic angular and staccato strokes. The quill pen used in manuscript illumination, cut from the wing-feathers of swans, geese and other birds, is more responsive and springy, moving easily across the paper; it has lately been superseded by the cheaper steel nib, in different widths and strengths.

CLAUDE LORRAINE (right)
Port scene, 1649–50
Claude has ruled up this small working drawing for transferring to canvas. Pen and wash are complementary: pen is used to establish spatial perspective, planar relationships and the main divisions of the composition; loosely applied washes indicate the final picture's dramatic tonal contrasts and magical watery light.

LEONARDO (left)
Lily, c. 1475
The pen is used like a scalpel to expose the plant's organic structure: fine brush-strokes define the lithe stem and blooms; white accents sharpen the petals' curling edges and project the floating pistils. The whole is washed over with a delicate sepia.

VAN GOGH (right)
Washerwomen on the canal, 1888
Van Gogh invented a supple calligraphy of dots, dashes, streaks, stabs and cross-hatchings in preparatory studies for oils. His reed-strokes expressing texture, tonal relationships and structural forms are also used to indicate reflections and radiating light in the manner of his impasto oils.

Pastel and Gouache

LIOTARD
Self-portrait with beard, 1749
The blunt pastel he holds is
for colour masses, but for
his prodigiously wiry beard
Liotard has used a pencil-
sharp edge. The alertness
of the pose reflects the
immediacy of the medium:
textural contrasts help to
offset the limited depth of
tone and the flat colours.

CARRIERA (above)
Louis XV, detail, 1720
Blending subtly to eliminate
individual chalk-strokes,
Carriera portrays the ten-
year-old king with exquisite
simplicity, the granular
nature of the pastel giving
his face a powdery softness.

DEGAS
(right) *Dancers in the wings*,
c. 1900; (above) detail
Abandoning the orthodoxy
of soft, waxy gradations,
Degas used a rough, tense,
linear handling to suggest
effects of movement and
light. The surface becomes
a vibrating patchwork of
dashes and scribbles, of
tracks crossing in slanting
diagonals and clashing hues.

REDON (above)
Roger and Angelica, c. 1910
Like Degas, Redon extended
pastel techniques by varying
his handling of the medium,
though to softer effect. He
gives shape to his ambiguous
visions by counterpointing
blocky contours and dense,
rich, chalky colours with
downy, smudged areas where
the side of the pastel is
rubbed deep into the paper.

Pastel chalks are the most easily applied and
responsive of all painting materials, putting pure
colour literally at the artist's fingertips. The chalks
are made by mixing ground pigment with water
and a binding agent to produce a stiff paste which
is then pressed into tubular moulds and dried;
white or black is added for tints or shades. The
medium is particularly associated with France and
the chalks are often called French pastels. They
can be used on any surface with sufficient tooth to
hold the pigment particles, but the medium is
fragile since the colour adheres only as a dry dust.
Varnish fixative diminishes the characteristic
granular freshness and pastels are therefore best
displayed within a deep mount and behind glass.

Although the opaque nature of the medium
restricts the range of tone and colour that can be
achieved, the ease and speed of execution and the
simplicity of its equipment made pastel a popular
portrait medium in eighteenth-century France
and Italy, especially with travelling professionals.
Pastel portraitists such as Nattier and Quentin de
La Tour achieved the fused, waxy softness of
highly-finished oil-paintings, blending the colours
by gentle rubbing with soft suede, a stump of
coiled paper, or with the thumb and fingers. The
spontaneity of the medium was exploited more
expressively by Chardin, Liotard and Rosalba
Carriera. But it was during the late nineteenth
century, in the individual experiments of Degas,
Toulouse-Lautrec and Redon, that the medium
was most brilliantly employed. Working on raw
strawboard or tinted, abrasive paper, they extracted a full range of tints, shades and hues with the
use of a few chalks. The influence of the tinted
ground was controlled by varying pressure on the
pastel; heavy strokes obliterated the ground colour, lighter touches allowed it to show through in
degrees and affect the colour of the chalks. Degas's
most vivid pastel works are perhaps those in which
his handling is most direct.

Degas and others also used pastels in combination with other media, and sometimes fixed
the chalk by working on turpentine-soaked paper
or over a pastel layer fixed with varnish. The more
recent development of oil pastels has enabled
artists to achieve the colour depth and adhesion of
wax crayons without losing the subtlety of pastels;
they can even be spread by washing over the chalk-
marks with brush and turpentine.

Gouache is a water-diluted medium which is
made, like watercolour, from powdered pigment
bound with gum arabic but is an opaque, denser
paint; the colours dry slightly lighter in key. As
with pastel, it is both a traditional material for
making life studies for paintings and a picture
medium in its own right. It, too, is a swift and
convenient method. Sometimes loosely termed
tempera, it is also marketed as "poster" and
"designer's" colour. Drying speed can be retarded
with the addition of honey or an acrylic medium
but, like tempera, gouache dries too quickly for
reliable tone and colour fusion. Instead, optical
blending is obtained with a pastel technique of
cross-hatched and overlapping brush-strokes of
different hues, often over a tinted ground. Impasto

ridges and whiskered colour boundaries are characteristics of gouaches painted with brushes of stiff hog bristle on canvas or rough paper. When the paint is prepared to the consistency of thin paste and applied directly with a broad, soft sable brush, flawless fields of unvarying colour can be achieved.

Until recently in Western art gouache has been generally used for preparatory sketches for oils. Among notable examples are the cartoons and colour sketches for tapestries and paintings by Raphael and Rubens. Since gouache is capable of delicate detail when applied with a fine pointed sable, it was the medium of the sixteenth-century miniaturists and was also used in France and Italy during the eighteenth century for fan decorations – Rococo pastoral scenes painted on paper, card and silk and mounted on exquisitely fretted sticks of ivory or wood. Modern artists who have used gouache as a picture medium for its qualities of rapid drying and application include Kandinsky, Picasso, Klee, Rouault and Sonia Delaunay. In his "Rose" period, Picasso often relied on gouache because it was cheap, but he continued to use it throughout his life and executed many of the sketches for his famous mural-size oil *Guernica*, in a monochrome gouache medium.

Gouache was the medium of Indian, Persian and Turkish "miniatures" – the court portraits and decorative illustrations to religious, historical and romantic narratives. Early album pictures were painted on palm leaves bound between wooden covers. The technique and approach of Hindu Indian painters, though influenced by the formal, ornate styles of Islamic manuscripts, were less inhibited, as demonstrated in the exuberant calligraphy of the Rajasthan schools.

KANDINSKY (above)
Russian beauty in a landscape, detail, 1905
Kandinsky has allowed the black paper ground to show through in places to provide contours and enhance the delicate harmonies of dry gouache colour. The blobs of quick-drying, flat paint create a shimmering mosaic.

RAJASTHAN, INDIA *(below)*
Raja Umed Singh of Kotah shooting tigers, c. 1790
Although gouache lacks the translucent softness of watercolour, its opacity and drying speed are advantages in elaborate decorative work such as this, where flat colour enhances a lively linear pattern. After the

design was outlined with a fine-pointed brush, a semi-transparent coat of white was laid over the whole and colouring and details were added, sometimes by a team of specialist artists. Apart from some softer areas where a swift wet-into-wet technique was used, brush-strokes are laid side by side, unblended.

Drawing

Drawing is associated intimately with painting,
both as a means of sketching or establishing the
design of a painting and as an independent medium which can clearly reveal the creative process
and the artist's temperament or sureness of hand.
Principal drawing media (apart from ink and
pastel) are charcoal, metal point, graphite pencil,
Conté crayon and chalk. The very limitations of
the materials used – their lack of fluidity and
restricted colour range – mean that drawing is
perhaps the most abstract medium of art, the least
illusionistic. Yet it is also the quickest and most
economical method of giving visual information,
developing concepts and expressing emotions.

A special aesthetic quality in a drawing may be
the conscious or intuitive placing of an isolated
image in relation to the frame or edge of its ground.
The empty spaces surrounding the image contribute to the overall pattern on the support (usually
paper) as "negative" shapes, and can also suggest
spatial recession. These spatial effects are not only
implied in representational drawings but seem to
occur, by optical effect, in non-figurative works
also, since all marks made on a bare surface appear
to advance from it. However, a drawing is not
always linear; when a massing of dark shapes
leaves isolated white patches of paper, these become the advancing planes.

Broad tonal masses are not easily achieved with
some drawing media, but linear hatching techniques can be used to create tonal patterns and
provide precise and subtle means of indicating
planar relationships and surface textures. Continuous, unvarying contours are used when an
accurate representation is required of sharp-edged
forms and interlocking flat planes. Illusions of
light, shade and substantial volume can be
achieved with chalk or charcoal by using the side
of the stick or smudging with the fingers.

RUBENS (below)
Young woman looking down,
detail, *c.* 1627–28
Working with three chalks
and using cream-tinted paper
as his general tone, Rubens
expresses volume, texture
and structure with masterly
economy. Rubbed white chalk
heightens the red and black
contours and shading; the
eyes are sharpened in ink.

KOLLWITZ (above)
Woman and Death, 1910
Emphatic contours, breadth
of modelling, and contrasted
grainy and smudged textures
are characteristic qualities
of charcoal drawings. The
medium is impermanent and
fragile, but its range of
effects – from thin, sharp
lines to broad, smoky
masses – and its erasability
enable it to be used with
unique expressive freedom.

Whether the primary expressive element is line
or mass, the physical presence of the drawing
surface is always apparent. Tinted paper and a
combination of coloured chalks facilitate a convincing rendering of space and solid form, the
paper tint being retained as an intermediate tone
between white highlights and darker chalk shading. The best papers are hand-made from hemp
and linen rag, as woodpulp paper soon yellows.
For smooth surfaces, suitable for the harder
grades of graphite pencil, the paper is dipped in a
glue solution.

Contributing to the comprehensive language of
drawing are the first, sketchy jottings of an idea,
experimental variations on a design, creative doo-
dles, calligraphic records of momentary movements, and incisive, investigative studies of form,
space and structure. Many drawings are made
solely for the artist's practice or pleasure; others
are executed as autonomous works of art or as
"presentation drawings" for a friend or patron.
The purpose of the drawing may determine the
artist's choice between various drawing materials,
some being suited to swift technique or broad
statements, others to fine detail and considered,
incisive execution.

Charcoal (charred willow twig is preferred) was
the earliest known drawing material. Metal point
(lead or silver) derived from the ancient stylus
technique and was primarily a linear Renaissance
medium; it has largely been supplanted by graphite pencil, in varying degrees of hardness and tonal
range. Conté (named after its eighteenth-century
inventor) is a grease-free, hard crayon, useful for
studies of tone and texture, and made by mixing
powdered graphite with a clay coloured with red
ochre, soot, or powdered blackstone. Chalks were
popular with Baroque and Rococo artists, who
achieved striking volumetric effects with red, black
and white chalks on a background of tinted paper.

HOCKNEY
Beach umbrella, Calvi,
detail, 1972
Directly and forcefully
used here for a finished
work, coloured pencil-
crayons are, like the felt-tip
pens and oil pastels, a rapid
means of colouring sketches
and preparatory designs.
They are made up from a
mixture of wax and powdered
pigment or dyestuff, with a
binder of gum or cellulose.

Painters and Printmaking

Blake developed his painting
from a monotype, beginning
with a design, in reverse,
painted on board in tacky
glue-tempera. From this he
took a print impression,
enriching it further while
it was still wet. Finally
he worked over the dry
monotype in pen and watercolour, wholly overpainting
some areas but retaining
the mottled and pitted
print impression where this
could suitably represent
natural surfaces. As the
detail shows, he used pen,
brush and ink to discover
and emphasize marine
imagery – sea-urchins,
anemones and seaweed
trailing across the rock.

Until fairly recently, printmaking was usually
regarded more as a means of reproducing paintings and drawings or illustrating books than as a
unique fine art form in its own right. Until the end
of the nineteenth century, the artist, or his printer,
pulled as many prints as could be sold. Prints are
now considered "original multiples" and are col-
lected as works of art for the very qualities which
distinguish them from other forms of expression.
Limited editions are individually signed and num-
bered by the artist and when the print or "run" is
completed, the printing surface is spoiled, to
ensure the commercial value of the edition.

There are three main groups of printmaking
process: relief, intaglio and surface, described in
greater detail overleaf. Relief methods (most commonly wood and linoleum-cutting, or wood-
engraving) involve the removal of some surface
areas, leaving raised areas to be inked with a roller.
Conversely, in intaglio techniques (metal-
engraving, etching, mezzotint and aquatint) the
ink is worked into lines and pits incised, or etched
with acid, into a metal plate. Surface (or planographic) methods include lithography, screen-
printing and monoprints, where the image is
drawn on to a flat plate or stencilled on a fabric
screen. Each print process has different characteristic linear and textural qualities, with distinctive
expressive possibilities. As in the history of painting, printing techniques have, from time to time,
been revitalized and given new directions by
individual artists.

In early European printmaking practice, the
plate or block was generally made, to the artist's
design, by craftsmen. Many of the Old Masters,
however, were themselves virtuoso craftsmen who
prepared their own printing surface, choosing the
medium and process which best enabled them to
extend particular expressive characteristics of
their painting. So, qualities of linear precision and
full tonal modelling in the paintings of Dürer,
Mantegna and Pollaiuolo are emphasized in the
hard, incisive line and elaborate cross-hatching of
their metal engravings; Rembrandt and Goya used
the very limitations of monochrome etching in
order to develop the dramatic chiaroscuro design
of their oils; The German Expressionists exploited
the raised long grain of wood to gouge splintery
cuts in character with the aggressive brush-strokes
of their oil-paintings.

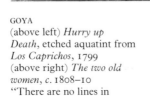

(above left) *Hurry up
Death*, etched aquatint from
Los Caprichos, 1799
(above right) *The two old
women*, c. 1808–10
"There are no lines in
nature", Goya said. His
prints and paintings were
both designed in broad
shapes of light and shadow.
While details were brought
into sharp focus by etching,
the first print impression
was made in aquatint (see
over) to produce a pattern
of harsh white and smoky
black masses. In a similar
way the painting began as
a stark design of scumbled
lights and glazed shadows.

NOLDE
(left) *The life of St Mary Aegyptiaca*, detail, 1912
(right) *The prophet*, 1912
The fierce colour conflicts of Nolde's oils parallel the harsh black white contrasts of his woodcuts. His direct and deliberately crude handling of tools denotes a frank acceptance of the physical nature of the two media: both the canvas weave and the wood grain are visible; the brush attacks with the savagery of the wood gouge.

Lithography can reproduce almost any kind of drawn mark and provides the widest range of gestural textures. Daumier (see over) pioneered the medium. His near-monochromatic oils and watercolours, essentially graphic in character, share with his prints qualities of calligraphic line drawn in counterpoint with powerful patterns of light and shade. The recent Abstract Expressionist lithographs of de Kooning and Motherwell extend their impetuous handling of oils and casein into skidding sweeps and explosive blots and splatters of fluid ink. In contrast, screenprints by Vasarély or Bridget Riley, with their precise knife-cut stencils, parallel some of their smaller Op Art paintings.

Painters have often used printmaking to work out problems met in their painting – either through the discipline imposed by a particular process or through the opportunities it offers for experimentation and unpredictable effects. A monotype, or decalcomania print, the single impression taken from a design painted on a flat surface, has provided the starting point for some paintings. William Blake's tempera monotypes created mottled textures he preserved in paintings completed with ink and watercolour. Other artists have employed monotype methods to experiment with various tone and colour schemes by painting over a preparatory sketch placed beneath a sheet of clear glass and then taking impressions to be worked over in their pictures. Degas kept some of his "one-off" prints in their original state; others he developed, with oil and gouache, working them up as finished paintings.

Just as the character of early European prints was governed largely by current styles of painting, prints and their characteristic effects in turn have affected the composition and textural range of many paintings and design forms. Japanese woodblock prints, for example, strongly influenced Impressionist painters such as Degas, Whistler and Monet, the book illustrations of Beardsley and Greenaway, and the poster designs of Toulouse-Lautrec, Bonnard, Vuillard, Steinlen and the Beggarstaff Brothers. Modern mixed-media painters have also combined different processes in mixed-media prints, juxtaposing shapes and textures created by relief, intaglio and stencil methods with images printed by commercial photographic processes.

HIROSHIGE (below)
The plum-tree garden, 1857
Many of the qualities that made the Japanese woodcut so influential in late 19th-century painting are seen here: flattened forms, broad colour areas, unorthodox use of empty space.

VAN GOGH
Oil based on Hiroshige's *The plum-tree garden*, 1886 Van Gogh has made an interpretative version of the print rather than a true copy. The tender optimism of the print, with its pale sky and soft explosion of

buds, is replaced by a more uneasy mood, a sense of forced and painful growth. The dominant silhouette of the foreground tree has been further thickened, and the abrupt tonal contrasts introduced in the sky hint at an approaching storm.

Printmaking Techniques

RELIEF PRINTING

Blocks for relief prints are cut away in the blank, or "negative", areas of the design, leaving "positive" lines and shapes standing proud for inking. The woodcut, made from a block sawn plank-wise, along the grain, was the earliest form of relief print, first developed in China, and fully established in Europe by the fifteenth century with the manufacture of paper and the introduction of typographical printing. Once the design is cut, the surface is rolled or dabbed with sticky ink and the paper print is pulled under a press or burnished by hand. Linocut prints have a softer appearance. The third major relief technique, wood engraving, which uses a small block of hardwood sawn across the grain rather than along it, can give finer detail and was widely used for book and magazine illustration before the introduction of photo-mechanical printing processes.

WOODCUTS, distinguished usually by a bold, forceful line, as in Holbein's *The Countess* (detail, left) from *The Dance of Death*, 1538, are gouged with "v" and "u" sectioned blades set in wooden handles. Wide-ended chisels remove the larger negative areas. Fine details, lines, and the contours of images are first incised with a knife to avoid whiskered or splintered edges where they cross the direction of the long grain. Progress impressions can be taken with wax rubbings on paper. Hardwood is preferred for fine details, though modern woodcutters have exploited raised grains of softwood.

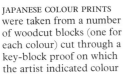

JAPANESE COLOUR PRINTS were taken from a number of woodcut blocks (one for each colour) cut through a key-block proof on which the artist indicated colour positions. Mulberry paper was then laid over each inked block in turn and rubbed with a twist of hemp, colours being modulated by varying pigment strength and pressure. Kunisada's triptych (1857) shows, from right to left, the key-block being cut, paper being soaked and hung to dry, and printing-off about to start.

LINOLEUM allows the artist to cut a freer, more spontaneous line than wood and to work unhampered by grain. In Gaudier-Brzeska's *Wrestlers*, 1914 (detail, above left), the cut-out areas print white. Picasso's exuberant lino-cuts, such as *Still life under the lamp*, 1962 (detail, above right) have helped to raise the status of the medium. By progressively removing areas of the design after completing each colour run, he was able to produce a number of polychrome prints from a single block.

WOOD ENGRAVINGS, on smooth, uniform end-grain, allow delicate detail and tonal cross-hatching. The block and print (above) by Thomas Bewick in his *History of British Birds* (1797) shows atmospheric effects created by chiselling down the block in background areas so that details cut on it took less ink and printed more lightly.

INTAGLIO PRINTING

An intaglio press forces dampened paper into ink-filled channels or pits in a metal plate that has been either directly scored with a tool or else etched with acid. Direct methods include engraving (the deeper the cut the wider and darker the printed line), drypoint, where the needle used leaves a fine, burred line, and mezzotint, where the effect is tonal rather than linear: the whole plate is burred and selected areas are smoothed down to print lighter. Etching, the other major intaglio technique, is often combined with the toning method known as aquatint. An acid bath is used to bite out the design drawn on an acid-resistant wax ground, the acid biting only where the metal plate has been exposed. The depth of line varies with the time and solution strength of the acid bath; the deeper the line the darker it will print. Etching allows more spontaneous handling than engraving.

METAL ENGRAVINGS are usually cut in copper, as in the detail of a lion by Dürer which shows the hard linear clarity of this slow and demanding technique.

MEZZOTINT plates are first uniformly roughened with a serrated "rocker". This ground prints as the overall soft, dense black seen behind the tiger by

Stubbs. Tones ranging from grey to white are managed by varying the degree to which the burred surface is then smoothed down with a burnisher or scraper.

ETCHING requires a metal plate (copper, zinc or aluminium) coated with two hard, acid-resistant grounds: wax on the working surface, varnish on the back. Designs are drawn by scratching the wax ground with a blunt steel needle set in a wooden holder. The plate is then immersed in a bath of acid solution, where the exposed lines are etched. The ground is removed with a solvent, but repeated "bites" can be taken by laying a new ground. The final print may be the last of many trial proofs. For printing, the inked plate is placed on the bed of a heavy intaglio press and covered with a sheet of damp paper, followed by felt blankets. Pressure

forcing the paper into the inked lines produces a slightly embossed surface. Etched line is combined with aquatint in both Arthur Boyd's *Lysistrata*, 1970 (detail, left) and Mary Cassatt's *The letter*, 1891 (detail, right); a separate plate was used for each colour and another for the etched lines. Aquatint is a quick way of creating broad dark-toned areas. Powdered rosin is dusted over the plate and fused by heating; the acid bites only between the dust particles, giving a pitted surface and a soft, granular tone when the plate is printed. In pure aquatint, without etched lines, the design is brushed over with stop-out varnish.

SURFACE PRINTING

The most direct surface prints are monotypes (see previous page), unique originals taken from a design painted on a non-absorbent plate. A more versatile planographic technique is lithography, which can give a number of prints. An alternative surface method is stencilling, the direct printing on to paper of an image formed by pushing ink through the open areas of a cut or painted mask, giving emphatic, hard-edged images.

LITHOGRAPHY can produce effects ranging from the soft granularity of the detail (top right) from Daumier's *The legislative paunch*, 1833-34, to the contrasted clear and stippled colour areas in Toulouse-Lautrec's *The passenger in cabin 54*, 1896 (detail, left). The process works by the natural antipathy of oil and water. The design is drawn with a greasy crayon or paint directly on a limestone block, a zinc or aluminium plate, or a sheet of coated paper. This greasy image is fixed with gum so that when water is sponged on the surface the unworked areas are dampened but the image remains dry. An oil-based ink is then rolled on and adheres only to the image. For colour lithography, separate stones are made for each colour run.

SILK-SCREEN PRINTING, or serigraphy in its fine-art form, uses a stencil made of paper or lacquered film stuck to a fine-mesh fabric stretched over a wooden frame. The printing ink is forced through the screen with a rubber squeegee. Cut stencils produce sharply defined images, but chalky lines and granular textures can be created by drawing on the screen with a waxy or waterproof medium. The mesh is then coated with gum and the medium in the image area is dissolved to allow the ink through. A design can also be painted directly on the screen with gum, varnish or plastic emulsion paint which masks negative areas. Warhol's *Marilyn*, 1962 (detail, left) is printed in acrylic ink using a stencil made from a half-tone film positive.

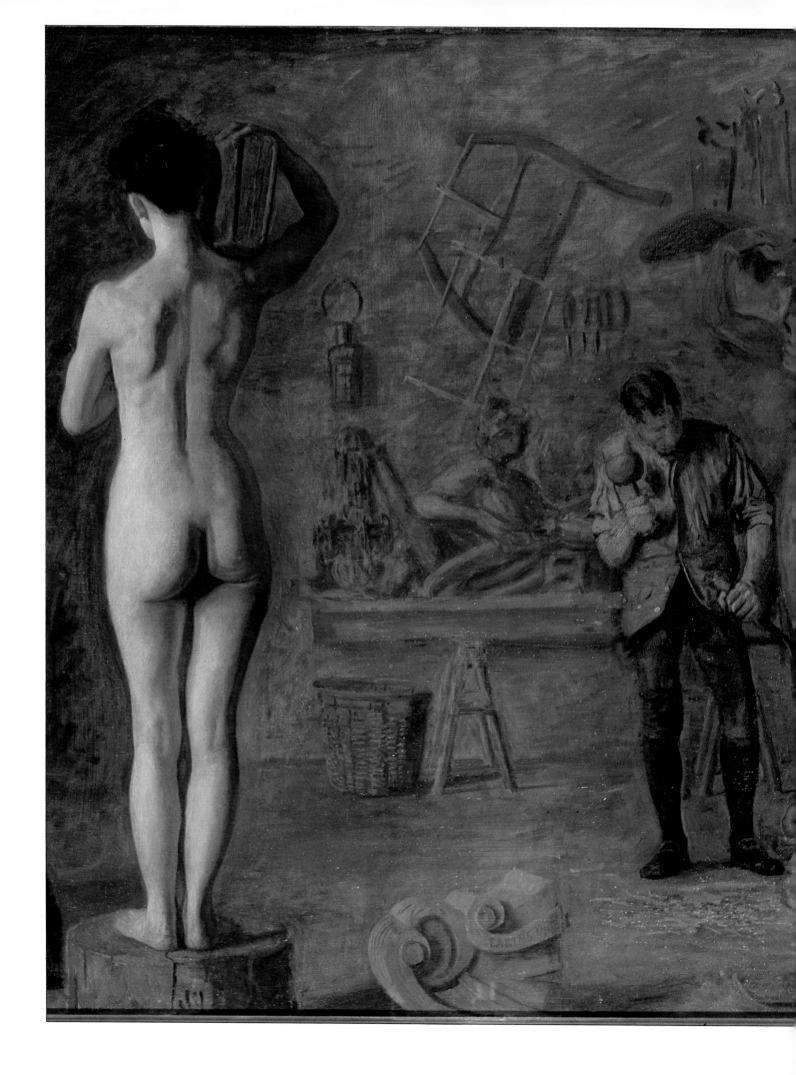

THE LANGUAGE AND METHODS OF SCULPTURE

"I say that the art of sculpture is eight
times as great as any other art based
on drawing, because a statue has eight views
and they must all be equally good"

— CELLINI

(above) ANDREA PISANO: *The art of sculpture*, mid-14th century, lower row of the Campanile, Florence
(left) EAKINS: *William Rush carving his allegorical figure of the Schuylkill River*, 1908;

Introduction

Because it occupies real, three-dimensional space, sculpture communicates with us quite differently from painting. For a start, it may have a weight and density – a sheer physical impact – that forces us to pay attention to it. At its best, figurative sculpture can also seem to give organic life to the material of which it is made, and we may sense a semi-magical presence even in works that are abstract. There is a difference, however, between responding to sculpture in this way and being fully alive to its expressive forms; unless we are sensitive to the sculptor's formal language, the very immediacy of our response may lead us to take a work for granted and prevent us from perceiving and enjoying its more subtle qualities.

The language of sculpture is best considered not on a theoretical basis but in the context of the materials and methods used, the function or format of the work and often its setting or background as well, and this is the approach adopted in the chapter that follows. As both designer and workman a sculptor has to take into account the physical and sensory properties of his materials and the limitations and possibilities of the available methods for working them. These always have some effect on the form and character of the finished work and often contribute a great deal to its beauty and expressiveness.

The elements of sculpture are also, in a sense, elements of painting but there, of course, they are always present in two dimensions. What we describe as volume or depth in a painting exists only in a notional spatial world that painters are able to conjure up by means of perspective or other pictorial devices. In sculpture the elements of line and shape, light and shade, colour and texture are ingredients of compositions which, from the shallowest reliefs to fully-in-the-round works, make use to some degree of three-dimensional mass and space, and it is these latter elements that provide sculptors with their most fundamental problem. For although they are working with actual volumes it is no easy matter to organize them with three-dimensional coherence.

Before the twentieth century, sculptors were concerned primarily with mass – with what Rodin called the "lump". In producing the images required for religious and commemorative purposes, or for the decoration of palaces and great houses, they were preoccupied with the human figure and, to a lesser extent, with animal forms. Space is not of much significance as an element in the composition of the human figure, whose shifting volumes, complex and subtle in both their structure and arrangement, provided a formidable and engrossing challenge.

Modern sculptors have broken away from the dominance of the human figure and greatly extended the range of forms available to them. In particular, they have become more interested in using space as a major element in design, creating sculptures that surround space as well as being surrounded by it, and in which space comes to have a substance and volume and expressive quality of its own. This development is closely linked with the exploration of form for its own sake in abstract art and with the emphasis on space and open structures in modern architecture.

The sculptor's primary concern with mass and space, whether expressed in natural forms or in works that create an order of their own, is emphatically illustrated in the work of Henry Moore, who has throughout his career been absorbed in an attempt to establish a satisfying balance between the "lump" and the void. His monumental *Sheep piece* is a reminder that sculpture is not a purely visual art but can also appeal strongly to our tactile senses. Its surfaces are smooth and continuous, encouraging the hand and eye to follow their movement round the solids and through the spaces of the sculpture. It is not necessary literally to touch such a work to sense its tactile qualities. As our eyes explore the forms we sense their hardness or softness, the fullness and tension or the slackness of their surfaces, and can feel – not merely see – the heavy passivity of the arched lower form and the lumbering contact of the massive form that rears above it.

Sculptural masses are, of course, contained in and defined by surfaces and any understanding we have of their shape or structure depends on our ability to read the clues provided by their surface qualities. In many sculptures, contour, line, colour or texture are significant elements of expression. Rodin (see over) concentrated much of his attention on the movement of surfaces and the play of light over them, often distorting anatomy to enhance these effects. Whereas Egyptian sculpture achieved its static, timeless quality largely through the density and power of heavy masses, in Romanesque sculpture line is often paramount. The great Romanesque relief of *The mission to the apostles* at Vézelay (see vol. 2 p. 73) formalizes the expression of religious excitement by means of a profusion of lines which spiral hypnotically, zig-zag, move in conflicting directions and converge to sharp, dagger-like points. Alternatively, line may be used to suggest a gentle, graceful movement, as in the wafted undulations of Greek drapery. These and similar ranges of variation in other surface qualities provide the sculptor with a highly versatile language of expressive form.

MOORE
Sheep piece, 1969-72
The shapes of the masses and the voids are conceived together in complete inter-dependence to achieve the power and serenity which characterize Henry Moore's work. In his monumental sculpture, the feeling of immense solidity is in no way contradicted by the knowledge that the bronze casting is hollow.

Introduction

RODIN
Nijinsky, 1910-11
The three-dimensionality of sculpture is full exploited by this tiny figure, only 18cm (7½in) high. The main forms of the body are contained within a large hexagon balanced on a single bent supporting leg. When the piece is turned round its energy becomes vividly apparent. Broken, faceted surfaces fragment the light (here reflected by a blue background), suggesting tense sinew and musculature in every ridge, boss and hollow, and creating a visual equivalent of movement in the static material of the sculpture.

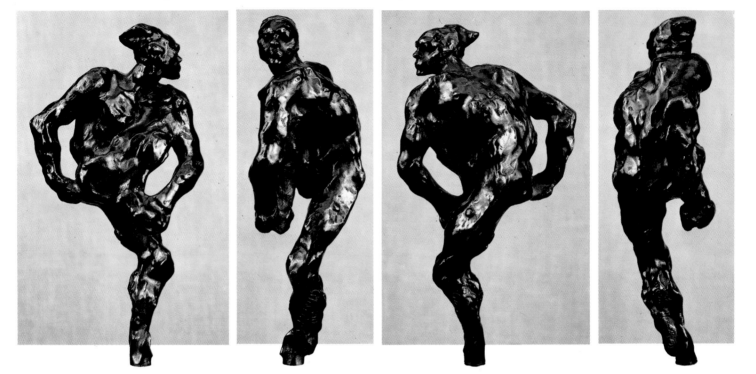

Sculptures are objects which have been fabricated, usually in an obstinate and resistant material, by a sculptor's hard concentrated labour. The intensely physical nature of the process was pungently described by Leonardo when he said that the sculptor's art was "a very mechanical exercise causing much perspiration which mingling with the grit turns into mud. His face is smeared all over with marble powder, making him look like a baker, and he is covered with minute chips as if emerging from a snowstorm."

The processes of making sculpture fall into three main groups: carving, in wood, stone or ivory, is essentially a reductive process – the sculptor begins with a block of more or less homogeneous solid material, and cuts away the surplus in order to reach the desired shape; modelling is a process by which forms are built up by manipulating malleable substances such as clay, wax or wet plaster; construction involves putting the sculpture together from previously formed pieces of material – sheets of plywood, metal and perspex, planks of wood, pipes, girders, ropes, wire. The range of materials is extremely wide and the methods of joining them include bolting, screwing, glueing, welding, and many other methods employed in manufacturing.

Each process and material will normally give rise to a kind of sculpture with its own special characteristics. To use a well-known phrase, it will be "true to its material", giving due recognition to its physical properties and bringing out its natural colour and texture. A clay or stone figure will look like a body made out of clay or stone and not be an attempt to reproduce the qualities of flesh or fabric. Some sculptors, however, look upon their material as a challenge, taking pride in a virtuosity of craftsmanship that enables them to push the material to its limits. Hellenistic, Baroque and Late Gothic carvers often achieve forms in wood or stone that contradict the nature of the material and are of such baffling intricacy that only the utmost skill and determination to bend the material to their will could bring the work to completion and prevent disaster. Much of the power of Michelangelo's work comes from a fruitful co-operation between material and idea, in which the artist is determined to impose his will on the stone but at the same time respects its qualities and limitations and allows it to have its say.

The surfaces of much second-rate sculpture are merely external features imposed on a mass of material without any organic connection with the interior shapes. But true surface quality should be visible as the outer limits of a structure of three-dimensional forms that appear to continue through the inner space of the sculpture, as in the great figures of the Classical European and Indian traditions. They have surfaces in which every feature is an external sign of a structure that informs the whole mass of the work. This translation of the anatomical structure of the figure into a completely ordered system of sculptural forms creates works which appeal to both the mind and the emotions as powerfully as the music of Bach or the architecture of Chartres.

A major determinant of sculptural style is the way that forms are organized in space. The arrangement may be along a straight, vertical axis, as in much archaic and primitive sculpture, or around a spiral, as in Giambologna's *Rape of the Sabine* (see p. 185) so that the eye is constantly led beyond any fixed viewpoint. Forms may be strictly confined within the cubic limits of a block of stone, or reach out freely into space in several directions; or, as in the magnificent *Victory of Samothrace* (see vol. 2 p. 38), everything may be caught up in, and made to contribute to, one surge of movement.

The organization of forms is often influenced significantly by the intended viewpoint of the onlooker. Some small sculptures, such as Japanese *netsuke*, or toggles, are completely free objects. Having no fixed base, they may be turned around in the hands like pebbles and viewed from any direction. Many larger works are designed to remain in a fixed position, either on the ground or on a base, but to be viewed all round so that their outlines and silhouettes continually change as we move round them. In figure sculptures of this kind, complex volumes of varied sizes, shapes and directions must be handled so that a fluent unity of design and expression is given to the whole composition, and it is only when the works are seen in rotation that the consummate skill of an artist such as Rodin can be fully appreciated.

Other sculptures in the round are intended to stand in a niche or against a background, and their composition is therefore designed to be effective from only a limited range of frontal views, as in much architectural sculpture. This is usually achieved, firstly, by avoiding any overlapping and foreshortening that might be confusing and, secondly, by ensuring that the actions of figures and the movements of lines and surfaces are resolved in the front aspect, and do not frustrate the viewer by making him want to move round the sculpture to see what is happening on the other side. Thus poses are usually kept simple, as in the gently swaying postures of Gothic statues, and compositions tend to be spread out across the viewer's line of vision, as in a relief or picture. Many sculptors, challenged by the limitations of this kind of work, have sought ways of giving the figure greater movement and tension without destroying its overall frontality. Michelangelo's *contrapposto*, in which the upper and lower halves of the figure are rotated well out of the front plane in opposite directions, is a well-known way of achieving this. Bernini, following precedents in Hellenistic sculpture, approached the problem in a more complex manner. His compositions often have considerable depth of space and recession of form, with figures moving violently towards and away from the viewer, but he takes great pains to ensure that the foreshortening and overlapping that result from this do not obscure any actions, facial expressions or gestures that have a bearing on the essential meaning of the work.

SOUTH INDIA
Parvati, c. 12th century
A paradoxical feature of most Indian sculpture is its fusion of rich, voluptuous forms and quiet spirituality. This figure is conceived in terms of curved, entirely convex volumes arranged in balanced asymmetry around a vertical axis. Their fullness is stressed by the encircling linear treatment of the head-dress, jewellery, robe and girdle. Unbroken curves over the projecting hip and across the shoulders, where all anatomical detail is suppressed, contribute to the figure's serene simplicity. Proportions conform to a strict canon which governs the relative dimensions of every part of the figure.

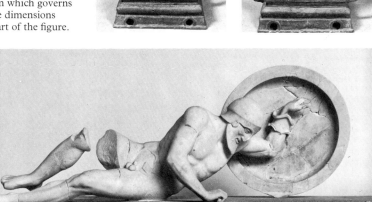

AEGINA (above)
Fallen warrior, c. 470 BC
The figure is designed to fit into the acute angle of a temple pediment and to be seen only from the front. Its forms are spread out across the viewer's line of vision, and make a bold silhouette against the background plane. The shoulders and hips are twisted in what could be regarded as a horizontal version of the *contrapposto* attitude. The up-and-down movements of the crisp forms against the straight line of the base are a major design feature.

BERNINI (right)
Pluto and Persephone, 1621–27
Bernini's mastery of the arduous process of carving is demonstrated by his ability to treat the marble with the spatial freedom of bronze. This early work has a number of more or less interesting subordinate views, but is primarily intended to be viewed from the front, where the violent dramatic action and the facial expressions and gestures of the participants are most clearly displayed.

Introduction

The problems of designing completely free-standing sculpture that is not only in the round but is also intended to be seen all round are solved by many sculptors by two methods that are often combined. Firstly, they may arrange and shape the forms so that they present interesting and well-composed aspects from at least a fair number of viewing positions. This more static method is well illustrated in Pilon's celebrated monument for the heart of Henry II, with its triangular composition of three similar figures. Secondly, they may create continuous movements of lines and surfaces which persuade viewers to move round the sculpture in order to complete their understanding of its forms and meaning – a notable example is the "serpentine" figure (*figura serpentinata*) of Mannerist sculpture. In many works by Cellini and Giambologna these two methods are cleverly combined. As the spiralling forms of their figures impel us to move round them they continually change their relationships, each time revealing a new aspect with a pleasing compositional pattern, but never, so to speak, giving us the complete picture.

While a work such as Cellini's *Virtue overcoming Vice* reaches out into space dynamically, moving through it with gyrating lines and surfaces, other types of free-standing sculpture take possession of space in a more static manner, by virtue of the inner structure and volume of their solid masses. The sculptural character of a great deal of tribal African, ancient Mexican and twentieth-century sculpture, including much of Brancusi's and Hepworth's, does not communicate itself to us by means of a kaleidoscopic sequence of views or aspects, and it is not primarily for the sake of these that we circulate around the sculpture. We do so mainly in an attempt to understand the inner structure of its solid forms as completely as we can grasp the structure of such simple solids as eggs or cubes – in an almost tactile manner.

Sculptures that are not attached to a wall, or suspended, usually have their weight supported in some way, and their relationship to the ground or base on which they stand is something that must be taken into account in their design. A base may be a mere slab that gives stability to a standing figure, or it may be developed into a feature which is an integral part of the design of the whole work. In some of Giacometti's works, for instance, the relatively large base has an expressive function emphasizing the emaciation of the figures.

Relationships with the ground plane or base are particularly important in horizontal sculptures such as recumbent figures. They may be mere reliefs, high or low, on a tomb slab, or they may be completely in the round but in contact with the ground plane along their whole length. It is only when they are lifted above the ground in some

HEPWORTH
Corinthos, 1954–55
Carved all round and lacking a base, this work is not merely free-standing but completely free. In spite of its size – nearly a metre in diameter – it is as self-contained as a seashell, and gives the impression that it could be picked up in the hand. The composition of its changing views has been carefully considered but is of less importance than the overall shape of the containing volume and the counterpoint of solids and hollows, of exterior and interior surfaces that make up its inner structure.

CELLINI
Virtue overcoming Vice,
c. 1550
Rotation and tilting of the main forms, together with complex linear rhythms and the varying directions of the arms, club, legs and whip-like tail set up a highly charged psychological relationship across space between the two figures. As a result, the meaning, form and composition of the work are clearly visible and effective from any point of view, yet the eye is constantly led onwards.

PILON (above)
Graces from the monument for the heart of Henry II, *c.* 1560
The three *Graces*, each only subtly different in pose and dress, create a multi-view composition by repeating a motif around a central axis.

parts and touching it in others that the relations between the sculpture and the ground plane become an important design feature. Then it becomes possible to connect one side of a sculpture to another by means of spaces beneath its forms and to exploit the different expressive characters of forms which merely touch the ground lightly at a single point, like spheres, and those which are firmly rooted over a wide area, like pyramids.

In most sculpture, the need to arrive at a satisfying balance in relation to gravity presents a fundamental challenge. To avoid a static effect in figurative sculpture the Greeks developed a pose with the weight mainly on one leg, the contrast between the tension of one side and the relaxation of the other giving a "living" balance. A sense of dynamic equilibrium is realized with astonishing skill in studies of dancers by Rodin (see preceding page) and Degas, the masses pressing outwards from the axis of the figure to achieve a stability that seems at once momentary and timeless.

Less deference is paid to gravity in twentieth-century constructions, where more abstract forms and greater structural strength have produced works that are not mass-based and give an effect of weightlessness. The aims and methods of Constructivists have led to several other radical changes in the language of sculpture – a frequent emphasis on open structure, on concave rather than convex surfaces, on transparent rather than opaque materials, on clear articulation of separate forms rather than the smooth transitions of much figurative sculpture, and on real motion rather than implied movement.

These elements of sculptural constructions are later examined separately, as are considerations of scale and proportion, which become particularly important in sculpture related to buildings or to specific outdoor settings. We will also look later at the special aspects of relief sculpture, in which there is some loss of real depth, and more linear, pictorial methods are used to suggest form and space. First, it will be helpful to study more closely the materials and methods of sculpture. As these inevitably affect the form and character of the finished work, there is much that we may miss or find inexplicable unless we know something about them. Of course, only certain kinds of technical knowledge contribute to an understanding; knowing how a sculptor tempers and sharpens his tools or what formula he uses for his modelling wax adds little to our enjoyment of his work. On the other hand, some knowledge of the stages in the production of a bronze figure, of the processes of modelling and carving, or of the physical properties of granite and the kinds of tools the ancient Egyptians had to carve it with, can give us a deeper understanding of why the sculpture is as it is.

HAWAII (below)
Food bowl, date unknown
The character of this lively little bowl with its carefully worked out pattern of solids and voids could hardly be more different from Pilon's elegance, but the principle of its design is similar.

GIACOMETTI
The palace at 4 a.m., 1932–33
Mass counts for little in this dreamlike Surrealist construction of wood, glass, wire and string. Space is defined by linear elements which become frames for the objects and cages within the main cage – a structure containing a female figure, a phallic form, a backbone and a skeletal flying bird. The three panels at the left determine the viewpoint as frontal and pictorial, yet there is a haunting sense of distance and isolation.

Preparatory Drawing

RODIN (left)
Seated female nude,
after 1906
Rodin said: "There is no
recipe for improving on
nature. The only thing is
to see". In swiftly drawn
sketches from life, he
captures, as if in a caress,
the natural, sometimes
momentary attitudes of the
nude female form at rest.

BERNINI (below)
Study for the Fontana
del Moro, 1652–53
Bernini creates an effect
of vigorous movement and
rippling light with deft,
freely drawn strokes overlaid by a light ink wash.
The group, of two Tritons
with fishes, was intended
for an existing fountain,
but was never carried out.

VEIT STOSS (above)
Drawing for the Bamberg
altarpiece, detail, *c.* 1520
In the main, the teeming
altarpiece follows this
drawing, requested in the
contract, but small changes
show that Stoss improvised
as the work proceeded.

ALFRED STEVENS (right)
Design for the Wellington
monument, *c.* 1856
A competition was held for
the monument's design with
lithographed paper supplied
to entrants showing the
setting. Stevens was a fine
draughtsman and his winning
sketch is unusually lively.

Artists' drawings give us the most intimate view of
the creative process in operation, and, although
there is naturally some overlapping of interest and
methods, drawings made by sculptors have certain
qualities which distinguish them from the drawings of painters and graphic artists. Not surprisingly, the sculptors' special strength lies in their
understanding of three-dimensional form and
structure, and their ability to describe and express
these in tone and line. They think of objects in the
round and have a strong sense of their solidity and
weight. For the most part they draw individual,
self-contained objects, rather than complete
scenes, and they are more likely to define them
with clear boundaries than to invest them with
atmosphere in an Impressionistic manner. Hence
they seldom show an interest in light and shade for
its own sake, although they may well make excellent use of it for descriptive purposes, as a means of
displaying and explaining form. And they tend to
treat the surface of the paper not as a coherent
picture space but as a field upon which forms are

put down side by side, each existing separately in a
space defined by its own volume.

Sculptors' drawings are made for a number of
reasons. Many of them may be regarded as a
search for information, explorations of the poses
and structure of the human figure. Rodin made
hundreds of such studies of the figure at rest and in
motion, capturing its spirit and contours in fluent,
rapidly drawn lines. Michelangelo, interested
more in the surfaces and volumes of the figure than
in its contours, explored them by means of his own
system of shading with a multitude of tiny hatched
lines, creating, as in the torso of the man shown
here, a marvellous sense of solid form.

These studies are part of the input side of a
sculptor's work, nourishment for his imagination.
But drawing also has its creative, output side as a
means of generating and developing ideas for
sculpture directly. Many sculptors' sketchbooks
are filled with page after page of spontaneous
drawings put down when the sculptor's mind is
relaxed and, in a sense, at play with forms and

MICHELANGELO (left)
Nude man turning away,
c. 1504–05
Michelangelo's first love was
sculpture, and he displays
an essentially sculptural
approach to form even when
working out ideas for paint.
This drawing for the lost
cartoon of the *Battle of
Cascina* (never realized)
is covered with a network
of hatched lines recalling
the marks of the chisel,
with which Michelangelo
"drew" the surface of most
of his carvings (see over).

DAVID SMITH (below)
Untitled, c. 1960
Smith worked out ideas for
some of his later work by
arranging rectangular cut-
outs on drawing paper and
spraying paint around them.
The sharpness of the pale,
blank shapes reproduces the
angular clarity of his later
Cubi sculptures, made of
burnished stainless steel.

ELISABETH FRINK (above)
Goggle head, c. 1965
Inspired by a magazine
photograph of a Moroccan
general, the small cranium
and massive jaw, combined
with the blinkering effect
of the glasses, give the
head an impersonal, brutal
quality. Frink later used
this drawing as the basis
of a powerful sculpture.

images, either in pursuit of ideas for a definite
commission or as a completely free activity. An
idea may emerge which will then be developed and
clarified either in further drawings or in a three-
dimensional medium such as clay or wax. Again,
these drawings for sculpture, like the studies from
life, are not ends in themselves, and their real value
lies in the sculptural ideas portrayed rather than in
the specific quality of the marks which describe
them; once the sculptor has grasped what he has
been studying or has a clear enough idea of the
form he is inventing, he need go no further. This is
why so many sculptors' drawings have a sketchy,
apparently unfinished quality.

There is another kind of sculptor's drawing,
however, which has to be fairly highly finished.
Intended to give a client some idea of what a work
will look like when finished and installed, "presentation drawings" are generally of lesser value
artistically, but occasionally they are fresh and
immediate, reflecting the sculptor's enthusiasm
for a project.

Stonecarving

MICHELANGELO (right)
"*Atlas*" *c.* 1513-20
Michelangelo made his own
stonecarving tools but the
basic equipment (left) has
changed little through the
ages. Using a metal hammer
(A) the carver strikes off edges
with a pitcher (B) and roughs
out main forms with a point
(C). A mallet (D) is used with
the finishing tools – the claw
chisel which "draws" the
forms in layers of powdered
stone, and the flat chisel
which cuts final detail.
Surface marks left by the
point and by a soft-stone
claw (E) and flat (F) chisel
are demonstrated (left). The
unfinished "Atlas" shows
Michelangelo's use of the
point and claw, and also
his habit of carving straight
into the block (here on the
diagonal) instead of working
evenly all round the figure.

Marble from the quarries at
Carrara (left) has a pure,
translucent whiteness and
was the chief material of
Michelangelo. The physical
properties of marble enable
it to be carved with great
freedom. A metamorphic
rock, it is less difficult to
work than igneous rock and
is finer and more durable
than most sedimentary rocks.
All three geological types
of rocks, differing in strength,
colour and texture, have been
used in carving. Hard igneous
rocks, such as granite and
basalt, are beautiful but
demanding, seen at their
best in ancient Egyptian
sculpture. The sedimentary
rocks include granular
sandstones (which provide
the warm, pink colours and
fine textures of much Indian
sculpture) and limestones,
usually grey or buff, which
are very workable and have
been the main materials of
architectural sculpture
throughout Northern Europe.

Whether in the temples of Athens and Angkor or the cathedrals at Chartres and Rheims, nearly all the major civilizations and religions have achieved their most complete artistic and spiritual expression in magnificent combinations of stone architecture and sculpture. Although stonecarvers sometimes use a natural boulder, a pebble, a nodule of agate or even an enormous outcrop of natural rock, as in the rock-cut temples of India, the most common starting point is a rectangular block taken from a quarry.

For the stonecarver a block of stone is both the raw material from which his work is carved and the space frame within which he has to conceive and shape it. This means that from the outset there are two major constraints on his freedom as designer and craftsman – the difficult physical nature of the material and the confined space of the rectangular block; but this may also act as a stimulus and much that is most expressive in stone sculpture arises from the sculptor's creative response to these very limitations.

The chief physical characteristics of stone affecting the design of sculpture are its lack of tensile strength, its weight and its hardness. A material with these qualities is not an ideal medium for representing the human figure with its thin ankles, long outstretched limbs, small projecting fingers, top-heaviness and inherent mobility. There must inevitably be some compromise between the demands of the material and the forms and poses of the figure. It is usual, therefore, in stonecarving to keep the arms tight against the body and the fingers bunched, or to find some way of attaching them so that they are not left unsupported. The ankles of standing figures are often strengthened by stone props representing sawn-off tree trunks, urns or masses of falling drapery. In all stonecarving, whether figurative or not, the natural tendency is to avoid fragile projections and unsupported shapes and keep the work compact.

This tendency is reinforced by the way stone is worked. Before power tools were invented all stonecarving was done either with a hammer and chisel or by pounding and abrading. These are slow, laborious processes even with softer stones, so the natural inclination of early carvers was to remove no more stone than was absolutely necessary for the purpose, leading to the simplification of form and the massiveness of so much ancient stonecarving.

It is extremely difficult to conceive, within a block of stone, forms that twist, tilt and bend in all directions, and to keep them clearly in mind throughout the whole process of carving. Such freedom of movement came as a gradual development in the history of sculpture. Early sculptors – Egyptian, Mesopotamian and Archaic Greek – clung to the four sides of the block as a frame of reference for their spatial imagination. They conceived the figure with its four sides strictly aligned with the four sides of the block, and carved it by working to elevations of its main views drawn on the faces of the block. The roughed out, foursquare figure was then developed by rounding out the forms and carving the details. The spatial

arrangement of the forms of figures carved in this manner is severely limited, but the main forms themselves and the surfaces and details are often extremely subtle and carved with great sensitivity. The stillness and intense withheld vitality of Egyptian and Archaic Greek stone figures owes much to this combination of confined space, rigid pose and richness of form.

As Greek sculptors learned more about carving the human figure, they began to create greater movement within the block and so extend the range of their composition. First they broke the rigid pose of the standing figure by placing the weight on one leg, which tilted the hips and shoulders and upset the bisymmetry of the figure, and then they rotated the torso slightly. In time the movements grew stronger, at first somewhat clumsily, but eventually more naturally as sculptors gained complete mastery of living forms and their movement. This knowledge, never completely lost, was the basis of Renaissance sculpture. In some of Michelangelo's unfinished work, where vigorous movement is compressed into the limits of the block with astonishing skill, the figures seem to be struggling to free themselves from confinement and to emerge from their matrix of stone. And in Baroque sculpture we find outstretched limbs and flying draperies courting disaster by defying the physical nature of the stone. The spatial restrictions of the single block were often overcome by jointing blocks together, enabling the sculptor to create more complex compositions.

CHARTRES CATHEDRAL (above)
Detail of the Royal Portal figures, *c.* 1150
Carved from long blocks set diagonally rather than squarely, these figures have a form consonant with the architecture and the angle from which they are viewed.

MICHELANGELO
"The Bruges Madonna",
c. 1506
The rough labour of carving is refined to a final waxen delicacy, but the sculpture is kept compact and the drapery establishes a unified contour without projections.

Stonecarving

Stonecarving is a medium that demands control and systematic planning rather then spontaneity. Yet much is decided as the work proceeds, and the sculptor leaves himself open to suggestions from the material. The sculptor may begin by blocking out the large masses and planes; then the next layer of smaller containing forms is carved in more detail, and so on down to the final surface. This orderly progression through containing and contained forms can be perceived in the finished work and gives unity to the whole design.

There are two main ways of carving stone: by cutting and by abrading. Much Archaic Greek, medieval and Indian sculpture – mostly of softish limestone – is cut with chisels, resulting in sharp-edged forms, and stylized details. In cultures that have lacked metal tools, the carving of hard stones was primarily a matter of wearing away the surface of the stone by pounding it to a powder and rubbing it with hard abrasives such as emery. This tedious process imparts a special quality to the work; there is a lack of deep cutting and strong projection and details are rendered by shallow ridges, flutes and bosses which do not interrupt the continuity of the main masses.

In strong contrast to the qualities of this abraded work are the deep drilling, undercutting, projections and broken, multifaceted surfaces of much Hellenistic, late Gothic and Baroque sculpture. A combination of highly developed skill and iron tools enabled the sculptor to explore the expressive possibilities of chiaroscuro and fragmentation of form. Violent emotions and vigorous

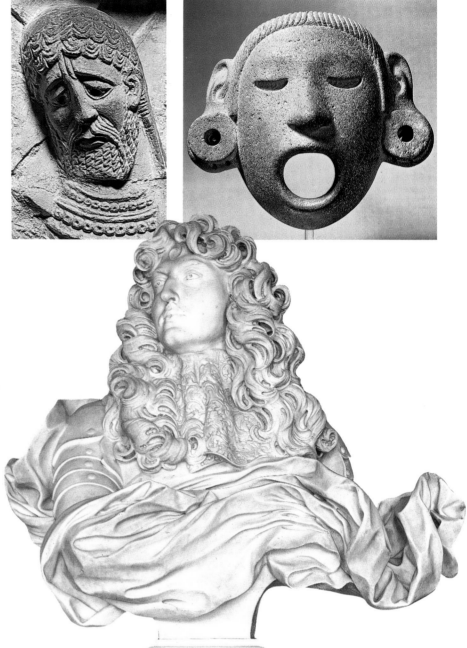

CHICHESTER (top left)
Head of Christ, c. 1100
MEXICO (top right)
Xipe Totec, 14th century
The crisp chiselling of Christ's hair and beard, in softish limestone, is in sharp contrast with the rubbed, pebble-like quality of the hard andesite mask.

BERNINI (right)
Louis XIV, 1665
The bust – a consummate essay in marble-carving – is a complex pattern of deep hollows, broken facets and highlighted edges, and lies at the opposite pole from the direct technique of the medieval relief.

movement can be expressed by these means, and the sculpture given a strong optical and painterly character by patterns of light and shade.

The desire for a high degree of naturalism and movement, and for methods of achieving it without undue risk to the block, or too much labour on the part of the sculptor, led to the development of indirect carving, which in the nineteenth century became the principal method of creating stone sculpture. A complete preliminary scale model in clay is cast in plaster and then reproduced in stone, usually by means of a pointing machine; sculpture produced in this way, brilliant though some of it is, easily loses the essential character of a design conceived for and executed in stone. If the sculptor has little direct experience of stone and leaves the actual carving to his assistants, the finished work may well degenerate into a mechanical copy in stone of an idea conceived entirely in terms of clay.

Although some twentieth-century sculptors have deliberately exploited the decorative and expressive potential of tool-marks, this was not common practice in the past. In general the surfaces of sculpture were smoothed with rasps and abrasives to remove the tool-marks and bring out the full beauty of the stone. Softish, granular stones will not take on a high degree of finish and most sculptors are content to leave their surface texture as it emerges from this final working over, but hard stones, especially marble, can be very highly finished and may even be wax-polished to bring out the surface lustre.

It is important to remember that most sculpture before the Renaissance was polychromed, and finish was therefore of lesser importance. We take a very different view of Greek sculpture, for example, when we realize it was once brightly coloured with strong hues, valued for their decorative effect, as well as for the naturalistic detail and the vivid presence they could impart to the figures on a frieze.

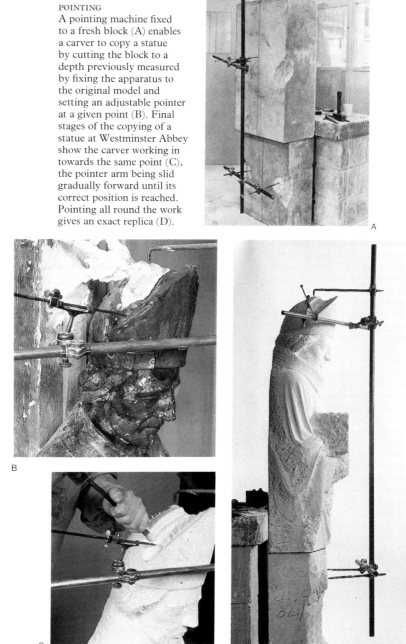

POINTING
A pointing machine fixed to a fresh block (A) enables a carver to copy a statue by cutting the block to a depth previously measured by fixing the apparatus to the original model and setting an adjustable pointer at a given point (B). Final stages of the copying of a statue at Westminster Abbey show the carver working in towards the same point (C), the pointer arm being slid gradually forward until its correct position is reached. Pointing all round the work gives an exact replica (D).

A

B

C

D

SIDON (left)
"The Alexander sarcophagus"
(with reconstructed colour)
c. 4th century BC
The Renaissance ideal of "classical purity" was undermined by late 19th-century archaeologists who revealed that classical sculpture was polychromed. Enough traces remain on the frieze to allow this tentative reconstruction of a section's original colouring, utterly startling to modern eyes, accustomed to smooth, plain stone. Six colours seem to have been used – blue, violet, purple, red, red-brown and yellow, applied for decorative effect, and also in order to supply details which the sculptor had left uncarved.

Carving in Wood and Ivory

The small amount of woodcarving that has survived from ancient civilizations may give the false impression that it was relatively unimportant as a medium for sculpture. Some superb work has been preserved in the dry climate of Egypt but there is little else from the Mediterranean area. Europe in the Middle Ages and the tribal societies of Africa, Oceania, and North America have provided the richest traditions of wood sculpture. The twentieth century, however, has produced several notable woodcarvers, amongst them Brancusi, Barlach, Zadkine, Moore and Hepworth.

The vastly different properties of wood and stone produce significant differences in sculptural forms. The fibrous nature of wood gives it considerable tensile strength along its grain and it is not unduly heavy. With due attention to the grain, it can be carved into thin and extended shapes and treated more openly than stone. Sculptors can use wood in boards for reliefs, in sawn blocks, and in its natural form as logs.

Forms are also influenced by the nature of the woods most widely used for sculpture – oak, lime, mahogany, walnut, pear, box, cedar and pine. Some, such as boxwood, may be carved very finely because they are hard and dense with no pronounced grain. Others, such as pine, which is soft and has an uneven grain, or elm, which is stringy and open-grained, respond less to a detailed treatment. The size of the block or log available depends upon the size of the tree: thus boxwood carvings are necessarily small, while those in pine may reach the gigantic size of North American Indian totem poles. Pieces of wood are more easily joined than pieces of stone, and many large composite woodcarvings are made up of numerous jointed blocks and slabs.

The colours of wood range from the black of ebony through the rich browns of oak, mahogany, and walnut to the pale, ivory-like quality of boxwood and sycamore. Sculptors today usually bring out the colour and grain of wood by polishing, but painting, gilding or inlaid decoration was common in earlier traditions. The surface effects of the carving process are often left in evidence. Central European Rococo woodcarving, for instance, owes much of its vigour and liveliness to the directly cut quality of its forms and the fluent "handwriting" of the sculptor.

Wood is widely used as a medium for decorative carving, especially in connection with furniture and interior fittings, and it is the preferred material for most popular, or folk, sculpture. Although large images have been produced, wood does not readily lend itself to the kind of monumental grandeur that can be achieved in stone. The warm nature of the material makes it particularly suitable for intimate, indoor sculpture. A cool, dry, constant temperature also minimizes the risk of decay always presented by an organic material which swells and contracts with changes of atmosphere. Large woodcarvings designed to stand in a niche or against a wall are often opened up at the back and hollowed out to help prevent the radial splitting common in old carvings, which is caused by shrinkage as the timber dries out.

SIERRA LEONE
Mende figure, 19th century
The slender, open, almost pole-like forms of this beautiful image (associated with magic healing) are in keeping with the fibrous nature and tensile strength of wood, and the straight, vertical axis reflects the cylindrical character of the log from which the figure was carved. The adze rather than the gouge is the principal tool of the African woodcarvers.

MOORE
Reclining figure (above) and detail (right), 1945–46
Moore has described the drama of carving this 1.9m (75in) figure "with its big, beating heart like a great pumping-station". The detail of the back shows the generous grain which makes elmwood such an attractive material to a woodcarver working on this unusually large scale. A fusion of landscape and female forms, a recurring theme in Moore's work, is suggested by the broad, undulating surfaces of the lower leg, the immense overhang of the upper leg and the cavernous openings.

GERMANY
Detail from a choir-stall, 1285
Woodcarvers use a variety of metal gouges and chisels, a selection of which can be seen on the wall of the monk's workshop. The curved edge of a gouge can cut through the bundles of wood fibre without splitting them. A round mallet is used for striking the wooden-handled tools; for delicate work the tool may be pushed with the hand. Chisels used at an early stage of a Moore reclining figure (right) suggest the rough labour of carving.

MICHEL ERHART
*Young woman in the
costume of the Burgundian
court, c.* 1475–80
The use of colour, rare on
monumental sculpture since
the Renaissance, has always
been important in wooden
sculpture. This exquisite,
somewhat wistful figure
was coated with gesso to
fill the grain and provide
a white ground for the
delicate flesh tints. The
jewellery and fabric were
richly gilded and painted.

LORRAINE, FRANCE (right)
Book cover, 11th century
Covers of medieval sacred
books often include panels
of carved ivory, usually set
in gold frames decorated
with enamels and precious
stones. These scenes from
the life of Christ are
carved with an exuberance
that is almost excessive,
the artist revelling in the
medium's scope for virtuosity
– the variety of botanical
motif in the borders, the
details of texture in the
draperies, the twisted
columns, the roof tiles and
stone walls of the buildings.
In spite of the small scale,
the relief is deeply undercut and rich in shadows.

Ivory is no longer an important material for art in
an age sensitive to conservation issues, but its use
for carving dates from the Palaeolithic period,
when animal and figure carvings of amazing
sensitivity were produced. The material is not
available in large pieces – elephant tusks reach a
diameter of about 17 centimetres (7in) – but its
hardness and close texture allow fine, detailed
carving. Medieval ecclesiastical objects in ivory
include many carvings which, in spite of their
smallness, are among the most spiritually profound and beautiful Christian works of art. In
addition to its widespread use for small, semi-
precious objects, ivory has sometimes been used
for the flesh parts of bronze figures, notably in
Greek sculpture.

Most ivory comes from elephant tusks but
sculptors have also carved from narwhal tusks,

CHINA (below)
Immortal Chang Kuo Lao,
17th century
The long, sweeping curve
preserves the natural
curvature of the tusk and
recalls the gentle sway of
many medieval Madonnas in
ivory. Contained within an
unbroken, simplified contour,
the figure owes much of its
elegance to the rhythmic
lines and repeated ovals of
its draperies. The patina of
age emphasizes the delicate
precision of the carving.

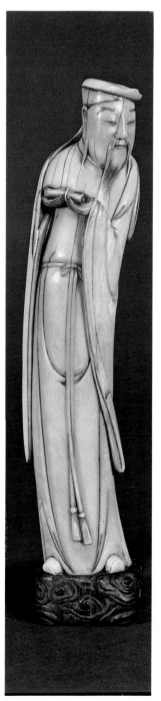

and hippopotamus and whale teeth. After the hard
outer layer of enamel has been removed, tusks are
sawn into panels for relief carving or blocks for
work in the round. Whole tusks hollowed out as
containers for holy relics or as drinking or hunting
horns (oliphants) were often carved with fine, all-
over relief patterns. After roughing out with a
coping saw, the bulk of the work is done with
chisels, knives, files and drills. The subtle grain
and colour of the material, varying from white to
yellow-brown, is brought out by polishing with
gentle abrasives, and grows richer with age.

Modelling

MARINI (right)
Stravinsky, 1951
The bronze cast records the
plasticity of the modelling
medium in contrasts between
the taut, bony structure
of the temples, and the
looser handling of the
scratched, encrusted cheeks.
The eyelids and brows are
cut into sharp planes with
a modelling tool. Portraits
are usually modelled over
an armature of looped lead.

In allowing the artist to work in a malleable
material, sometimes shaped by hand alone,
modelling is the most direct of all sculptural
techniques – a process by which every element of
the final form can be carefully ordered, built up
layer upon layer from a very basic statement of
volume to the most intricate detail of surface
finish. Compared with carving, where the spatial
and material limitations are apparent from the
outset, modelling provides greater freedom to
experiment with extended forms, energetic composition and expressive texture. The plasticity of
the materials – clay, wax, plaster or modern
synthetics – means that at every stage a model can
be changed and remoulded.

As one painter may produce an eggshell finish
while another prefers vigorous impasto, so
modelling styles vary. Many sculptors enjoy the
responsiveness of clay – the way it registers every
impression of fingers and tools as it is worked – and
like to preserve this in the finished model. Others
eliminate all traces of handling to give the work a

JAPAN
Haniwa figure, 8th century
In form and in decoration
ceramic tomb figures like
this reflect their kinship
with pottery; they were built
hollow from coils and slabs
of coarse, sandy clay.

smooth, clearly defined surface. Apart from the
sculptor's thumbs and fingers, clay is worked
usually with shaped hardwood tools or wire loops
attached to wooden handles. For modelled sculptures in which forms extend into space an armature of metal and wood is used to construct the
basic axes of the composition and provide internal
strength. Works too massive for solid modelling
are sometimes modelled over an armature constructed as a hollow shell approximating to the
final shape of the sculpture.

Natural clays, the most widely used of all
modelling materials are found in almost every part
of the world. When clay is moistened and kneaded
it becomes extremely plastic and is delightful to
handle. For durability, it can be either fired in a
kiln or reproduced as a cast in metal, concrete or
plaster. Firing subjects the clay to an irreversible
physical change which converts it into a substance
varying (according to the temperature of the firing
and the composition of the material) from porous
earthenware to hard, impervious stoneware and
fine, translucent porcelain. This *ceramic* property
has been exploited by sculptors, potters and builders throughout history since it was first discovered in Neolithic times. Sculpture in fired clay
is often called *terracotta* (baked earth). The natural colours of clay range from white, yellow and
buff through to rich pinks, reds and browns, which

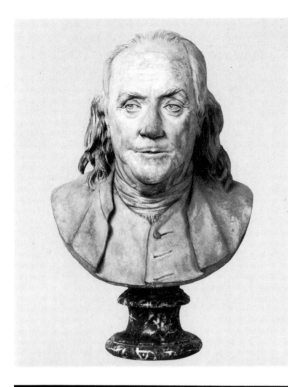

HOUDON (left)
Benjamin Franklin, 1778
Committed to naturalism, Houdon used the immediacy of modelling in clay to catch with extraordinary accuracy the expressive mobility of his sitter's face. From this original model, later preserved by being hollowed out and fired, countless copies were made in terracotta, plaster, marble and bronze.

CHINA (left)
Groom and horse, c. 750
Tomb figurines of the T'ang dynasty were made, usually in earthenware, from moulds and were either decorated with coloured glazes or left unglazed, and painted.

KAENDLER (left)
Cockatoo, c. 1735
Though porcelain sculpture had been produced in China for centuries, a European formula for hard porcelain was invented only in 1709. Kaendler's work at the Meissen factory was amongst the first and most spirited in a medium admirably suited to the Rococo taste for small-scale, decorative and imaginative sculpture.

ROSSO (above)
"Ecce Puer," 1906–07
The influence of material on form is striking in the "painterly" sculpture of Rosso, who modelled in wax over plaster to create elusive images in which the flow and play of light was more important than clear definition of detail. The blurred, barely materialized face suggests the flux and malleability of personality.

can be enhanced by burnishing and transparent glazes or decorated with coloured slips (liquid clay), enamels and coloured glazes. By the use of plaster moulds made from the original model, works can be cheaply reproduced, either by pressing plastic clay into the mould or by pouring in liquid clay and allowing time for the plaster to absorb enough moisture for a layer of stiffer clay to be formed on the inside of the mould.

A clay model shrinks by about one tenth when water is driven off during firing. To prevent cracking or shattering caused by shrinkage and escaping steam, clay models intended for firing are made hollow, with walls of an even thickness. The model can be made hollow from the start, by techniques closely allied to the craft of pottery, sometimes characterized by the pot-like final form of the work. Another method is to make the model solid and to hollow it out later, when the clay is stiff

but not quite dry. This is a sculptural tradition, in which the purpose of modelling is usually to produce a casting in metal.

Although Etruscan, Chinese and Renaissance artists have produced life-size figures in ceramic, it is not a suitable material for monumental sculpture; and the size of the kiln is itself a limitation. Modelling is of major importance, however, as a sculptor's sketching medium. The Greeks made considerable steps forward in their understanding of the human figure through making small models and translating what they learned into their stone sculpture. Superb examples of such "sketches" (or *maquettes*) have been preserved, in wax or clay, among the works of most great sculptors since the Renaissance. They often have a freshness and vigour difficult to preserve in larger, more laboriously executed sculpture. Wax is also widely used as the finishing layer for large models to be cast in metal.

GIAMBOLOGNA
Model for *Rape of the Sabine*, c. 1579
Such complex and violently spiralling compositions could hardly have been worked out without a sketch model, here wax over wire.

Casting

Casting

CELLINI (above)
The *Perseus*, which Cellini
believed would prove him a
sculptor in the rank of
Michelangelo, was the
largest and most complex
statue cast in Florence in
living memory. During its
casting the foundry was
swept by wind, rain and
fire, and just as the bronze
was being prepared, Cellini
was forced to bed with a
fever. The extracts (right)
from his *Autobiography* of
1558-66 describe his
efforts to avert a disaster.

"In the middle of this dreadful suffering, I
caught sight of someone making his way into
my room ... and he began to moan, 'Poor
Benvenuto! Your work is all ruined' ... I went
at once to inspect the furnace and found that
the metal had all curdled, caked as they say. I
ordered two of the hands to go ... for a load of
young oak ... When they carried in the first
armfuls, I began to stuff them under the grate
... You should have seen how that curdled
metal begin to glow and sparkle! Then I had
someone bring me a lump of pewter ... which
I threw inside the furnace on to the caked
metal ... By this means and by piling on the
fuel ... the metal soon became molten ... I
saw that despite the despair of my ignorant
assistants, I had brought a corpse back to life
... At this point there was a sudden explosion
and a tremendous flash of fire ... When the
glare and noise had died away we ... realized
that the furnace had cracked open and the
bronze was pouring out, I hastily opened the
mouths of the mould ... Then seeing that the
bronze was not running as easily as it should, I
realized that the alloy must have been con-
sumed in that terrific heat. So I sent for all my
pewter plates, bowls and salvers, which num-
bered about 200, and put them one by one in
front of the channels, throwing some straight
into the furnace. This expedient succeeded,
and every one could now perceive that my
bronze was in most perfect liquefaction, and
my mould was filling, whereupon they all with
heartiness and happy cheer assisted and
obeyed my bidding ... And then in an instant
my mould was filled."

CASTING THE PERSEUS
The statue began as a clay
model, which Cellini baked
well and covered with a
finely modelled layer of
wax to be melted out and
replaced by one finger's
thickness of bronze. Pins
were inserted (A) to hold
the clay core at the right
distance from the mould
once the wax melted. To
provide exit points for the
wax, entry points for the
bronze and vents for air,

a system of wax-filled cane
pipes was attached (B) and
the whole covered with an
investment mould of three
layers of clay (C). This
was bound with iron bands
and fired to bake the mould
and let the wax run off,
then gently lowered into
the foundry pit by two
windlasses. Before casting,
the mould was packed round
with earth, through which
Cellini laid pipes leading
up from the air vents (D).

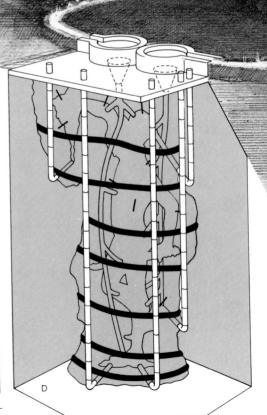

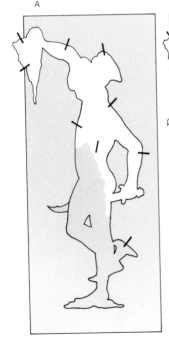

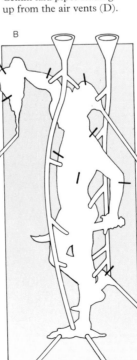

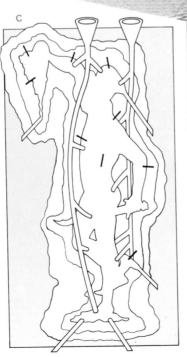

When a modelled sculpture is cast in metal it acquires a tensile strength permitting slender, open types of composition that would not be feasible in wood, ceramic or stone. Though the extension into space of modelled sculpture is not limited, as it is in stone or wood, by the given dimensions or shape of the lump, the modeller of ceramic cannot take full advantage of this freedom because his material is friable. Cast metal sculpture is subject to no such restriction; the artist may represent the human figure in a variety of graceful poses, including even the most fleeting movements of dancers or athletes, and he is able to extend limbs and draperies into space without the need for props or supports. Celebrated examples of the compositional arrangements possible are Giambologna's *Mercury* and Alfred Gilbert's *Eros*, balanced on one foot as if poised for flight, or, equally daring in its structural engineering, the outstretched arm of Cellini's *Perseus* terminating in the weighty mass of Medusa's head.

The favoured means of casting metal has always been the lost-wax process. Though difficult in practice, the principle of the method is relatively straightforward: the sculpture is first modelled in wax and surrounded by a mould of refractory (heat-resisting) material; the mould is then baked to dry it and melt out the wax, leaving a negative impression of the work, to be filled in with molten metal. After the whole has been allowed to cool, the mould is broken open and the sculpture cleaned, chased and polished. Small sculpture can be cast solid by this method but larger objects are cast from models consisting of a layer of wax over a core of refractory material which, once casting is complete, can be poked out through holes left in the surface for that purpose. This was the method used by Cellini in the casting of his *Perseus*.

These "direct" casting methods have the disadvantage that the original model does not survive, and a third method of lost-wax casting, the most sophisticated and laborious of all, is the indirect process, in which a negative piece mould made from the original model may be reused for as many copies as are needed. For each casting the mould is lined with a thin layer of wax, reassembled and then filled in with a core before the wax is melted out to make room for the bronze.

It is interesting that Cellini considered using an indirect method for the casting of the very large *Perseus*, but abandoned it as too time-consuming. He was well aware that the casting of such a large statue would be exceedingly difficult whatever process he used, but not, as his patron Duke Cosimo I feared, impossible. He constructed a special furnace with two outlets for the molten bronze, hoping that the metal would flow into the mould at a greater rate. Nevertheless, he was prepared for the right foot to be ill-formed since the metal had to travel such a distance down the figure that it was likely to be caked by the time it reached the base. As it happened, the mould filled up perfectly and only a small part of the toes had to be retouched; such was Cellini's self-esteem that he was pleased at this blemish, since he had predicted that the foot would need retouching.

CELLINI (above):
Perseus and Medusa, 1545-54
The body of Medusa, which Perseus bestrides, was cast before the main figure.

Cast Metal Sculpture

The metal most widely used for casting sculpture is bronze, an alloy mainly of copper and tin. Apart from more precious metals, such as gold and silver, used in small-scale works, other casting metals include lead, copper, brass and, more recently, aluminium, but none has the special combination of qualities that makes bronze such an excellent sculptural material. Its tendency to expand as it solidifies forces it against the surface of the mould, enabling even the most intricate, detailed modelling to be reproduced accurately. The fine, hard surface can be chased, filed and polished to a high degree of finish, and, in addition to its own range of rich golden and brown colours, bronze can take a variety of attractive surface treatments. It also has great structural strength and a high resistance to atmospheric corrosion which makes it especially suitable for outdoor sculpture, including fountains.

Some modellers work towards bronze sculptures that will bring out the texture and lustre of the metal itself; they carry their modelling to a high level of finish and then spend much time working directly on the surface of the bronze cast, perfecting the forms and details, sometimes until a mirror-like finish has been achieved, as in Brancusi's gleaming bronzes of birds (see vol. 3 p. 146). Others, such as Rodin, use bronze primarily as a durable material for fixing the character of the plastic modelling medium and for reproducing their personal way of handling it.

The natural colours of bronze may be changed by the corrosive effects of prolonged burial or immersion in water, giving the beautiful patinas of many ancient bronzes. Attempts to imitate these effects have led to the development of artificial patination by means of chemicals: the rich blacks, dark greens and reds, and powdery light blues and greens of modern bronzes are all achieved in this way. More sumptuous effects have been achieved by gilding and silvering bronze; Ghiberti's "Gates of Paradise" (see p. 194) is a celebrated example of gilded bronze.

Next in importance to bronze as a metal for casting sculpture is lead, which has a low melting point and is relatively easy to cast. Its soft, slightly blurred quality, its resistance to corrosion (except in highly industrial areas) and the way it blends well with foliage make it a material particularly suited to pleasure sculpture in gardens.

Many twentieth-century sculptors, including Picasso and Paolozzi, have used casting in a direct manner to create witty or surrealistic works from assemblages of found objects rather than casting from modelled forms. Others have explored new and more rapid techniques of producing cast metal sculpture. The widely used industrial method of casting metals in moulds made from hardened sand is not refined or accurate enough for most kinds of metal sculpture, but some sculptors have been prepared to work within its limitations. A recent development, cheaper and less laborious than traditional methods of sand-casting, involves the production of an original pattern in expanded polystyrene foam, which is burned away to leave a negative for the metal.

GREECE
Youth, c. 350 BC
The modelling is highly finished, and the original surface of this fine bronze would have been smooth and golden. It owes its patina to centuries of immersion in sea-water off the coast of Marathon where it was found in 1925 – part of a consignment bound for Italy.

TORRIGIANO (below)
Tomb of Henry VII, completed in 1518
The king "dwelt more richly dead than he did alive in any of his palaces", wrote Bacon of this splendidly detailed bronze sarcophagus. The gilding of the flowing draperies creates an almost flamelike effect around the effigies of Henry and his Queen, Elizabeth. Death masks were used to assist in modelling the heads.

RODIN (left)
The burghers of Calais,
detail, 1884–88

NIGERIA (below)
Human head, 15th century
The classically pure head
from Ife almost seems cut
clean from the bronze in
which it is cast. Rodin's
romantic, expressive bronze
records, in contrast, its
origins as a clay model.

PAOLOZZI (right)
Japanese war god, detail,
1958
The rich texture of this
nightmarish bronze was
created by casting assembled
sheets of wax made from
clay pressings and plaster
mouldings of a miscellany
of found objects, mostly
electronic and other junk.

GEOFFREY CLARKE (left)
Toroidal vortex, 1968
The "lost pattern" for this
aluminium architectural
sculpture was of expanded
polystyrene foam, a material
easily shaped by cutting
with a hot wire, rasping
and sandpapering. It was
buried in foundry sand and
burned out as the metal was
poured in to take its place.
Lost pattern casting is
principally used for broadly
executed sculpture, mainly
abstract, rather than for
detailed figurative work.

PICASSO (below)
Baboon and young, detail,
1951
Toy cars make up the head,
a large pot the body. A
master of visual punning,

Picasso gives these found
objects an entirely new
existence and context by
transforming them, together
with plaster modelling, into
the same material – bronze.

Construction

Construction, building up a form by putting together various component parts, is a fundamental technical process by which a vast range of artefacts has been produced, from animal traps to space rockets. Yet although the process is at least as ancient and widespread as carving or modelling it is only in the twentieth century, with the development of abstract art, that it has become a primary method of producing sculpture.

The processes of modelling organic shapes or carving them from a homogeneous mass of stone or wood, so suited to sculpting the human figure, were less relevant to sculptors' aims once their interest had shifted to a preoccupation with non-representational form and in particular, with the role of space as a positive element in three-dimensional design. Modern architecture, with its steel frames, glass walls, concrete shell construction, open planning and raised or suspended structures, has broken down the distinct division between the interior and exterior spaces of buildings, reduced to a minimum their substantial mass and weight, and made their construction a prominent rather than a hidden aspect of their visual design. The relations between architecture and sculpture have always been close and these new concepts and attitudes have inevitably been reflected in the opening up of solid sculptural forms.

Modern industrial technology has made available a vast range of new materials and processes which can be adapted to this purpose. Outstandingly important among these have been new techniques for cutting and welding metals. The oxy-acetylene torch can be used as a sculptor's tool for making rigid and durable work directly in metals, especially iron and steel. Using ready-made sheets, rods and bars of metal, or metal components which they may fabricate themselves, sculptors are able to practise a kind of drawing in real space with the solid materials.

The components of Anthony Caro's welded metal sculptures, for instance, describe a series of movements in space like the diagrammatic traces of a dancer's movements. They relate also across space, opposing and complementing each other in shape, size and direction and creating powerful silhouettes in relationships changing continuously as a viewer moves round them. The removal of the spatial limitations of a block or armature has made constructed sculptures potentially infinite in size and spatial extension. They range from structures of the utmost geometric simplicity to twisting, involuted and interpenetrating surfaces or shimmering linear constructions that could have been woven by a giant, mathematically-minded spider. Actual motion – natural or mechanical – rather than illusory movement has also become a feature of this new universe of sculptural form. Not all constructions are devoid of representational or emotive content, but the viewer must often be ready to respond to more abstract qualities of shape, texture or design, and to paradoxical or unexpected treatment of elements such as balance and proportion; it is the interest of their ideas rather than their technical virtuosity which has become most important in evaluating artists.

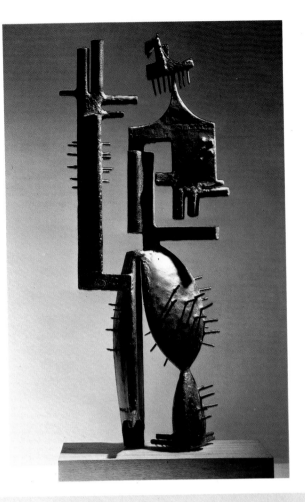

GONZALEZ (right)
Cactus man, 1939–40
González, called by his foremost successor, David Smith, "the first master of the torch", here welds at right angles separately shaped iron parts (including real nails) to achieve an expressive, original form which traditional methods could never have produced.

CALDER (below)
Antennae with red and blue dots, 1960
The components are balanced so sensitively that they are moved by surrounding air currents in a gentle, endless round of inter-weaving arabesques which we watch with the same tranquillized fascination induced by following the movement of gulls in the air or fish in water. Calder was not the first Kinetic sculptor but few have used mass and motion with such judgment; his "moving Mondrians" have inspired a whole new form of folk art.

DAVID SMITH (below)
Cubi XII, 1963
Constructed from welded
sheet stainless steel, these
basic, geometric units seem
at once provisional and
final, balanced with the
utmost confidence in a kind
of dynamic instability. The
mainly frontal projection
stresses the silhouette and
the rough-polished surface.

CARO (above)
Deep north, 1969–70
Caro (left) welds together
disparate shapes that are in
themselves primarily two-
dimensional to create a
kind of graphic design in
three dimensions. As the
silhouette diagram shows,
the components of this work
look alternately compressed
or sprawling, sheet-like or
linear depending on the
viewpoint. Everything is light,
strong, centreless, baseless.

CESAR (above)
Torso, 1954
The attempt to build up
traditional "solid" form
is relatively uncommon in
welded sculpture, but junk
metal has been used to
create powerful works. Here

plates and rods of iron,
joined and fused by arc-
welding, produce a surface
that suggests corruption,
complementing the broken,
fragmentary forms. Polished
areas seem to reassert the
nature of the material.

Construction

Once the freedom to explore materials and processes outside the traditional boundaries of sculpture had been acquired, no limit could be set to the range of techniques and variety of components that could be brought into service. Indeed it is no longer meaningful to speak of the materials or forms of sculpture as though they were a class apart; the term sculpture is now applied to almost anything from smoke trailed from an aeroplane to a pyramid of oranges or a pile of folded pieces of felt. Yet two distinct approaches can be discerned in constructed sculpture, one concerned with purely formal elements, the other with imagery, symbolism and the more subjective aspects of art.

In the variant of the constructive method known as "assemblage" the components are not standard pieces of raw material but objects or parts of objects which already exist in their own right, and which are chosen usually for their expressive significance, their effect on our feelings. Surrealist artists such as Miró or Cornell use this method to project an intensely personal, dreamlike visual poetry; in more ironic or humorous vein the Dadaists and, later, Pop artists such as Claes Oldenburg force us to re-examine familiar objects by giving them inappropriate contexts or shapes. Assemblage has also been used in a theatrical way to present tableaux which make a social comment, as in the often savage work of Edward Kienholz, or to construct environments that involve the viewer physically. The idea that sculpture can be a system rather than an object is pursued by many Kinetic sculptors who create spectacles using light and motorized movement, often with reflective or

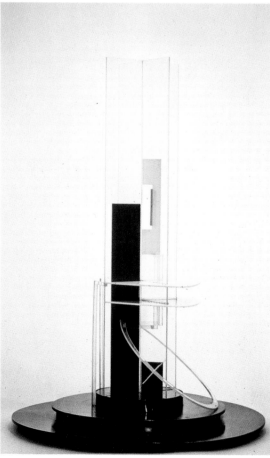

CORNELL (above)
Bird in a box, 1943
Box sculptures, with their sense of seclusion and of secrecy, their references back to the reliquaries of medieval times, have been an important form of assemblage. Cornell's boxes enclose a small world of found objects chosen partly for their texture and colour, partly for the poetry of their associative imagery.

GABO (left)
Column, 1923
Glass and transparent plastic are used to divide and unite space simultaneously in a work of classical purity that has the impersonal polish of a scientific instrument.

KIENHOLZ (right)
Portable war museum, 1968
The components of this 10-metre tableau are listed as propaganda figures, photographs, working Coca-Cola machine, stuffed dog, wood, metal, fibreglass etc. A staged representation which almost dismantles the old boundaries between sculpture and reality, it shows both the range of materials for assemblages and the new scope they offer for satire.

transparent materials, and with sound effects.

On the other wing of constructed sculpture are those artists who prefer a formal, abstract and somewhat severe approach. The austere spatial constructions of Naum Gabo are the products of an intellectually controlled imagination exploring the possibilities of spatial design for its own sake, and they have a kind of cool, mathematical, objective beauty. One limit of this approach is reached in the large, clear-drawn, deliberately empty "primary structures" of Minimal sculptors which, in the words of the critic Clement Greenberg, are "just nudgeable into art". Their impersonality is often enhanced by the gloss of technical perfection they acquire through being fabricated for the sculptor by expert industrial tradesmen. The aim is to present objects as pure material facts, shorn equally of functional purpose and of any associative or emotive content.

The effects of the unprecedented expansion of techniques, subject matter and range of form and expression in recent sculpture have been extremely mixed. Though something new and stimulating is always happening, young sculptors have no traditional values, skills or commonly accepted images to inherit and develop. Modern societies with their lack of deeply-held common beliefs can hardly find appropriate expression in the transcendent and idealized sculptural imagery of the great religions, and it may well be argued that the present condition of mankind finds its true reflection not in any particular style of sculpture but in the diversity and chaotically individualistic state of the art.

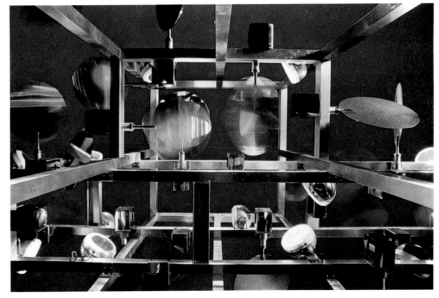

SCHOFFER (above)
Chronos, 1962
Sculpture takes on dynamic modern forms in the work of a Kinetic artist such as Schöffer, who has created complex spectacles of movement and coloured light, sometimes with music added. His sculptures are virtually machines directed towards aesthetic ends and incorporating electronics and even cybernetic control systems, but with random elements.

OLDENBURG (left)
Soft blue drain-pipe, 1967
The translation of hard pipe into limp, gathered canvas is characteristic of the wry Pop art of Oldenburg, whose soft sculptures, often in fabric stuffed with foam plastic, also introduce unexpected changes of scale.

Relief

Sculptural forms are influenced not only by the materials and methods used to produce them but also by their setting, function or scale. In reliefs, for instance, the essential three-dimensionality of sculpture (discussed in the introduction) is modified by the fact that forms do not lead a separate existence but are created on or against an underlying surface. The images exist in a real, if condensed, space, and have in some degree the weight, volume and responsiveness to light of free-standing works. However, as they are presented in a single view, and in a space that is to a certain degree notional and illusory, such pictorial means of expression as outlines, foreshortening and perspective may be used to suggest receding space and atmospheric effects beyond the scope of free-standing sculpture, which is necessarily limited to the real space it occupies.

The double nature of relief makes it a complex, difficult, but richly versatile and expressive art form, requiring ability in both drawing and sculpture. Low reliefs tend to be pictorial above all. Indeed, some are clearly conceived as a development of drawing and painting rather than as a contraction of sculpture, for example the low reliefs of Pre-Columbian America, with their raised, flat silhouettes, or the incised outline reliefs of ancient Western Asia, both of which superbly exploit the expressive possibilities of pattern and texture rather than form in depth.

The conception of the field of the relief as a receding picture space which the images inhabit was not unknown to early sculptors, but it is most thoroughly realized in works that postdate the development of systematic perspective in the fifteenth century. The type of relief invented by Donatello and known as *stiacciato* (flattened) relief depends for its highly pictorial atmospheric effect on a carefully controlled combination of engraved lines and the merest degree of projection. The extreme delicacy of the engraving and surface modelling in Donatello's pure white marble reliefs has never been surpassed, and his influence can still be seen in the eloquent work of the modern Italian sculptor Giacomo Manzù.

As the represented depth of elements in a relief cannot correspond with the actual physical depth in the stone, the creation of an apparently correct order of receding overlapping forms is one of the most difficult aspects of relief carving. In order to arrive at a solution that works optically from the front, the sculptor has to distort the forms, as becomes apparent when the relief is viewed obliquely. Frequently, shapes have to be cut back or hollowed out to make room for a shape in front, and the suggestive power of line has to be used to the full. Sometimes the effect of recession is supplemented by considerable variations in the degree to which figures project. In Ghiberti's "Gates of Paradise", modelled at a time when systematic perspective was a new and exciting discovery, distant figures and other components in the narrative are hardly raised at all from the background, while the nearer figures are in medium or high relief, or even virtually detached from the matrix and fully in the round.

DONATELLO (right)
The Ascension with Christ giving the keys to St Peter, detail, *c.* 1430
The modelling is so flat that the figures have no independent corporeality. Some parts of the forms are defined only by incised lines and others are faded off into the matrix, producing a subtle, atmospheric effect with a soft pattern of light and shade. Background and figures form a continuous flowing surface, yet with a clear order of recession.

MANZU (below)
St Notburga and the beheading of the Blessed Engelbert Knolland, panel from a bronze door for Salzburg Cathedral, 1958
Broad and simple handling of the clay modelling is combined with a subtlety and sensitivity of outline which recalls Donatello's draughtsmanship. Though the low relief and the thin outline framing the composition suggest a pictorial treatment, the background is blank without implied recession. The hen and raven in very high relief have associations with charity, the theme of the whole door.

GHIBERTI (left)
The Isaac panel from "The Gates of Paradise",
c. 1425–47
Upon a panel with an actual depth measured in inches, Ghiberti creates a notional depth of some 14m (45ft), plotted in the diagram above. Using architectural features to separate the scenes, he shows seven different incidents in the story of Jacob and Esau, each clearly visible within a coherently designed system of linear perspective. The implied recession of forms is reinforced by the actual diminishing both of the scale of the figures and of their degree of modelling, those in the foreground being almost fully in the round, a masterly fusion of the pictorial and sculptural.

NINEVEH (left)
King Assurbanipal killing a lion, c. 668–627 BC
The low, flat reliefs on stone slabs from the palaces of the Assyrian kings show movement only along a horizontal line, with no attempt to represent depth. Yet the bodies of animals especially are subtly modelled to suggest their underlying structure, as in the tense musculature of this lion, contrasting with the stiff impassivity of the king.

GUATEMALA (right)
Toltec stela, *c.* AD 1000
The bold pattern revealed by strong sunlight striking the sharply cut outlines of raised shapes is paramount in many Pre-Columbian reliefs. There is decorative texture here but almost no modelling of the surface.

Medium and High Relief

In reliefs that are primarily sculptural rather than pictorial the background is conceived not as a notional picture space within which the forms exist, but as a solid, impenetrable backdrop against which they are placed. The space inhabited by the figures becomes a kind of shallow stage, the depth of which is defined by the solid mass or volume of the figures themselves. And the forms and movements of the figures are centred upon axes of their own and not subordinated to the demands of the matrix. This essentially sculptural approach can be seen clearly in Greek, Indian and Gothic sculpture even where the actual depth of relief is quite shallow.

The manner in which forms are accommodated in the limited depth of a medium relief has a profound effect on the visual character of the work. The whole form may either be compressed or flattened, or the front of the form may be fully modelled with the back sunk into the matrix as if immersed in water. When a form such as a sphere or even a head in profile is sunk as far as the half round, its contour may coincide exactly with the level of the background. Complex forms, including the human figure, present a more convoluted profile, however, and if the figure is to be represented as an independent entity with any degree of natural movement, some of its contours will project from the background, making some undercutting inevitable. The masterly handling of the articulation of forms in relation to, but independently of, the background is one of the most admired and imitated qualities of Classical Greek relief carvings (see pp. 180–181).

Where several figures are shown one behind the other the sculptor has to find a simultaneous solution to two main problems: first, how to make all the figures visible and, secondly, how to compress overlapping figures into a restricted depth. Visibility is usually ensured by a bird's-eye viewpoint with each row of figures higher than the one in front, as in a group photograph of people standing on steps. The problem of overlap is solved by keeping all the heads on the same level of the front plane of the relief and tapering the rear figures downwards to fit behind those in front. The shallow space of medium reliefs also affects the way in which movement is represented. In almost all reliefs before the age of Baroque, movement is lateral; figures bend at the waist or stretch out their arms or legs sideways rather than outwards. This restriction of movement contributes greatly to the calm, somewhat remote, self-contained quality of many of the finest Classical reliefs. Totally different in spirit are Baroque high reliefs such as Algardi's huge *Meeting of Pope Leo I and Attila*, where turbulent figures project out of the space of the relief and invade the space of the viewer, drawing him into their drama.

The composite woodcarved altarpieces of late Gothic northern Europe, in which many of the figures are fully in the round, are among the most remarkable examples of high relief. Though each scene is presented as a separate tableau on a sloping stage within a box-like space, their depth is balanced by canopies and a framework of fantastically carved tracery, which maintains the continuity of the frontal plane – important in the architectural context. There are some parallels in the work of the modern sculptor Louise Nevelson, who also exploits the power of small enclosures to give significance to the objects within them, and whose monumental assemblages of found objects have a haunting presence.

MATHURA, INDIA
Yakshi, c. AD 100
Though only some of the limbs are undercut, the figure seems to exist in the round, embedded in the stone. Its fullness is emphasized by the line of the girdle and necklace which, like much drapery in Greek medium relief sculpture, follows the form to suggest a roundness the real depth cannot provide.

ALGARDI (left)
The meeting of Pope Leo I and Attila, 1646–53
The receding space of the Ghiberti on the previous page is here reversed as the figures press forward, their gesticulating arms and spiralling draperies compelling our involvement. Algardi brilliantly combines traditional devices such as vertical banks of figures and lateral disposition of the flying Apostles with diagonal outward momentum.

NEVELSON (right)
Golden gate, 1961
Nevelson's assemblages recall the general composition and appearance of altarpieces. But in place of sacred figures are mere wooden oddments redeemed from banality by their setting.

BRUGGEMANN (left)
The Brodesholm altarpiece:
details, (below) *The scourging
of Christ*, (bottom) *Pontius
Pilate washing his hands*,
1515–21
The sloping floors of the
stage-like compartments
give each scene maximum
visibility and an illusion
of increased depth. Yet the
space is finite, bounded by
an impenetrable backdrop.
As the details show, most of
the figures are free-standing
and all are vividly individual.
The strong pattern of light
and shade created by the
overlapping forms heightens
the drama, Christ's heavily
fragmented robe contrasting
expressively with the tight
costuming of the soldiery.

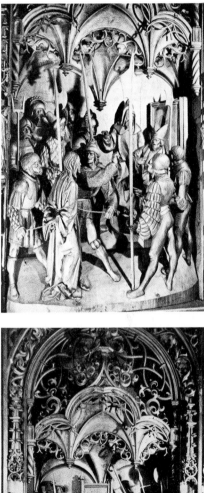

Sculpture and Architecture

ELURA, INDIA (right)
The Kailasanatha temple,
c. AD 900
"How is it possible that
I built this other than by
magic?", exclaimed Krishna
II, who sponsored this most
awesome of all Indian rock-
cut temples. Carved out of
volcanic rock, it stands
about 29m (96ft) high,
and the total excavation
from the hillside measures
84 by 47m (276 by 154ft).

AUTUN, ST LAZARE
The Flight into Egypt,
c. 1125–35
Here, at the height of
Romanesque sculpture, the
narrative group has almost
freed itself from the
basket shape of the more
basic medieval capital. Yet
the forward lean of Joseph's
body as he leads the donkey
onward is adapted to its
swell without breaking the
overall architectural line.

The association between sculpture and architecture is inevitably close – and not only because it is
natural that the images of gods, spirits, saints,
heroes or kings should be connected with the
buildings in which they dwelt or were worshipped.
Fundamental to both arts is a concern for space
and solid form. Perhaps the most astonishing
application of sculptural methods and principles
to architecture is in the rock-cut temples of India;
at Elura a whole building – exterior shape, interior
space and sculptural decoration – is cut from living
rock like a huge carving. Other building styles may
be described as sculptural because of the attention
devoted to the shapes and composition of masses.

The post-and-lintel stone buildings of the
Graeco-Roman world are an example not only of
such a style but also of the way in which architecture can present many different opportunities for
sculptural decoration. The triangular pediments
of Greek temples suggested compositions of considerable ingenuity, the repeated squares of the
metopes were ideal for separate scenes and incidents, and the long horizontal bands of the
friezes lent themselves readily to processions and
battle scenes.

Perhaps nowhere in the world has the fusion of
architecture and sculpture come nearer to perfection than in the great churches of medieval
Europe. The medieval imagination was able to
adapt human figures, animals, plants and fantastic
creatures of its own invention to occupy spaces of
any shape. Door jambs, lintels, tympana, archi-
volts, corbels, capitals, window mullions, roof
bosses, water spouts and finials all came alive
under the sculptor's chisel.

In the development from Romanesque to

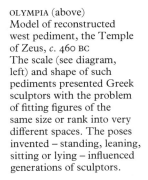

OLYMPIA (above)
Model of reconstructed
west pediment, the Temple
of Zeus, *c.* 460 BC
The scale (see diagram,
left) and shape of such
pediments presented Greek
sculptors with the problem
of fitting figures of the
same size or rank into very
different spaces. The poses
invented – standing, leaning,
sitting or lying – influenced
generations of sculptors.

WESTMINSTER ABBEY (right)
Censing angel, c. 1250
The fluency with which the
angel's wings, draperies
and swinging censer are
adapted to fill an awkward
space make this one of the
finest achievements of
medieval English sculpture.
A long, gently swaying
rhythm pervades the whole
figure, its sweetness and
graceful presence softening
the forms of the architecture.

Gothic we can trace the increasing independence
of sculpture from the matrix of the building. At
first the lines, forms and compositions of the
sculpture tend to follow and underline the architectural shapes and to preserve unbroken the unity
of the wall or column. But as Romanesque gives
way to Gothic, figures cease to behave like so many
motifs adapted and transformed to fit the surfaces
they decorate. Emerging from the wall to assume a
freer, more organic life of their own, they acquire
greater mass, their draperies deepen, changing
from shallow grooves and ridges to thick folds,
their shadows intensify and their movements
become more fluid.

The association between sculpture and architecture is most complete when building components themselves become sculptures. The cary-
atids of the Athenian Erechtheum, the "Atlas"
figures of ancient Mexico, the lions supporting the
columns of a Pisano pulpit (see over) all serve a
similar dual role as image of support and as
support. This functional use of sculpture is developed more freely in applied arts when the structural risks are not so great, as in mirror handles
shaped like figures or furniture legs carved or
moulded in the shape of sphinxes.

In the twentieth century, though sculpture and
architecture have interacted, the movement away
from applied ornamentation has reduced the opportunities for sculptural decoration of buildings.
Yet a work such as Barbara Hepworth's *Winged
figure* for the John Lewis building in Oxford
Street, London, shows a sculptor responding to
the challenge of designing a work suited to an
existing building while at the same time satisfying
her personal criteria and feelings about sculpture.

HEPWORTH (above)
Winged figure, 1962
The inward curving shell-
like aluminium structure with
its large open spaces and
taut linear components is

designed to contrast both
in form and materials with
the building's flat side and
to create ever-changing
patterns of light and shade
within itself and on the wall.

TULA, MEXICO (above)
Toltec warrior, Temple
of Quetzalcoatl, *c.* 900–1168
This 3m (15ft) high figure
was one of four similar
statues supporting the roof
of the sanctuary on the
pyramid at Tula. Details
are suggested by shallow
relief carving on the sides
of the four massive blocks
from which it is made, but
with minimal alteration in
the essential columnar shape.

Sculpture and Architecture

The forms and decoration invented for their own purposes by architects have entered the vocabularies of many of the other arts and become a major source of motifs for a vast array of artefacts. These include, besides such relatively small objects as candlesticks, a number of grander independent indoor structures – tombs, pulpits, fonts, tabernacles, altars – in which sculpture also plays an important, sometimes a dominant, role. The elements of classical, Gothic and other building styles are used freely, both as structural components and as decorative motifs, along with figurative and ornamental sculpture to create highly imaginative composite works of art.

The use of architectural motifs for tombs was not, of course, arbitrary or merely decorative. A main function of tombs, from great mausoleums and pyramids to the more modest house-shaped sarcophagus with its roof-like lid and gables, has been to provide a "home" for the dead, projecting the illusion that they inhabit it still. Other functions – the expression of hope for the salvation of the dead in the next world and their commemoration in this world – were fulfilled by sculpture, in symbolic religious images and human effigies. Many tombs are extremely rich in sculpture; indeed, much of the world's greatest sculpture is associated with them.

The great series of humanist wall-tombs of the Florentine Renaissance, beginning with those of Donatello and Michelozzo and including superb works by the Rossellino brothers and Desiderio da Settignano, afford a rare opportunity for seeing how the skill and imaginative powers of a group of highly gifted artists can manipulate and vary the architectural and sculptural elements of a particular compositional scheme.

Central to many tombs are the effigies of the dead, whether they are the affectionate half-reclining married couples on the lids of Etruscan

DESIDERIO (above)
Marsuppini monument, c.1453
The delicate carving forms a unity with the mouldings, panels and columns; it is the triumphal arch rather than the effigy which expresses the meaning.

NICOLA PISANO (left)
The pulpit of Siena Cathedral, 1265–68
Composite works of this kind should be viewed as complete designs in which the proportions of the architecture, the placing of the figures in relation to it and the combination of materials are as relevant aesthetically as are the qualities of individual sculptural groups (detail above). Nicola was both the sculptor and architect.

SOLESMES ABBEY (left)
The entombment of Christ,
1496
Despite its complex religious symbolism the group makes a strong, simple statement. The marrying of sculpture and architecture is as skilful as the psychological subtlety with which figures (details below and right) are carved and placed. A major design aspect is the treatment of drapery, which sculptors use both for its endless variety of pattern and for compositional and

expressive effects. The arrangement of folds may suggest either agitated movement or – as here – a calm gravity. The unusual placing of the Magdalen in the foreground adds depth and variety of height, and breaks the hammock-like sweep of the shroud which might otherwise echo too obviously the curve of the arch. Carved with sensitive restraint and enclosed in her private grief, this figure has an individuality rare in Gothic sculpture.

GIUSTI BROTHERS (left)
Tomb of Louis XII and Anne of Brittany, completed 1531
The Giusti's tomb set a pattern for others, and has a wealth of figure sculpture showing the variation in quality often found in this kind of large architectural commission. The Apostles beneath the arches and the Virtues at each corner are the work of several hands and cannot compare in quality with either the kneeling royal couple or their reclining effigies within the arcaded space – haunting images of death.

sarcophagi, the Elizabethan English gentleman kneeling with his wife and row of children, the recumbent medieval knight with his lady at his side and his dog at his feet, or the simple marble commemorative portrait medallion popular in the nineteenth century.

A particularly striking treatment occurs in a magnificent group of sixteenth-century French free-standing royal tombs, the first that of Louis XII. Recumbent figures in the round representing the dead couple nude and *en transis* (as corpses in varying states of emaciation or decay) are often carved with remarkable skill and an almost poetic realism which does not flinch at showing embalming incisions. Above the central, chapel-like space in which they are housed, the couple appear again, clothed in royal robes and kneeling in prayer. Panels of relief and free-standing figures of *Virtues* also form part of the composition. Like the Italian humanist tombs, these complex works of art are planned as a fusion of architecture and sculpture.

Throughout the fifteenth century, representations of the entombment of Christ were placed as private monuments in churches all over France. These sculptured groups are made up of several life-size free-standing figures which usually represent Joseph of Arimathaea and Nicodemus lowering the body of Christ into a sarcophagus while the chief mourners – the Virgin, St John, Mary Magdalen and others – look on in various attitudes of grief. The dramatic impact of many of these groups is enhanced by placing them in large stage-like niches representing the burial chamber, framed with Gothic architecture. The most splendid of these architectural settings, at Solesmes Abbey, surrounds what is also generally regarded as the greatest of the Entombment groups. The burial chamber is sited at the bottom of a high structure containing other figures and a wealth of architectural detail, sculpture and architecture making up a completely integrated formal design.

Sculpture in its Setting

MOCHI (right)
Duke Alexander Farnese,
1620–25
The suggestion of withheld
energy, managed with such
skill, is created largely by
the rider's swirling cloak,
which echoes the powerful
waves of the mane and tail.
The cloak also connects the

rider to the mass of the
horse and converts his
vertical shape into a more
dynamic, oblique shape. The
diagram indicates the less
impressive appearance of a
horse and rider shorn of
the proportional devices that
Mochi has employed to
increase the sense of power.

Some of the special considerations that affect the
nature and forms of sculpture associated with
buildings continue to apply when sculpture is
freed from a matrix and placed outdoors. The
scale and position of the work must often be
carefully related to its site. How will it fit into and
show up against its surroundings in the changing
light that falls upon it? In which direction should it
face, how high should it be placed and what size
should it be in relation to the surrounding space,
the viewing distances and positions, and the scale
of nearby buildings or vistas?

The purpose of much outdoor sculpture
throughout history has been to perpetuate the
memory of individuals or events in durable three-
dimensional images which command attention in
the environment by the sheer physical presence
they exert. Such public monuments are usually set
apart from their surroundings by means of a plinth
or other feature serving a function similar to that
of a picture frame; the height and shape of this
support and the relations between its forms and
those of the sculpture are significant.

A sculptural format that in many ways typifies
the challenges of designing monuments is the free-
standing equestrian statue. Its development can be
traced in a wealth of noble examples from the
statue of Marcus Aurelius (the supreme survivor
of hundreds of similar statues erected throughout
the Roman Empire), through its revival in
fifteenth-century Italy and its heyday in the seventeenth and eighteenth centuries, to its almost
complete demise in the modern age when horse-
riding became little more than a picturesque
pastime. The physical problems of supporting the
large bulk of a horse and rider on the four slender
columns of a horse's legs make bronze, rather than
stone, the natural choice of medium. Apart from
the problems of mastering the complex anatomy of
the horse, the technical problems of modelling and
casting such statues are formidable.

A general problem in the siting of outdoor
sculpture, especially when it is placed above eye-
level, is the effect of foreshortening, often solved
by elongating and enlarging the upper parts of the

GOERITZ (left)
The square of towers, 1957
The simple, geometric forms
of these five triangular
towers (ranging up to a
height of 6om (195ft)
attempt to blend sculpture
with modern architecture
in a setting unsuited to
the traditional kind of
town square statuary. In
reinforced concrete, they
mark the entry to a satellite
town outside Mexico City.

J. H. FOLEY (right)
Prince Albert, 1868–73
More than double life-size and originally gilded, this seated figure presented severe problems of fore-shortening from the low viewing angle, and the sculptor was not permitted to falsify the proportions as a remedy. His solution was an open, turned pose with the upper body and head inclined forwards as the silhouette of the memorial shows (lower right). The sculptural decoration of this grand High Victorian monument, designed by Gilbert Scott, is developed around the four sides and diagonals of a square to be taken in slowly as a viewer explores each aspect. The buttress-like compositions of the marble groups at the corners of the base give visual support to the canopy and begin the movement out to groups representing the four continents placed at the corners of the steps.

ZADKINE (left)
The destroyed city, 1953
The outspread, broken forms of this massive bronze are designed to make a powerful silhouette against the open sky, communicating instantly the message of the memorial – outrage against the bombing of Rotterdam.

BORGLUM (below)
American presidents in Mt Rushmore, 1927–41
The colossal heads, each some 20m (60ft) high, of Presidents Washington, Jefferson, Lincoln and Theodore Roosevelt, are intended to be viewed from considerable distances. The carving (much of it using dynamite and power tools) is appropriately bold, with clear definition of form.

figure or inclining them forwards towards the onlooker, as in many seated figures. The tendency is for a naturally proportioned equestrian figure to appear ridiculous, as though sunk into his mount. The usual remedy is to make the rider taller and to sit him abnormally high in the saddle; this also serves the expressive purpose of making him seem dominant. The difficulties of relating the lighter, vertical shape of the rider to the great horizontal mass of the horse are frequently overcome by using the rider's cloak to increase his bulk and to ease the transition from one form to another.

Another problem common to outdoor sculptures, especially when they are made of dark material, is the apparent reduction in the mass of forms seen against the sky. To counteract this effect, to which the legs of a horse are particularly vulnerable, the sculptor usually gives them a greater than natural thickness. Both these proportional aspects of design are sometimes noticeable when a statue is removed from its site and placed indoors at eye-level. A further departure from natural proportions may be seen in the size of the horse's head, which is often reduced in order to give more mass and power to its body; Verrocchio's Colleoni monument (see p. 68) is a brilliant example.

Outdoor settings enable sculptors to work on a colossal scale where the proportional problems may be overcome by the sheer distance of the viewer from the sculpture. Such famous examples as the Statue of Liberty are surpassed in ambition by Borglum's conversion of a whole section of Mt Rushmore into a memorial in portrait form of four American presidents. At least in the Western democracies, however, the image that modern man has of himself is no longer one that lends itself to expression in terms of monumental sculpture. The taste for triumphal arches, huge columns and such splendidly confident celebrations of imperial power as the Albert Memorial in London has given way to a preference for symbolic monuments that do not particularize men or events, and are conceived in the more generalized expressive language of abstract form.

Sculpture in its Setting

Outdoor sculpture is perhaps uniquely capable of persuading us that its forms are alive. The interaction between natural and sculptural materials is particularly close in fountains and in park and garden sculptures, the designs and imagery of which are intimately related both to their setting and to their purpose. They may be intended to encourage meditation or simply to delight and amuse. Gardens – essentially contrived landscapes – are ideal places for the play of fantasy: for monsters, mythical beings, grotesque and *tableaux vivants*, groups of sculpted figures posed within the landscape without plinths, as though living there, unexpectedly encountered.

The popularity of fountains is not surprising in view of their manifold appeal to our senses. They can not only call on an almost infinite variety of sculptural forms in their solid structure but are also enhanced by the movement and sounds of the water – the gleam of wet stone and bronze, the iridescence of drifting mist or the reflections in a still basin when the fountain is at rest. Modern preoccupations with non-figurative, spatial or Kinetic forms of art have influenced the design of recent fountains, and a revolutionary development is sculpture in which water is the only material, describing spectacular arabesques under pressure applied intermittently to give it an independent life in the air, or illumined by constantly-changing coloured lights.

NOGUCHI (right)
Courtyard at Yale, 1960–64
The austere geometry of this stone garden and the whiteness of its marble surfaces give the courtyard an aura of intellectual calm which complements perfectly its position in a library and the plain character of the building itself. Precedents include the sand gardens of Japan, Indian astronomical gardens and Italian paved squares.

BRANCUSI (left)
Endless column, at Tirgu Jiu, Romania, 1937
Brancusi carefully planned a large clear area around this huge sculpture, for the appearance and relationships of the modules (each the size of a man) continually change as a viewer moves in relation to it. Gradually the finite character emerges – the insistent verticality and monumental abstraction.

CHRISTO (right)
Wrapped coast, 1969
The capacity of sculpture to modify the environment has been extended by the Land sculptor who, in seeking to fuse art with reality, alters the landscape itself. Christo's packaging of an entire stretch of Australian coastline with polythene sheets transformed commonplace rocks into forms of sudden mystery.

ROME (left)
The Fountain of the Naiads, detail: "*The Nymph of Subterranean Waters*", 1900
Fountains were truly multi-media works long before that term was coined; the languorous arching movement of the nymph – one of four large bronze figures decorating the basin of this grandiose fountain – is echoed by the arcing jets of water.

GIAMBOLOGNA (left)
Appennino, 1577–81
The colossal mountain god, a 10-metre (32ft) high construction in brick and stone, crouches above a pool in the Medici villa at Pratolino. The subject is brilliantly interpreted by the fusion of geological and human elements and by the compact, triangular shape, seeming to have just emerged from the earth.

ITALY, NEAR NAPLES (right)
Diana and nymphs, c. 1770
The sumptuous gardens of the Villa Reale at Caserta feature a cascade falling some 16 metres (52ft) into a pool, on either side of which are placed groups of figures like inhabitants of an escapist paradise. Diana and her nymphs, in a tableau of playful eroticism, are disturbed at their toilet by the hunter Actaeon.

Small Portable Sculpture

Sculpture in such materials as jade, ivory, quartz, semi-precious stones, gold and silver is necessarily small, either because the materials are available only in small pieces or because they are rare and valuable. However, the careful detail and exquisite craftsmanship found in so many small-scale works are influenced not only by the fine nature of these materials but also by the function or purpose of the sculptures; for they were often intended to be held in the hand and inspected at leisure. A corresponding care and loving treatment of detail is typical of book illuminations, similarly intended to be enjoyed at close quarters.

Work on a small scale provides sculptors with opportunities not available in monumental sculpture, lending itself more readily to a light-hearted approach, to experiment with form, composition, and movement, and to the free play of fantasy: it is more likely to delight and amuse than to overwhelm. The unfortunate corollary is that small-scale sculpture can and often does fall into the trap of excessive fussiness and trivial prettiness.

Small sculptures are often addressed to the hand as much as to the eye; many are completely self-contained objects, which can be picked up and turned in any direction, so our response to their sculptural qualities is likely to be especially vivid and direct. Also, they are less at the mercy of specific lighting conditions than larger, more fixed sculpture: a piece of table sculpture or a figurine can be turned to the light which best suits it, or light can be brought to it; and because small sculptures are easily carried from place to place, they have acted as important agents in the dissemination of sculptural styles and iconographic motifs. Their self-sufficient quality may also be imparted to larger works, such as Henry Moore's *Reclining figures* (see p. 182), which have no fixed base or background and which are created, Moore has said, by thinking of the solid shape, whatever its size, as if he were holding it completely enclosed in the hollow of his hand.

Coins and medals of all ages have been especially important in the dissemination of artistic ideas. Earlier coins, such as those of the Greeks, were impressed with designs cut in intaglio on the end of a metal punch, which was then hammered into a blank metal disc: the result was a variable, but vigorously alive coin, sometimes a miniature sculptural masterpiece, very different from the mechanically reproduced coins of today.

Though the commemorative medal was an invention of the early Renaissance, emulation of the Antique played a vital role here, as in other arts of the period, and almost every medal produced by the masters who took up the medium – notably Pisanello and Niccolò Fiorentino in Italy, and Dürer in Germany – bears a portrait on the obverse, in the manner of Greek and Roman coinage. The popularity of the medal as an art form is increasing today, possibly because it can be produced in batches and so reach more people, but also because it allows the sculptor more freedom than large-scale commissioned work. Medals may be struck like coins, carved in boxwood or cast from originals modelled in wax or clay.

Each square represents 2cm

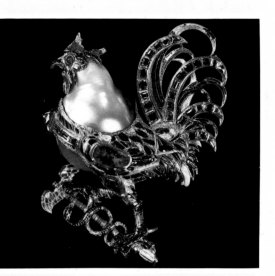

NICCOLO FIORENTINO (right)
Medal of *Giovanna Albizzi*,
c. 1486
The medal was made by a
sand-casting process: a
negative mould of casting-
sand was prepared from a
wax original and molten
bronze poured in; when
cool, the medal was chased.
Any number of casts can be
taken from a single mould.

NORTH ITALY (above)
16th/17th century
The goldsmith has used the
natural shape of a baroque
(blister) pearl to fashion
a miniaturized sculpture of
almost surrealist fantasy.

The head and part of the
body with the tail are
richly embellished with
enamels and gems – a huge
ruby and several diamonds.
The bird holds an enamelled
wand between its claws.

PERSIA (left)
Libation vessel,
c. 5th century BC
This gold python was made
of sheet-metal by beating
and embossing techniques.
The decorative treatment
of the wings and mane and
the definition of form by
means of puckers and
ridges are typical of direct
metalworking techniques.

CENTRAL GERMANY (right)
Eltenberg shrine, *c.* 1150
Shrines were occasionally
carried in procession; so,
despite its relatively greater
bulk (see scale diagram),
this magnificent example –
of gilt bronze, decorated
with enamels – perhaps
more truly merits the epi-
thet 'portable' than any
other object on the page.

RICCIO (right)
Seated satyr, c. 1500
Riccio's fluent, tactile
modelling and imaginative
feeling for the mythical
creatures of the ancient
world clearly emerge in this
piece, which like many of
his bronze figurines has a
functional aspect: on its
right shoulder it carries
an oil-lamp in the shape
of a conch shell, and in
the other arm, an inkwell.

RAINO HEINO (above)
SALT *Conference medal*,
1969
Traditionally the designs
on commemorative medals
have been representational,
but recently medallists

have experimented with
abstract forms. In this
bronze-struck medal the
artist resolves, in the
unified design of the
principal face, a conflict
of forms on the reverse.

List of Illustrations and Acknowledgments

Works of art illustrated are listed in the order in which they appear in the book. In general, the order runs from top to bottom and left to right on each page, though works by the same artist or of the same origin are grouped together.

The name of the artist (or, if the artist is not known, the place or origin) and the title or description of each work are followed by its medium, its dimensions (metric) and its present location and ownership. Photographic credits are given in brackets, unless the photograph has been supplied by the owner.

Though every effort has been made to check the accuracy of these specifications, it has not always been possible to verify all of the information at source.

10–19 Looking at Art
RENOIR: *The theatre box* (La loge), 1874, oil on canvas, 80 × 60 cm, London, Courtauld Institute Galleries.
MASTER OF MARY OF BURGUNDY: *Maximilian and Mary of Burgundy before the Virgin*, from the Book of Hours of Charles the Bold, c. 1477, Cod. 1857, fol. 14v. Vienna, Österreichische Nationalbibliothek.

20–21 Variations on Twelve Themes
TITIAN: "*The Concert Champêtre*" (Pastoral music making), oil on canvas, 110 × 138 cm, Paris, Louvre (Scala).
LEONARDO: *A woman pointing*, after 1513, black chalk, 21 × 13.5 cm, Windsor, Royal Library (by gracious permission of Her Majesty the Queen).

20–23 The Human Figure
MICHELANGELO: *David*, 1501-04, marble, height 434 cm, Florence, Accademia (Scala).

24–25 The Human Figure
TANZANIA: Rock-painting of a bushman painting a mountain, from a Neolithic site in S.W. Africa, dimensions unrecorded, *in situ* (Gerald Cubitt).
EGYPT: *Fowling in the marshes*, from the Tomb of Nebamun, 1400 BC, fresco, London, British Museum (Michael Holford).
ANAVYSOS, ATTICA: Kouros, c. 540-515 BC, marble, height 193 cm, Athens, National Museum (Scala).
DURER: *Nude woman*, 1493, drawing, Bayonne, Musée Bonnat (Photo Bulloz); *Eve*, c. 1506, both versions pen and bistre on wash, 26 × 16.5 cm, Vienna, Albertina.
GREECE: "*The Venus de Milo*", c. 100 BC, marble, height 180 cm, Paris, Louvre (Alinari).
KHAJURAHO, INDIA: Sculptural decoration from the Kandarya Mahadeva Temple, c. 1000 (René Roland).
RAPHAEL: *The three Graces*, 1504-05, oil on panel, 17 × 17 cm, Chantilly, Musée Condé (Giraudon).

26–27 The Human Figure
TINTORETTO: *Susannah and the Elders*, c. 1550, oil on canvas, 143.5 × 193 cm, Vienna, Kunsthistorisches Museum (Scala).
REMBRANDT: *Bathsheba at her toilet*, 1654, oil on canvas, 142 × 142 cm, Paris, Louvre (Documentation Photographique de la Réunion des Musées Nationaux).
RUBENS: *Bathsheba reading David's letter*, c. 1636-38, oil on panel, 167 × 125 cm, Dresden, Gemäldegalerie (Cooper-Bridgeman Library).
BOUCHER: *Miss O'Murphy*, 1732, oil on canvas, 59 × 73 cm, Munich, Alte Pinakothek (Scala).
COURBET: *The artist's studio*, 1854-55, oil on canvas, 361 × 598 cm, Paris, Louvre (Scala).
BOCCIONI: *Unique forms of continuity in space*, 1913, bronze, height 109.5 cm, New York, Museum of Modern Art, Lillie P. Bliss Bequest.
BRANCUSI: *Male torso*, after 1924, brass, height 45.5 cm, Ohio, Cleveland Museum of Art, Hinman B. Hurlbut collection.
DE KOONING: *Woman IV*, 1952-53, oil and enamel on canvas, 150 × 118.5 cm, Kansas City, Missouri, Nelson Gallery-Atkins Museum, Gift of Mr William Inge.
PICASSO: *Nude in an armchair*, 1932, oil on canvas, 130 × 97 cm, London, Tate Gallery.

28–29 The Human Face
LEONARDO: *Mona Lisa*, c. 1503-06, oil on panel, 77 × 53 cm, Paris, Louvre (Scala).

30–31 The Human Face
JOSEPH WRIGHT: *The Corinthian Maid*, 1784, oil on canvas, 106.7 × 127 cm, Upperville, Virginia, Mr and Mrs Paul Mellon Collection.
AMMAN: *Jericho skull*, c. 6000 BC, skull, shell and clay, Amman, Archaeological Museum (Scala).
RUBENS: *Susanna Lunden*, c. 1622-25, oil on panel, 79 × 54 cm, London, National Gallery.
J. S. DEVILLE: Life-mask of William Blake, c. 1825, plaster, height 29 cm, Cambridge, Fitzwilliam Museum.
POLYEUKTOS: Detail of head from the statue of *Demosthenes*, original c. 280 BC, marble, height 202 cm, Copenhagen, Ny Carlsberg Glyptotek.
DAVID: *Napoleon in his study*, 1812, oil on canvas, 202 × 124 cm, Washington, National Gallery of Art, Samuel H. Kress collection.
GILLRAY: *Maniac ravings*, 24th May 1805, lithograph, London, British Museum (John Freeman).
BRAQUE: *Man with a guitar*, 1911, oil on canvas, 116 × 81 cm, New York, Museum of Modern Art, Lillie P. Bliss Bequest.
DIX: *Sylvia von Harden*, 1926, oil on panel, 121 × 89 cm, Paris, Musée National d'Art Moderne.

32–33 The Human Face
DURER: *Self-portrait naked*, c. 1510, pen and brush, heightened with white on green paper, 19.5 × 15.5 cm, Weimar, Kunstsammlungen (Eberhard Renno).
REMBRANDT: *Self-portrait*, 1669, oil on canvas, 86 × 70.5 cm, London, National Gallery.
HOKUSAI: *Self-portrait*, c. 1843, drawing, Leyden, Rijksmuseum voor Volkerkunde.
COURBET: *The meeting*, 1854, oil on canvas, 129 × 149 cm, Montpellier, Musée Fabre (Photo Bulloz).
VAN GOGH: *Self-portrait*, 1890, oil on canvas, 63 × 53 cm, Paris, Louvre, Musée Jeu de Paume (Scala).
CEZANNE: *Self-portrait in a hat*, 1880, oil on canvas, 65 × 51 cm, Berne, Kunstmuseum (Colorphoto Hans Hinz).
CLOSE: *Self-portrait*, 1968, acrylic on canvas, 273 × 212 cm, Minneapolis, Walker Art Center.
KOKOSCHKA: *Self-portrait*, 1913, oil on canvas, 80 × 48 cm, New York, Museum of Modern Art.

34–35 Couples
RODIN: *The kiss*, 1901-04, marble, 184 × 122 × 149 cm, London, Tate Gallery.

36–37 Couples
DURER: *Adam and Eve*, 1507, diptych, oil on panel, *Adam* 209 × 81 cm, *Eve* 209 × 83 cm, Madrid, Prado (Scala).
VAN EYCK: "*The Arnolfini Marriage*", 1434, oil on panel, 81.5 × 59.5 cm, London, National Gallery.
EGYPT, MEIDUM: *Prince Rahotep and his wife Nofret*, c. 2550 BC, painted limestone with inlaid eyes, height 120 cm, Cairo, Egyptian Museum (Kuhnert and Landrock); A panel of Tutankhamun's throne, before 1361 BC, wood plated with gold and silver, inlays of glass and paste, height 104 cm, Cairo, Egyptian Museum (Werner Forman Archive).
IRAN: *Salaman and Absal reach the shore of the sea*, 1556-65, manuscript fol. 194b from the *Haft Awrang* of Jami, 34 × 23 cm, Washington, DC, Freer Gallery of Art.
REMBRANDT: "*The Jewish Bride*", c. 1665, oil on canvas, 121.5 × 166.5 cm, Amsterdam, Rijksmuseum (Scala).
DOGON: *Male and female principals*, undated, wood, height 85 cm, New York, Schindler Collection (Werner Forman Archive).
MOORE: *King and Queen*, 1952-53, bronze, height 161 cm, Washington DC, Hirshhorn Museum and Sculpture Garden, Smithsonian Institution (John Tennant).
GROSZ: *A married couple*, 1930, watercolour, 66 × 47.5 cm, London, Tate Gallery.
WOOD: *American Gothic*, 1930, oil on board, 76 × 63 cm, Chicago, Art Institute of Chicago.

38–39 Couples
KHAJURAHO, INDIA: The Kandarya Mahadeva Temple, c. 1000, sandstone (Werner Forman Archive).
TITIAN: *Venus and the organ player*, c. 1550, oil on canvas, 148 × 217 cm, Madrid, Prado (Scala); *Io and Jupiter*, c. 1560, charcoal, 25 × 26 cm, Cambridge, Fitzwilliam Museum.
KORYUSAI, JAPAN: *Shunga*, second half of 18th century, woodcut, London, Victoria and Albert Museum (Cooper-Bridgeman Library).
HOGARTH: *Before the Seduction* and *After*, 1731, oil on canvas, 35.5 × 44.5 cm, Malibu, J. Paul Getty Museum.
COURBET: *The sleepers*, 1862, oil on canvas, 75 × 95 cm, Paris, Petit Palais (Scala).
MUNCH: *Vampire*, 1895-1902, lithograph, 38.5 × 54.5 cm, Oslo, Munch Museet (Scala).
SCHIELE: *The embrace*, 1917, oil on canvas, 100 × 170.5 cm, Vienna, Österreiches Galerie.

40–41 Life and Work
THE LIMBOURG BROTHERS: *Les Très Riches Heures du Duc de Berri; February, October* and *June*, 1413-16, colour on vellum, 21.5 × 14 cm, Chantilly, Musée Condé (Giraudon).

42–43 Life and Work
DELLA QUERCIA: *Labours of Adam and Eve*, c. 1428, marble relief, height 99 cm, Bologna, S. Petronio (Giraudon).
THEBES: *Harvesting*, c. 1450 BC, wall-painting, Thebes, Tomb of Menna (Ronald Sheridan).
BRUEGEL: *August (The corn harvest)*, 1565, oil on panel, 118 × 160.5 cm, New York, Metropolitan Museum of Art, Rogers Fund.
ANTELAMI: *June* and *September*, c. 1200, stone, Parma, Baptistery (Scala).
CRETE: The Harvesters' Vase, c. 1550 BC, diameter 11.5 cm, London, British Museum (Ronald Sheridan).
STUBBS: *The reapers*, 1795, enamel on a Wedgwood plaque, 77 × 103 cm, Yale Center for British Art, Paul Mellon collection.
MILLET: *The reaper*, c. 1866-68, wood engraving, New York, Metropolitan Museum of Art, Harris Brisbane Dick Fund.
VAN GOGH: *The reaper*, 1889, oil on canvas, 43.5 × 33.5 cm, Amsterdam, National Museum Vincent van Gogh.

44–45 Life and Work
REMBRANDT: *The anatomy lesson of Dr Tulp*, 1632, oil on canvas, 169.5 × 216.5 cm, The Hague, Mauritshuis (Scala).

EAKINS: *The Gross Clinic*, 1875, oil on canvas, 244 × 198 cm, Philadelphia, Jefferson Medical College of Jefferson University (Cooper-Bridgeman Library).
VERMEER: *Servant girl pouring milk*, c. 1663, oil on canvas, 43.5 × 41 cm, Amsterdam, Rijksmuseum (Cooper-Bridgeman Library).
REYNOLDS: *Dr Johnson*, 1756, oil on canvas, 122 × 97 cm, London, National Portrait Gallery.
HODLER: *The woodcutter*, 1910, oil on canvas, 261 × 212 cm, Sao Paulo, Museum of Art (Giraudon).
DEGAS: *The Cotton Exchange at New Orleans*, 1873, oil on canvas, 73 × 92 cm, Pau, Musée des Beaux-Arts (Giraudon).
LEGER: *The builders*, 1950, oil on canvas, 300 × 200 cm, Biot, Musée Fernand Léger.

46–47 Life and Leisure
RENOIR: *The luncheon of the boating party*, 1881, oil on canvas, Washington DC, Phillips Collection.

48–49 Life and Leisure
EXEKIAS: *Dionysos sailing*, c. 550 BC, black-figure *kylix*, Munich, Antikensammlung.
HARUNOBU: *Girl with a lantern on a balcony viewing plum-blossoms at night*, c. 1768, woodcut, 32.5 × 21 cm, New York, Metropolitan Museum of Art.
GIOVANNI BELLINI: *The feast of the gods*, 1514, oil on canvas, 170 × 188 cm, Washington, National Gallery, Widener collection.
BRUEGEL: *The peasant wedding*, c. 1567, oil on oak, 114 × 163 cm, Vienna, Kunsthistorisches Museum (Cooper-Bridgeman Library).
WATTEAU: *Les Champs-Elysées*, 1717, oil on canvas, 40.5 × 31.5 cm, London, Wallace Collection (John Freeman).
FRITH: *Derby Day*, 1856-58, oil on canvas, 101 × 223 cm, London, Tate Gallery.
KIENHOLZ: *Barney's Beanery*, 1965, mixed-media environment, life-size, Amsterdam, Stedelijk Museum.
MATISSE: "*La Joie de Vivre*", 1905-06, oil on canvas, 174 × 238 cm, Merion, Pennsylvania, Barnes Foundation.

50–51 Life and Leisure
AFTER MYRON: "*Diskobolos*" (The discus thrower), original c. 450 BC, marble, height 147 cm, Rome, Museo della Terme (Scala).
DE HOOGH: *Skittle-players*, c. 1663-66, oil on canvas, 66 × 70 cm, Aylesbury, Waddesdon Manor (National Trust).
ROUSSEAU: *The ball-players*, 1908, oil on canvas, 100 × 80 cm, New York, Solomon R. Guggenheim Museum.
TERBORCH: *The concert*, shortly after 1675, oil on wood, 56 × 44 cm, West Berlin, Staatliche Museen (Bildarchiv Preussischer Kulturbesitz).
AFTER CARAVAGGIO: *The card-players*, 17th century, oil on canvas, 96.5 × 117 cm, Cambridge, Mass., Fogg Art Museum (Gift: Friends of the Fogg

Art Museum).
KHNOPFF: *Memories*, 1889, pastel, 127 × 200 cm, Brussels, Musées Royaux des Beaux-Arts.
SHAHN: *Handball*, 1939, tempera on paper, mounted on board, 58 × 79.5 cm, New York, Museum of Modern Art (Scala).
CEZANNE: *The card-players*, 1890-92, oil on canvas, 45 × 57 cm, Paris, Louvre, Musée Jeu de Paume (Scala).

52–53 Narration
ALTDORFER: *The battle of Alexander and Darius on the Issus*, 1529, oil on panel, 158.5 × 120.5 cm, Munich, Alte Pinakothek (Scala).

54–55 Narration
CANTERBURY: The Bayeux Tapestry: *Construction of the fleet*, c. 1080, embroidered cotton, height 50 cm, length 69 metres, Bayeux, Musée (Scala).
GIOVANNI DI PAOLO: *St John entering the wilderness*, c. 1450, tempera on panel, 31 × 39 cm, London, National Gallery.
RUBENS: *The marriage* from the Marie de' Médicis cycle, c. 1622-25, oil on canvas, 394 × 295 cm, Paris, Louvre (Scala).
LICHTENSTEIN: *Whaam!*, 1963, 172.5 × 406.5 cm, acrylic on canvas, London, Tate Gallery.
HOGARTH: *The arrest* and *The prison*, from *The Rake's Progress*, c. 1733, oil on canvas, 62 × 75 cm, London, Sir John Soane's Museum (Cooper-Bridgeman Library).
GREECE: Sepulchral monument, 5th century BC, marble, Athens, National Museum (Scala).
HUGHES: *Home from the sea*, 1862, oil on panel, 51 × 65 cm, Oxford, Ashmolean Museum.
RIVERA: Mural, c. 1924-27, Chapingo, Mexico, National School of Agriculture.

56–57 Narration
POMPEII, AFTER PHILOXENES?: The Alexander mosaic, *Alexander meets Darius in battle*, original c. 300 BC, mosaic, height 3.7 m, Naples, Museo Nazionale (Scala).
GERMANY: *Alexander the Great in single combat*, 13th century, manuscript illumination, Hanover, Kestner Museum.
RUBENS: *The battle of the Amazons*, c. 1618, oil on canvas, 121 × 165 cm, Munich, Alte Pinakothek (Scala).
RUDE: "*La Marseillaise*" (The departure of the volunteers), 1833-36, stone, 12.7 × 6 metres, Paris, Arc de Triomphe (Giraudon).
PICASSO: *Guernica*, 1937, oil on canvas, 351 × 782 cm, New York, Museum of Modern Art, on loan from the artist's estate.
VELAZQUEZ: *The surrender of Breda*, 1634-35, oil on canvas, 307 × 370 cm, Madrid, Prado (Scala).
LEUTZE: *Washington crossing the Delaware*, 1850, oil on canvas, 387.5 × 644.5 cm, New York, Metropolitan Museum of Art, Gift of John Stuart Kennedy.
GOYA: *The same*, from *The Disasters

of War*, 1810-15, etching, 16 × 22 cm (The Mansell Collection).
GROSZ: *Republican automatons*, 1920, watercolour, 60 × 50 cm, New York, Museum of Modern Art, Advisory Committee Fund.

58–59 Landscape
HOKUSAI: *Southerly wind and fine weather* from *Thirty-six views of Mt Fuji*, c. 1823-29, woodcut, 25.5 × 38 cm (Tokyo, Heibonsha Publishers Ltd).

60–61 Landscape
LI CHENG?: *Buddhist temple in the mountains after rain*, c. 1000, ink and light colour on silk, 110 × 55 cm, Kansas City, Missouri, Nelson Gallery-Atkins Museum, Nelson Fund.
POMPEII: *Landscape with villa*, c. 50 BC, wall-painting, House of the Vettii (Scala).
GIOVANNI DI PAOLO: *Madonna and Child in a landscape*, c. 1432, tempera on panel, 56 × 43 cm, Boston, Museum of Fine Arts.
DURER: *The piece of turf*, 1503, watercolour and gouache on paper, 41 × 31.5 cm, Vienna, Albertina.
VAN EYCK: *The Madonna with Chancellor Rolin*, c. 1435, oil on panel, 66 × 62 cm, Paris, Louvre (Scala).
BRUEGEL: *The hunters in the snow (January)*, 1565, oil on oak, 117 × 162 cm, Vienna, Kunsthistorisches Museum (Cooper-Bridgeman Library).
JACOB VAN RUISDAEL: *Wheatfields*, c. 1670, oil on canvas, 100 × 130 cm, New York, Metropolitan Museum of Art.

62–63 Landscape
GAINSBOROUGH: *Mr and Mrs Andrews*, c. 1748, oil on canvas, 69 × 119 cm, London, National Gallery.
CLAUDE: *Egeria mourning over Numa*, 1669, oil on canvas, 155 × 199 cm, Naples, Museo di Capodimonte (Scala).
TURNER: *Burning of the Houses of Parliament*, 1834, oil on canvas, 92.5 × 113 cm, Cleveland Museum of Fine Art, Gift of Hanna Fund.
CONSTABLE: *Fording the river, showery weather*, 1831, oil on canvas, 136 × 188 cm, London, Guildhall (Cooper-Bridgeman Library).
COURBET: *Seaside at Palavas*, 1854, oil on canvas, 39 × 46 cm, Montpellier, Musée Gustave Courbet (Claude O'Sughrue).
MONDRIAN: *The sea*, 1914, charcoal and gouache on paper, 90 × 123 cm, New York, Solomon R. Guggenheim Museum.
HOPPER: *Highland light*, 1930, watercolour, 40.6 × 63.5 cm, Harvard University, Fogg Art Museum, Louise E. Bettens Fund.

64–65 Animals
LASCAUX, FRANCE: "The Hall of Bulls", in use c. 15000 BC, cave-paintings (Colorphoto Hans Hinz).

66–67 Animals
CONSTANTINOPLE: *Adam naming the

beasts*, 4th/5th century AD, ivory, Florence, Bargello (Scala).
SAQQARA, EGYPT: Bronze *Cat*, after 30 BC, bronze, nose and ear-rings gold, breast inlaid with silver, height 33 cm, London, British Museum (Ronald Sheridan).
CRETE: Bull's head *rhyton*, c. 1500 BC, stone, wood, crystal and shell, height 21 cm, Heraklion, Archaeological Museum (Sonia Halliday).
COURBET: *The death of the stag*, 1867, oil on canvas, 355 × 500 cm, Besançon, Musée des Beaux-Arts (Giraudon).
CANOVA: *Theseus and the Minotaur*, c. 1781-82, marble, height 147 cm, London, Victoria and Albert Museum.
FRANCE: *To my sole desire*, from *The Lady of the Unicorn*, c. 1480-90, tapestry, Paris, Musée Cluny (Scala).
PICASSO: Vollard Suite no. 85, *Drinking Minotaur and sculptor with two models*, 1933, etching (Christie's/A. C. Cooper).
REMBRANDT: *Three elephants*, c. 1637, black chalk, 23 × 34 cm, Vienna, Albertina.
DURER: *The young hare*, 1502, watercolour, 25 × 22.5 cm, Vienna, Albertina.

68–69 Animals
VERROCCHIO: *Bartolommeo Colleoni*, 1481-90, height about 4 metres, Venice, Campo SS. Giovanni e Paolo (Scala).
LEONARDO: *Study of a rearing horse*, c. 1498-90, red chalk, 15.5 × 14 cm, Florence, Gabinetto Nazionale dei Disegni e Stampe (Scala).
WUWEI, EASTERN CHINA: "*Flying Horse*", 2nd century AD, bronze, length 45 cm, from tomb at Leit'ai, Gansu, China (Robert Harding Associates).
PISANELLO: *Horses*, c. 1433-38, pen on paper, height 20 × 16.5 cm, Paris, Louvre (Photo Bulloz).
STUBBS: *Mares and foals*, 1762, oil on canvas, 89 × 200.5 cm, London, Earl Fitzwilliam Collection (Cooper-Bridgeman Library).
GERICAULT: *A horse frightened by lightning*, c. 1820, oil on canvas, 49 × 60.5 cm, London, National Gallery.
DEGAS: *A carriage at the races*, 1877-80, oil on canvas, 66 × 82 cm, Paris, Louvre, Musée Jeu de Paume (Scala).
MUYBRIDGE: *Sally Gardner running*, 1878, New York, International Museum of Photography.
MARINI: *Little rider*, 1946, bronze, height 49 cm, Rome, Galleria Nazionale d'Arte Moderna (Scala).
DUCHAMP-VILLON: *The horse*, 1914, bronze, height 100 cm, New York, Museum of Modern Art, Van Gogh Purchase Fund.

70–71 Still Life
VAN GOGH: *Still life with drawing board*, 1889, oil on canvas, 50 × 63 cm, Otterlo, Rijksmuseum Kröller-Müller; *Self-portrait*, January 1889, oil on canvas, 60 × 49 cm, London, Courtauld Institute Galleries (Cooper-Bridgeman Library).

72–73 Still Life
ROME: *A basket of flowers*, 2nd century AD, floor mosaic, Vatican, Museo Pio Clementino (Scala).
ZHAO JI: *Birds and flowers*, early 12th century, ink and colours on silk, London, British Museum (Cooper-Bridgeman Library).
VAN EYCK: *St Jerome*, 1442, oil on panel, 20 × 13 cm, Detroit, Detroit Institute of Arts.
CARAVAGGIO: *A basket of fruit*, 1596, oil on canvas, 46 × 64.5 cm, Milan, Pinacoteca Ambrosiana (Scala).
VAN BEYEREN: *Still life with wine ewer*, after 1655, oil on canvas, 79.5 × 63.5 cm, Ohio, Toledo Museum of Art, Gift of Edward Drummond Library.
COORTE: *A bundle of asparagus*, 1703, oil on canvas, 30 × 23 cm, Oxford, Ashmolean Museum.
BAUGIN: *Still life with a chequerboard (The five senses)*, c. 1630, oil on panel, 55 × 73 cm, Paris, Louvre (Documentation Photographique de la Réunion des Musées Nationaux).

74–75 Still Life
REMBRANDT: *The flayed ox*, 1655, oil on panel, 94 × 68 cm, Paris, Louvre (Scala).
CHARDIN: *The white tablecloth*, c. 1737, oil on canvas, 99 × 119 cm, Chicago, The Art Institute of Chicago.
REDON: *Wild flowers*, after 1912, pastel, 57 × 35 cm, Paris, Louvre (Scala).
RAPHAELLE PEALE: *After the bath*, 1823, oil on canvas, 73.5 × 61 cm, Kansas City, Missouri, Nelson Gallery-Atkins Museum, Nelson Fund.
CEZANNE: *Still life with apples and oranges*, 1895-1900, oil on canvas, 73 × 93 cm, Paris, Louvre, Musée Jeu de Paume (Scala).
GRIS: *Breakfast*, 1914, oil, pasted paper and crayon, 81 × 59.5 cm, New York, Museum of Modern Art, Lillie P. Bliss Bequest.
JOHNS: *Painted bronze II: ale cans*, 1964, painted bronze, 13.5 × 12 cm, New York, the artist's collection.

76–77 Images of Divinity
REMBRANDT: *The three crosses*, 1653 and c. 1662, etching in the 2nd and 4th states, 38.7 × 45 cm, London, British Museum.
PISANELLO: *Gianfrancesco Gonzaga*, c. 1439, bronze, diameter 8.5 cm, Brescia, Museo Civico (The Mansell Collection).

78–79 Images of Divinity
ENGLAND: Crucifix, 10th/11th century, ivory, London, Victoria and Albert Museum (Cooper-Bridgeman Library).
GERMANY: Abbess Mathilde's Cross, 974-982, gold, gems, pearls, enamels and silver gilt, height 45 cm, Essen, Cathedral Treasury (Bildarchiv Foto Marburg).
GERMANY: Plague Cross, 1304, wood, Cologne, Schnutzen Museum (Rheinisches Bildarchiv).
GRUNEWALD: Isenheim altarpiece,

1515, oil on panel, 269 × 593 cm, Colmar, Unterlinden Museum (Scala).
RAPHAEL: "*The Mond Crucifixion*", 1502-03, oil on wood, 280.5 × 165 cm, London, National Gallery.
EL GRECO: *Crucifixion with a landscape*, 1600-10, oil on canvas, 193 × 116 cm, Cleveland Museum of Art, Gift of Hanna Fund.
GAUGUIN: "*The Yellow Christ*", 1889, oil on canvas, 92 × 73 cm, Buffalo, Albright-Knox Art Gallery (Scala).

80–81 Images of Divinity
CZECHOSLOVAKIA: "*The Venus of Věstonice*", Upper Aurignacian period (14000-13500 BC), terracotta, height 11.5 cm, Brno, Moravian Museum (Werner Forman Archive).
MEXICO: *Aztec goddess of life and death*, undated, stone, Mexico City, Anthropological Museum (Michael Holford).
DAHOMEY: *Gu, god of war*, undated, iron, height 165 cm, Paris, Musée de l'Homme.
JAVA: *Seated Jambhala*, undated, bronze, Paris, Musée Guimet (Michael Holford).
INDIA: *Shiva as Nataraja*, undated, bronze, Paris, Musée Guimet (Michael Holford).
RAPHAEL: "*The Alba Madonna*", c. 1511, wood transferred to canvas, diameter 95 cm, Washington, National Gallery of Art, Andrew Mellon collection.
AMIDA, JAPAN: "*The Kamakura Buddha*", 1252, bronze, *in situ*, height 11.3 m (Werner Forman Archive).
GREECE: *Head of Aphrodite*, 2nd century BC, bronze, height 38 cm, London, British Museum (Michael Holford).
TURKEY: *Name of Allah*, undated, Istanbul, Hagia Sophia (Sonia Halliday).

82–83 Allegory, Myth and Fantasy
GIOVANNI BELLINI: "*The Sacred Allegory*", c. 1490, oil and tempera on panel, 72 × 117 cm, Florence, Uffizi (Scala).

84–85 Allegory, Myth and Fantasy
RAIMONDI: *The Judgment of Paris*, c. 1516, 29 × 43 cm, engraving after Raphael, London, British Museum.
EWORTH: *Queen Elizabeth confounding the three goddesses*, 1569, oil on panel, 71 × 84.5 cm, Windsor, Royal Collection (by gracious permission of Her Majesty the Queen).
BLAKE: *The Judgment of Paris*, 1817, watercolour, 39.5 × 47 cm, London, British Museum.
RUBENS: *The Judgment of Paris*, c. 1632-35, oil on wood, 145 × 193.5 cm, London, National Gallery.
ROWLANDSON: *Englishman in Paris*, 1807, ink and watercolour over pencil, height 15 × 24 cm, London, Wellington Museum.
MANET: "*Le Déjeuner sur l'Herbe*", 1863, oil on canvas, 208 × 264 cm, Paris, Louvre, Musée Jeu de Paume (Scala).

PICASSO: "*Le Déjeuner sur l'Herbe*", 1962, lithograph, 25 × 32 cm, Private collection (Christie, Manson and Wood).

86–87 Myth and Allegory
KUNIYOSHI: From "*The Heroes of Suikoden*", *Tameijiro dan Shogo grapples with his enemy under water*, 1828-29, woodcut, B. W. Robinson Collection (Cooper-Bridgeman Library).
GIAMBOLOGNA: *The rape of the Sabine*, 1579-83, marble, 410 cm, Florence, Loggia dei Lanzi (Scala).
TIEPOLO: *Apollo pursuing Daphne*, c. 1755-60, oil on canvas, 69 × 87 cm, Washington, National Gallery of Art, Samuel H. Kress Collection.
BOTTICELLI: *Venus and Mars*, c. 1485, tempera on panel, 69 × 173 cm, London, National Gallery.
BLAKE: *The great red dragon and the woman clothed with the sun*, c. 1800-10, watercolour, 34 × 50 cm, New York, Brooklyn Museum, Gift of William Augustus White.
BROWN: *Work*, 1852-63, oil on canvas, 134.5 × 196 cm, Manchester, City Art Gallery.
DAUMIER: *The triumph of Menelaus*, 1842, lithograph, London, British Library.
MAGRITTE: *The house of glass*, 1939, gouache, 32 × 38.5 cm, Rotterdam, Museum Boymans-van Beuningen. (Edward James Foundation.)
ROUSSEAU: *The dream*, 1910, oil on canvas, 204.5 × 298 cm, New York, Museum of Modern Art, Gift of Nelson A. Rockefeller.

88–89 The Inward Eye
ROTHKO: *Black on maroon*, 1958, oil on canvas, 266.5 × 366 cm, London, Tate Gallery.

90–91 The Inward Eye
VAN DER WEYDEN: *The Last Judgment*, detail, c. 1450?, oil on panel, width 560 cm, Beaune, Musée de l'Hôtel-Dieu (Photo Bulloz).
BOSCH: *The Garden of Earthly Delights*, detail, c. 1505-10, oil on wood, 220 × 195 cm, Madrid, Prado (Scala).
MICHELANGELO: *The Last Judgment*, detail, 1534-41, fresco, Vatican, Sistine Chapel (Scala).
GOYA: *The colossus*, 1808-12, mezzotint, 25 × 20.5 cm, Paris, Bibliothèque Nationale (Immédiate 2).
DALI: *3 Young Surrealist women holding in their arms the skins of an orchestra*, 1936, oil on canvas, St Petersburg, Florida, Salvador Dali Foundation, Inc.
CHIRICO: *The enigma of the hour*, 1912, canvas, 55 × 71 cm, Milan, Mattioli Collection.
BACON: *Study after Velazquez*, 1953, oil on canvas, 152 × 117.5 cm, New York, Museum of Modern Art, Gift of Mr and Mrs William A. M. Burden.

92–93 The Inward Eye
BERNINI: *St Theresa*, 1646-52, marble, altarpiece figures life-size, Rome, S. Maria della Vittoria

(Scala).
EL GRECO: *The Fifth Seal of the Apocalypse*, c. 1608-14, oil on canvas, 224.8 × 193 cm, New York, Metropolitan Museum of Art, Rogers Fund.
JAN AND HUBERT VAN EYCK: The Ghent altarpiece, finished 1432, oil and tempera on panel, overall height 340 cm, Ghent, St Bavo (Scala).
FRA ANGELICO: The Linaiuoli triptych, 1433, tempera on panel, 260 × 330 cm, Florence, S. Marco (Scala).
FRIEDRICH: *Moonrise over the sea*, 1822, oil on canvas, 55 × 71 cm, West Berlin, Staatliche Museen.
SPENCER: *The resurrection of the soldiers*, 1928-29, oil on canvas, 640 × 533 cm, Burghclere, Sandham Memorial Chapel (Jeremy Whitaker/National Trust).
MONDRIAN: *Composition in red, yellow and blue*, 1921, oil on canvas, 103 × 100 cm, The Hague, Gemeentemuseum.

94–95 The Language of Painting
FRA ANGELICO: *The Annunciation*, c. 1451-55, tempera on panel, 39 × 39 cm, Florence, Museo di S. Marco (Scala).
DAUMIER: *The connoisseurs*, 1860-63, oil on canvas, 23.5 × 31 cm, Rotterdam, Museum Boymans-van Beuningen.

96–97 Introduction
TITIAN: *Bacchus and Ariadne*, 1522-23, oil on canvas, 175 × 190 cm, London, National Gallery.
Diagrams: (top) Alan Brown, (lower) Alan Suttie.

98–99 Scale and Space
BLAKE: *Glad day*, c. 1794, print worked up with watercolour, 27.5 × 20 cm, London, British Museum (Cooper-Bridgeman Library).
MUNCH: *Puberty*, 1895, oil on canvas, 151 × 110 cm, Oslo, National Gallery (Scala).
BECKMANN: *The trapeze*, 1923, oil on canvas, 193 × 84 cm, St Louis, Art Museum, Marton D. May collection.
MALEVICH: *Suprematist composition*, c. 1917, oil on canvas, 96.5 × 52 cm, New York, Museum of Modern Art.
COROT: *A view near Volterra*, 1838, oil on canvas, 69.5 × 95 cm, Washington, National Gallery of Art, Chester Dale collection.
Diagrams: Alan Suttie.
RUBENS: *The fall of the damned*, c. 1614-18, oil on panel, 281.5 × 222 cm, Munich, Alte Pinakothek.
DELACROIX: *Liberty leading the people*, 1830, oil on canvas, 216 × 325 cm, Paris, Louvre (Scala).
Diagrams: Alan Suttie.

100–101 Types of Pictorial Space
VAN DER GOES: *The Adoration of the shepherds*, from the Portinari altarpiece, c. 1474-76, panel, 245 × 297 cm, Florence, Uffizi (Scala).
NORTH AMERICA, TLINGIT TRIBE: Bear screen, c. 1840, incised wood and paint, 4.57 × 2.47 metres, Denver, Art Museum.

AUSTRIAN SCHOOL: *The Trinity with Christ crucified*, 15th century, panel, 118 × 114 cm, London, National Gallery.
HARUNOBU: *The evening bell of the clock*, c. 1766, woodcut, 29 × 22 cm, Chicago, Art Institute (Cooper-Bridgeman Library).
TINTORETTO: *Bacchus and Ariadne*, 1578, oil on canvas, 146 × 157 cm, Venice, Palazzo Ducale (Scala).
TURNER: *Norham Castle: sunrise*, c. 1835-40, oil on canvas, 89.5 × 120 cm, London, Tate Gallery (Angelo Hornak).

102–103 Projection
PERSIA: *Khosroe and his courtiers*, 1524-25, gouache miniature, New York, Metropolitan Museum of Art.
CHAGALL: *The birthday*, 1915, oil on cardboard, 79.5 × 98 cm, New York, Museum of Modern Art, Lillie P. Bliss Bequest.
THEBES: *Garden with pond*, c. 1400 BC, wall-painting, London, British Museum.
BRAQUE: *Pitcher and violin*, 1910, oil on canvas, 117 × 73.5 cm, Basel, Kunstmuseum (Colorphoto Hans Hinz).
CHINA: *Winding veranda and porches of a palace*, c.1679, ink-drawing from *The Mustard Seed Garden Manual of Painting*.
Diagrams: Alan Suttie.

104–105 Perspective
CHIRICO: *Sinister Muses*, 1917, gouache on board, 94 × 62 cm, Munich, Bayerische Staatsgemäldesammlung (Scala).
RAPHAEL: *"The School of Athens"*, in the Stanza della Segnatura, fresco, about 770 cm wide at base, Vatican (David Lees/Colorific!).
Diagrams: (top) Michael McGuinness, (middle and bottom left) Alan Suttie, (right) Harry Clow.

106–107 Viewpoint
TINTORETTO: *The Ascension*, 1583-87, fresco, Venice, Scuola di San Rocco (Scala).
RUBENS: *The Madonna adored by SS. Gregory and Domitilla*, 1607, oil on canvas, 165 × 220 cm, Grenoble, Musée des Beaux-Arts (Scala).
DE HOOGH: *The courtyard of a house in Delft*, 1658, oil on canvas, 67 × 53.5 cm, Edinburgh, National Gallery of Scotland.
BRUEGEL: *Netherlandish proverbs*, 1559, oil on canvas, 117 × 163 cm, West Berlin, Staatliche Museen (Scala).
DUBUFFET: *Business prospers*, 1961, oil on canvas, 165 × 220 cm, New York, Museum of Modern Art.
Diagrams: Michael McGuinness.

108–109 Volume, Mass and Gravity
VELAZQUEZ: *The water-carrier of Seville*, c. 1619, oil on canvas, 105 × 80 cm, London, Wellington Museum (Cooper-Bridgeman Library).
WATTEAU: *Love in the French theatre*, c. 1719, oil on canvas, 36.5 × 53 cm, West Berlin, Staatliche Museen (Bildarchiv Preussischer Kulturbesitz).
MILLET: *The gleaners*, 1857, oil on canvas, 84 × 111 cm, Paris, Louvre (Scala).
HARTUNG: *Composition*, 1936, oil on canvas, 171 × 115 cm, Philadelphia Museum of Art, A. E. Gallatin collection.
PICASSO: *Daniel Henry Kahnweiler*, 1910, oil on canvas, 100 × 73 cm, Chicago, Art Institute, Mrs Charles B. Goodspeed collection.
Diagrams: (top and right) Alan Suttie, (bottom) Keith Palmer.

110–111 Line, Shape, Contour, Articulation
BOTTICELLI: *Venus and Mars*, c. 1485, tempera on wood, 69 × 173 cm, London, National Gallery.
VELAZQUEZ: *Portrait of a man*, c. 1640, oil on canvas, 76 × 65 cm, London, Wellington Museum.
STABIAE, ITALY: *Maiden gathering flowers*, 1st century AD, fresco, Naples, Museo Nazionale (Scala).
MICHELANGELO: *The creation of Adam*, detail of the Sistine Chapel ceiling, 1511, fresco, Vatican, Sistine Chapel (Scala).
BUFFET: *Artist and model*, 1948, oil on canvas, Paris, Musée d'Art Moderne (Giraudon).
MODIGLIANI: *Reclining nude*, c. 1919, oil on canvas, 70 × 114 cm, New York, Museum of Modern Art, Mrs Simon Guggenheim Fund.
Diagram: Alan Suttie.

112–113 Visual Dynamics
ARP: *Configuration: navel, shirt and head*, 1926, painted wood relief, 145.5 × 115.5 cm, Basel, Offentliche Kunstsammlung (Colorphoto Hans Hinz).
TITIAN: *"Noli Me Tangere"* (Christ with Mary Magdalen), c. 1512, oil on canvas, 109 × 91 cm, London, National Gallery.
Diagrams: Fehmi Cômert.

114–115 Movement
VASARELY: *Lomblin*, 1951-56, 65 × 60 cm, Annet-sur-Marne, the artist's collection.
MONDRIAN: *Broadway Boogie-Woogie*, 1942-43, oil on canvas, 127 × 127 cm, New York, Museum of Modern Art.
TINTORETTO: *Bacchus and Ariadne*, 1578, oil on canvas, 146 × 157 cm, Venice, Palazzo Ducale (Scala).
DUCHAMP: *Nude descending a staircase no. 2*, 1912, oil on canvas, 148 × 90 cm, Philadelphia Museum of Art, The Louise and Walter Arensberg collection.
GOYA: *The stilt-walkers*, c. 1788, oil on canvas, 268 × 320 cm, Madrid, Prado (Scala).
Diagram: Dinah Lone.

116–117 Illumination and Tonality
CHARTRES, FRANCE: *"Our Lady of the Beautiful Glass"*, mid-12th century, stained glass, Chartres Cathedral (Robert Harding Associates).
VELAZQUEZ: *The water-carrier of Seville*, c. 1619, oil on canvas, 105.5 × 80 cm, London, Wellington

Museum (Cooper-Bridgeman Library).
REMBRANDT: *A scholar*, c. 1630, oil on wood, 55 × 46.5 cm, London, National Gallery.
CHARDIN: *Still life with a marmite*, c. 1762, oil on canvas, 30.5 × 38 cm, Oxford, Ashmolean Museum.
MONET: *Beach at Ste-Adresse*, 1867, oil on canvas, 71.5 × 103 cm, Chicago, Art Institute.
KLEE: *Painting on black background*, 1940, oil on canvas, 100 × 80.5 cm, Berne, Felix Klee Collection.
Diagrams: (top) Alan Suttie, (bottom) Keith Palmer.

118–119 Texture and Surface
GOINGS: *Airstream trailer*, 1970, acrylic on canvas, 152 × 214 cm, Aachen, Neue Galerie (Anne Gold).
TOBEY: *Barth rhythmus*, 1961, mixed materials on board, Lugano, Thyssen Collection (Scala).
CONSTABLE: *The leaping horse*, 1825, oil on canvas, 142 × 187 cm, London, Royal Academy of Arts.
INGRES: *The spring*, 1856, oil on canvas, 164 × 82 cm, Paris, Louvre (Scala).
VAN GOGH: *Chair and pipe*, 1888-89, oil on canvas, 92 × 72 cm, London, Tate Gallery.
CEZANNE: *Mont Ste-Victoire from Bibémus Quarry*, 1898, oil on canvas, 64 × 80 cm, Baltimore Museum of Art.

120–121 Edge Qualities
JAMMU, INDIA: *Mian Brij Raj Dev with attendants*, c. 1765, gouache on paper, 216 × 295 mm, London, Victoria and Albert Museum.
MANTEGNA: *The Agony in the Garden*, c. 1460, tempera on panel, 63 × 80 cm, London, National Gallery.
ROTHKO: *Red, white and brown*, 1957, oil on canvas, 252.5 × 207 cm, Basel, Kunstmuseum (Colorphoto Hans Hinz).
LEGER: *The mechanic*, 1920, oil on canvas, 155.5 × 88.5 cm, Ottawa, National Gallery of Canada.
REMBRANDT: *Self-portrait*, 1660, oil on canvas, 111 × 85 cm, Paris, Louvre (Documentation Photographique de la Réunion des Musées Nationaux).
RENOIR: *Bather drying her leg*, 1910, oil on canvas, 84 × 65 cm, São Paulo, Museum of Art.
LEONARDO: *The Virgin of the rocks* (2nd version), c. 1505, oil on panel, 189.5 × 120 cm, London, National Gallery.
Diagram: Mitchell Beazley Studio.

122–123 Pattern
HOKUSAI: *Carp leaping in a pool*, late 18th century, colour woodcut, 36 × 16.5 cm, London, Victoria and Albert Museum.
BRAQUE: *Still life on a red tablecloth*, 1936, oil on canvas, 197 × 129.5 cm, West Palm Beach, Florida, Norton Gallery and School of Art.
MATISSE: *Odalisque*, 1922, oil on canvas, 57 × 84cm, Paris, Musée National de l'Art Moderne (Scala).
HILLIARD: *Young man in a garden*, c. 1588, watercolour on vellum, 13.5

× 7 cm, London, Victoria and Albert Museum.
WARHOL: *Marilyn Monroe*, 1962, silk-screen, Paris, René Montagu Collection (Leo Castelli).
SPENCER: *Swan-upping*, 1914-15, finished 1919, oil on canvas, 117 × 142 cm, London, Tate Gallery. Diagram: Derek Carmichael.

124–125 The Dimensions of Colour
POUSSIN: *Lamentation over the dead Christ*, c. 1655, oil on canvas, 100 × 134 cm, Dublin, National Gallery of Ireland.
MATISSE: *The red studio*, 1911, oil on canvas, 181 × 219 cm, New York, Museum of Modern Art, Mrs Simon Guggenheim Fund.
PUVIS DE CHAVANNES: *The poor fisherman*, 1881, oil on canvas, 155 × 192.5 cm, Paris, Louvre (Documentation Photographique de la Réunion des Musées Nationaux).
BONNARD: *Self-portrait*, 1940, oil on canvas, 63 × 47 cm, New York, Private Collection (Photo: Wildenstein and Co.).
CEZANNE: *Self-portrait*, c. 1880, oil on canvas, 33.5 × 26 cm, London, National Gallery.
Diagram: Alan Suttie.

126–127 Ways of Using Colour
NOVGOROD, RUSSIA: *The Archangel Michael*, early 14th century, tempera on panel, formerly G. Hann Collection, Pennsylvania (Christie's, New York).
SEURAT: *Fishing fleet at Port-en-Bessin*, 1888, oil on canvas, 55 × 65 cm, New York, Museum of Modern Art, Lillie P. Bliss Bequest.
TIEPOLO: *The marriage of Frederick and Beatrice*, 1753, fresco from the Residenz at Würzburg (Scala).
TISSOT: *The ball on shipboard*, 1874, oil on canvas, 85.5 × 127.5 cm, London, Tate Gallery (Cooper-Bridgeman Library).
PIERO DELLA FRANCESCA: *The baptism of Christ*, c. 1440-50, tempera on wood, 167 × 116 cm, London, National Gallery.
FRIEDRICH: *Man and woman gazing at the moon*, c. 1830-35, oil on canvas, 34.5 × 45.5 cm, West Berlin, Nationalgalerie (Scala).
Diagram: Alan Suttie.

128–129 Pictorial Organization
VASARELY: *Betelgeuse-I*, 1957, 195 × 130 cm, Paris, Collection Denise René.
TITIAN: *Bacchus and Ariadne*, 1522-23, oil on canvas, 175 × 190 cm, London, National Gallery.
Diagrams: (top) Alan Suttie, (bottom) Dinah Lone.

130–131 Proportion
KLEE: *Individualized measurement of strata*, 1930, pastel, 48.5 × 35.5 cm, Berne, Paul Klee Foundation (Hamlyn Picture Library).
TITIAN: *The Presentation of the Virgin*, c. 1534-38, oil on canvas, 136 × 295 cm, Venice, Accademia (Scala).
RAEBURN: *The Rev. Robert Walker*

skating, c.1784, oil on canvas, 76.2 × 63.5 cm, Edinburgh, National Gallery of Scotland.
Diagrams: (centre and right) Dinah Lone, (bottom) Christopher Cornford.

132–133 Abstraction
MONDRIAN: *Composition*, 1921, oil on canvas, 47.5 × 41.5 cm, Basel, Kunstmuseum (Colorphoto Hans Hinz).
KANDINSKY: Study for *Composition no. 7*, 1913, oil on canvas, 78 × 100 cm, Berne, Felix Klee Collection.
MIRO: *Catalonian landscape (The hunter)*, 1923-24, oil on canvas, 63 × 99 cm, New York, Museum of Modern Art.
RAJASTHAN, INDIA: *Sri Yantra*, 18th century, 33 × 33 cm, Paris, Ravi Kumar Collection (Angelo Hornak).
LOHSE: *30 vertical systematic shades with red diagonals*, 1943-70, oil on canvas, 165 × 165 cm, Zurich, the artist's collection.
FRANKENTHALER: *Madridscape*, 1959, oil on canvas, 255 × 403 cm, Baltimore Museum of Art.

134–135 Language and Style
RUBENS: *The Adoration of the Magi*, c. 1624, oil on panel, 440 × 330 cm, Madrid, Prado (Cooper-Bridgeman Library).
PUNJAB, INDIA: *Emperor Akbar being entertained by his foster-brother Azim Khan*, 1571, gouache, 18 × 30 cm, London, Victoria and Albert Museum.
Diagram: Alan Suttie.

136–137 Materials and Methods of Painting
CHARDIN: *The attributes of the arts*, 1766, oil on canvas, 133 × 140 cm, Minneapolis Institute of Arts, William H. Dunwoody Fund.
BRUEGEL: *The painter and the connoisseur*, 1566-68, pen and bistre, Vienna, Albertina.

138–139 Introduction
BOTTICELLI: *Venus and the Graces bringing presents to a bride*, c. 1486, detail of a fresco from the Villa Lemni, Paris, Louvre (Documentation Photographique de la Réunion des Musées Nationaux).
Diagrams: Michael McGuinness.

140–141 Tempera and Encaustic
JOHNS: *Numbers in colour*, 1958-59, encaustic and collage on canvas, 170 × 126 cm, Buffalo, New York, Albright-Knox Art Gallery.
ORCAGNA: *The Adoration of the shepherds*, c. 1370-71, tempera on wood, 95.5 × 49.5 cm, London, National Gallery.
ANDREA PISANO: *Painting*, c. 1431, marble, 83 × 69 cm, Florence, Museo dell' Opera del Duomo (Scala).
SHAHN: *Handball*, 1939, tempera on paper over composition board, 58 × 79.5 cm, New York, Museum of Modern Art, Abby Aldrich Rockefeller Fund.
Diagrams: (centre) Byron Harvey, (right) Graham Marks.

142–143 Wall-painting
MICHELANGELO: *Adam*, detail from the Sistine Chapel ceiling, 1510-12, fresco, Vatican, Sistine Chapel (Scala).
LEONARDO: *The Last Supper*, c. 1495, 420 × 910 cm, probably oil and tempera on plaster, Milan, S. Maria delle Grazie (Scala).
Diagram: Michael McGuinness and Byron Harvey, based on Castagno's frescos of *The Crucifixion, Deposition and Resurrection of Christ*, c. 1445-50, in the Convent of S. Apollonia, Florence (Scala).

144–145 Early Oil Techniques
MASTER OF THE VIEW OF SAINT GUDULE: *A young man*, c. 1480, oil and tempera on panel, 22 × 14.5 cm, London, National Gallery.
MILLAIS: *Mariana*, 1851, oil on panel, 59 × 49.5 cm, Basingstoke, Lord Sherwood Collection (Cooper-Bridgeman Library).
MEMLINC: The Nieuwenhove diptych, 1487, each panel 44 × 33 cm, Bruges, Memlinc Museum (Scala).
EDDY: *Untitled*, 1971, oil on canvas, 122 × 167 cm, Aachen, Neue Galerie, Ludwig collection (Ann Münchow).
ANTONELLO DA MESSINA: The S. Cassiano altarpiece, 1476, oil on panel, height of fragment 63 cm, Vienna, Kunsthistorisches Museum (Scala).
Diagrams: Byron Harvey, Michael McGuinness.

146–147 Oils on Coloured Grounds
TITIAN: *Bacchus and Ariadne*, 1522-23, oil on canvas, 175 × 190 cm, London, National Gallery; *The death of Actaeon*, c. 1559, oil on canvas, 178.5 × 198 cm, London, National Gallery.
ZURBARAN: *A painter at the foot of the Cross*, c. 1635-40?, oil on canvas, 105 × 84 cm, Madrid, Prado (Scala).
GAINSBOROUGH: *The painter's daughters with a cat*, c. 1759, oil on canvas, 74.5 × 62 cm, London, National Gallery.
RUBENS: Sketch for *The Annunciation*, 1620-21, oil on panel, Oxford, Ashmolean Museum.

148–149 Oils: Surface Effects
CANALETTO: *The harbour of St Mark's towards the west*, c. 1760-66?, oil on canvas, 51 × 66 cm, Princeton University, The Art Museum, Gift of Henry W. Cannon Jnr. in memory of his father; *The harbour of St Mark's from the east*, 1740, oil on canvas, 129 × 187 cm, London, Wallace Collection.
HALS: *A member of the Coymans family*, 1645, oil on canvas, 77 × 64 cm, Washington, National Gallery of Art, Andrew W. Mellon collection.
REMBRANDT: *Belshazzar's Feast*, 1635, oil on canvas, 167.5 × 209 cm, London, National Gallery (Angelo Hornak).

150–151 Oils: Direct Methods
WHISTLER: *Symphony in white no. 3*,

1867, oil on canvas, 52 × 76.5 cm, Birmingham, Barber Institute of Fine Arts, University of Birmingham.
CEZANNE: *Woodland scene*, 1882-85, oil on canvas, 62 × 51.5 cm, Cambridge, Fitzwilliam Museum.
PISSARRO: *The Oise near Pontoise*, 1873, oil on canvas, 45.5 × 55 cm, Williamstown, Sterling and Francine Clark Institute.
MUNCH: *Death in the room*, 1892, oil on canvas, 149.5 × 167.5 cm, Oslo, National Gallery.
JORN: *Green ballet*, 1960, oil on canvas, 144 × 199.5 cm, New York, Solomon R. Guggenheim Museum.

152–153 Twentieth-Century Developments
ERNST: *Forest*, 1929, frottage, 81 × 100 cm, Milan, Dr A. Mazzotta Collection (Scala).
DUCHAMP: *Tu m'*, 1918, oil and pencil on canvas, with collage, 70 × 31.5 cm, New Haven, Yale University Art Gallery, Bequest of Katherine S. Dreier.
TAPIES: *Ochre gris*, 1958, oil, latex and marble dust on canvas, 256.5 × 191.5 cm, London, Tate Gallery.
RICHARD SMITH: *Sudden country*, 1972, acrylic on canvas, 203 × 310 cm, Cardiff, National Museum of Wales.
FRANK STELLA: *Agbatana 3*, 1968, fluorescent acrylic on canvas, 305 × 457 cm, Ohio, Allen Memorial Art Museum.
HOYLAND: *Drape*, 1978, acrylic on cotton duck, 125 × 100 cm, London, Waddington Galleries Ltd.
LOUIS: *Theta*, 1960, acrylic resin on canvas, 255 × 420 cm, Boston, Museum of Fine Arts.

154–155 Mixed Media
CRIVELLI: *St Peter* from the Demidoff altarpiece, 1476, panel, 40 × 135 cm, London, National Gallery.
SCHWITTERS: *Opened by Customs*, c. 1937, collage, 33 × 25.5 cm, London, Tate Gallery (Angelo Hornak).
HAMILTON: *My Marilyn*, 1965, photographs and oil on paper, 50.5 × 61 cm, Cologne, Wallraf-Richartz Museum.
WESSELMAN: *Bath-tub collage no. 3*, 1963, 213 × 270 × 45 cm, Cologne, Wallraf-Richartz Museum.
MATISSE: *Sorrows of the king*, 1952, cut paper, 287.5 × 398.5 cm, Paris, Musée National de l'Art Moderne.
RAUSCHENBERG: *Reservoir*, 1961, oil, wood, graphite, fabric, metal and rubber on canvas, 117 × 58.5 × 37.5 cm, Washington DC, The National Collection of Fine Arts, Smithsonian Institution, Gift of S. C. Johnson & Son Inc.

156–157 Watercolour
TURNER: *Sunset on the Jura*, 1841, watercolour and pencil, 22.5 × 29.5 cm, London, British Museum (The Fotomas Index); *Tintern Abbey*, 1794, watercolour and pencil, 36 × 25.5 cm, London, British Museum. Turner's paintbox, London, Victoria and Albert

Museum (Angelo Hornak).
KLEE: *Hamammet motif*, 1914, watercolour, 20 × 15.5 cm, Basel, Kunstmuseum, Kupferstichkabinett.
CEZANNE: *The black château*, c. 1895, pencil and watercolour, 36 × 52.5 cm, Rotterdam, Museum Boymans-van Beuningen.
EAKINS: *John Biglen in a single scull*, 1876, watercolour, 42 × 57.5 cm, New York, Metropolitan Museum of Art.
NOLDE: *Summer flowers*, c. 1930, watercolour, 35 × 47.5 cm, Lugano, Thyssen Collection (Scala).

158–159 Ink
TAN-AN: *Heron*, c. 1570, ink on paper, 32 × 49 cm, Tokyo, National Museum.
HAN GAN: *Night shining white*, 8th century, ink on paper, 29.5 × 35 cm, New York, Metropolitan Museum of Art.
XIA GUI: *Landscape*, c. 1200-25, ink on silk, Boston, Museum of Fine Arts.
TOSA MITSUYOSHI: *The battle of Uji river*, 16th/17th century, screen panels with colour on paper, London, Victoria and Albert Museum.
LEONARDO: *Lily*, c. 1475, pen and ink and brown wash over black chalk, heightened with white, 31.5 × 17.5 cm, Windsor, Royal Library (by gracious permission of Her Majesty The Queen).
CLAUDE LORRAINE: *Port scene*, 1649-50, pen and wash, London, British Museum.
VAN GOGH: *Washerwomen on the canal*, 1888, pen and ink, 31.5 × 24 cm, Otterlo, Rijksmuseum Kröller-Müller.

160–161 Pastel and Gouache
LIOTARD: *Self-portrait with beard*, 1749, pastel, 97 × 71 cm, Geneva, Musée de l'Art et de l'Histoire.
DEGAS: *Dancers in the wings*, c. 1900, pastel, 71 × 66 cm, St Louis, Missouri, The St Louis Art Museum.
CARRIERA: *Louis XV*, 1720, pastel, 50.5 × 38.5 cm, Dresden, Staatliche Kunstsammlung.
REDON: *Roger and Angelica*, c. 1910, pastel, 91.5 × 71 cm, New York, Museum of Modern Art, Lillie P. Bliss Bequest.
KANDINSKY: *Russian beauty in a landscape*, 1905, gouache, Munich, Staatliche Museen.
RAJASTHAN, INDIA: *Raja Umed Singh of Kotah shooting tigers*, c. 1790, gouache, 32.5 × 39.5, London, Victoria and Albert Museum.

162–163 Drawing
LEONARDO: *Head and bust of a woman*, c. 1486-88, silverpoint on pinkish prepared surface, 32 × 20 cm, Windsor, Royal Library (by gracious permission of Her Majesty The Queen).
INGRES: *The Stamaty family*, 1818, pencil on paper, 46 × 37 cm, Paris, Louvre (Documentation Photographique de la Réunion des Musées Nationaux).
SEURAT: *Place de la Concorde, winter*,

c. 1882-83, Conté crayon, 23 × 30.5 cm, New York, Solomon R. Guggenheim Museum.
KLIMT: *Woman lying down*, 1904, pencil, 34.5 × 54 cm, Stuttgart, Staatsgalerie.
RUBENS: *Young woman looking down*, *c.* 1627-28, black, white and red chalk, 41.5 × 28.5 cm, Florence, Uffizi (Scala).
KOLLWITZ: *Woman and Death*, 1910, charcoal, 47 × 61 cm, Washington, DC, National Gallery of Art, Rosenwald collection.
HOCKNEY: *Beach umbrella, Calvi*, 1972, crayon, 42 × 35 cm, London, British Museum (copyright David Hockney 1979, courtesy Petersburg Press).

164–165 Painters and Printmaking
BLAKE: *Newton*, 1795, monotype finished in pen and watercolour, 45.5 × 59 cm, London, Tate Gallery.
GOYA: *The two old women, c.* 1808-10, oil on canvas, 181 × 125 cm, Lille, Musée des Beaux-Arts (Giraudon); *Hurry up Death*, 1799, etching on copper-plate, 21.5 × 15 cm, London, British Museum (Fotomas Index).
NOLDE: *The life of St Mary Aegyptiaca*, 1912, oil on canvas, Hamburg, Kunsthalle (Ada and Emil Nolde Foundation); *The Prophet*, 1912, woodcut, 32 × 22.5 cm, Washington, National Gallery of Art, Rosenwald collection.
HIROSHIGE: *The plum-tree garden*, 1857, woodcut, Amsterdam, National Museum Vincent van Gogh.
VAN GOGH: *The plum-tree garden*, 1886, oil on canvas, 55 × 46 cm, Amsterdam, National Museum Vincent van Gogh.

166–167 Printmaking techniques
KUNISADA: *Making colour prints*, 1857, woodcut, London, Victoria and Albert Museum.
GAUDIER-BRZESKA: *Wrestlers*, 1914, linocut, 41.5 × 35.5 cm, London, Victoria and Albert Museum.
PICASSO: *Still life under the lamp*, 1962, coloured linocut, 52 × 64.5 cm, New York Museum, Museum of Modern Art, Gift of Mrs Donald B. Strauss.
HOLBEIN: *The Countess*, from *The Dance of Death*, 1538, woodcut, 5 × 7.5 cm, London, British Library (The Fotomas Index).
BEWICK: *Pelican*, from *History of British Birds*, 1797, wood engraving and block, Newcastle upon Tyne, Public Library.
BOYD: *Lysistrata*, from *Welcome Lampito*, 1970, etching and aquatint, 34.5 × 39.5 cm, London, Ganymed Ltd.
TOULOUSE-LAUTREC: *The passenger in cabin 54*, 1896, coloured lithograph, 61 × 40.5 cm, Paris, Cabinet des Estampes (Giraudon).
DURER: *St Jerome in his study*, 1514, metal engraving, 24.5 × 19 cm, London, British Museum.
STUBBS: *A tiger and a sleeping leopard, c.* 1788, mezzotint, 25 × 32 cm, London, British Museum (The Fotomas Index).

CASSATT: *The letter*, 1891, etching, drypoint and aquatint, 34 × 22.5 cm, Chicago Art Institute, Mr and Mrs A. Ryerson collection.
DAUMIER: *The legislative paunch*, 1833-34, lithograph, 280 × 431 cm, Paris, Bibliothèque Nationale (Immédiate 2).
WARHOL: *Marilyn*, 1962, silk-screen, acrylic and oil on canvas, 208 × 142.5 cm, New York, Museum of Modern Art, Gift of Philip Johnson.

168–169 The Language and Methods of Sculpture
EAKINS: *William Rush carving his allegorical figure of the Schuylkill River*, 1908, version of an earlier work of 1877, oil on canvas, 89.5 × 121.5 cm, New York, Brooklyn Museum, The Dick S. Ramsey Fund.
ANDREA PISANO: *The art of sculpture*, mid-14th century, marble, lower row of the Campanile, Florence (Scala).

170–171 Introduction
MOORE: *Sheep piece*, 1969-72, bronze, height 5.6 metres, Much Hadham, Hertfordshire, England (John Hedgecoe).

172–173 Introduction
RODIN: *Nijinsky*, 1910-11, bronze, height 19 cm, London, Roland Collection (Harold Bridge).
SOUTH INDIA: *Parvati, c.* 12th century, bronze, height 66.5 cm, London, Victoria and Albert Museum.
AEGINA, GREECE: *Fallen warrior, c.* 470 BC, marble, height 62.5 cm, Munich, Glypothek (Hirmer Verlag).
BERNINI: *The rape of Proserpina*, 1621-27, marble, over life-size, Rome, Galleria Borghese (Scala).

174–175 Introduction
PILON: *Graces*, from the monument for the heart of Henry II, *c.* 1560, marble, height 150 cm, Paris, Louvre (Documentation Photographique de la Réunion des Musées Nationaux).
HEPWORTH: *Corinthos*, 1954-55, wood and oil, 102.5 × 105 × 101.5 cm, London, Tate Gallery (John Webb).
CELLINI: *Virtue overcoming Vice*, *c.* 1550, bronze with black lacquer patina, 24.5 × 17.5 × 9 cm, Washington, National Gallery of Art, Widener collection.
HAWAII: Food bowl, undated, wood, shell and bone, diameter 20.5 cm, London, British Museum.
GIACOMETTI: *The palace at 4 a.m.*, 1932-33, wood, glass, wire and string, 62.5 × 71.2 × 39.4 cm, New York, Museum of Modern Art.

176–177 Preparatory drawing
VIET STOSS: Design for the Bamberg altarpiece, *c.* 1520, ink, Cracow, University Archaeology Department.
RODIN: *Seated female nude*, after 1906, pencil, 34 × 27 cm, London, Courtauld Institute Galleries.
STEVENS: Design for the Wellington monument, *c.* 1856, ink, London, Victoria and Albert Museum.
BERNINI: Study for the Fontana del Moro, 1652-53, pen and wash,

Windsor, Royal Library (by gracious permission of Her Majesty The Queen).
MICHELANGELO: *Nude man turning away, c.* 1504-05, pen and brush with two coloured inks heightened with white, 42 × 28.5 cm, London, British Museum.
FRINK: *Goggle head, c.* 1965, pencil and watercolour, 76 × 56 cm, London, Waddington Galleries.
DAVID SMITH: *Untitled, c.* 1960, spray-painted stencil on paper, 50 × 66 cm, New York, Estate of David Smith, courtesy of M. Knoedler & Co. (Geoffrey Clements).

178–179 Stonecarving
MICHELANGELO: "*Atlas*", *c.* 1513-20, marble, height 259 cm, Florence, Accademia (Scala); *The Bruges Madonna, c.* 1506, marble, height 125 cm, Bruges, Notre Dame (Scala).
CHARTRES, FRANCE: Royal Portal figures, *c.* 1150, stone, height about 5.5 metres, Chartres Cathedral (Sonia Halliday).
Photographs: (top) Angelo Hornak, (bottom) John Hedgecoe.

180–181 Stonecarving
CHICHESTER, ENGLAND: *Head of Christ, c.* 1100, Caen stone, Chichester Cathedral (A. F. Kersting).
MEXICO: *Xipe Totec*, 14th century, andesite, height 22.9 cm, London, British Museum.
BERNINI: *Louis XIV*, 1665, marble, height 98.5 cm, Versailles Palace (Documentation Photographique de la Réunion des Musées Nationaux).
SIDON: "The Alexander sarcophagus", *Battle scene, c.*4th century BC, marble, Istanbul, Archaeological Museum (Mike Fear).
WESTMINSTER: *Abbot Litlington*, 1351, stone; replica stonecarver Arthur Ayres (Photos: Angelo Hornak).
Diagram: Byron Harvey.

182–183 Carving in wood and ivory
SIERRA LEONE: *Mende* figure, early 19th century, wood, height 117.5 cm, London, British Museum.
MOORE: *Reclining figure*, 1945-46, elmwood, length 187.5 cm, London, Fischer Fine Art (John Hedgecoe).
GERMANY: Detail from a choir-stall, 1285, wood panel, Hanover, Provinzial Museum (Bildarchiv Foto Marburg).
MICHEL ERHART: *Young woman in the costume of the Burgundian court*, *c.* 1475-80, polychromed linden-wood, 53.5 × 30.5 × 22 cm, Ulm Museum.
LORRAINE, FRANCE: Book cover, 11th century, ivory, 25 × 15 cm, London, Victoria and Albert Museum.
CHINA: *Immortal Chang Kuo Lao*, 17th century, ivory, London, British Museum.
Photograph of carver's tools: John Hedgecoe.

184–185 Modelling
GREECE: Tanagra figure, *c.* 300 BC,

painted terracotta, London, British Museum.
JAPAN: *Haniwa* warrior figure, 5th century, terracotta, Paris, Musée Guimet (Documentation Photographique de la Réunion des Musées Nationaux).
MARINI: *Stravinsky*, 1951, bronze, height 36 cm, Milan, Galleria d'Arte Moderna.
HOUDON: *Benjamin Franklin*, 1778, terracotta, life-size, Paris, Louvre (Documentation Photographique de la Réunion des Musées Nationaux).
CHINA: *Groom and horse, c.* 750, glazed terracotta, London, British Museum.
KAENDLER: *Cockatoo, c.* 1735, painted porcelain, Meissen, Staatliche Porzellanmanufaktur, Schauhalle.
ROSSO: "*Ecce Puer*", 1906-07, wax over plaster, height 43 cm, Piacenza, Galleria d'Arte Moderna (Scala).
GIAMBOLOGNA: Model for *The rape of the Sabine, c.* 1579, wax, height 30 cm, London, Victoria and Albert Museum.
Diagram: Alan Suttie.

186–187 Casting
ITALY: *Cellini*, 16th century, engraving, London, British Museum.
CELLINI: *Perseus and Medusa*, 1545-54, bronze, height 5.5 metres, Florence, Loggia dei Lanzi (The Mansell Collection).
Diagrams: (centre) Michael McGuinness, (bottom) Keith Palmer.

188–189 Cast metal sculpture
GREECE: *Youth, c.* 350 BC, bronze, height 130 cm, Athens, National Museum (Scala).
TORRIGIANO: Tomb of Henry VII, completed 1518, gilded bronze, figures life-size, London, Westminster Abbey (Angelo Hornak).
RODIN: *The burghers of Calais*, 1884-86, bronze, height about 2 metres, Paris, Musée Rodin.
IFE, NIGERIA: *Human head*, 15th century, bronze, London, British Museum (Werner Forman Archive).
GEOFFREY CLARKE: *Toroidal vortex*, 1968, aluminium, height 12.5 metres, Exeter University (Floyd Picture Library).
PAOLOZZI: *Japanese war god*, 1958, bronze, height 153 cm, Buffalo, New York, Albright-Knox Art Gallery.
PICASSO: *Baboon and young*, 1951, bronze, height 52.5 cm, New York, Museum of Modern Art, Mrs Simon Guggenheim Fund.

190–191 Construction
GONZALEZ: *Cactus man*, 1939-40, bronze, height 80 cm, Paris, Louvre (Documentation Photographique de la Réunion des Musées Nationaux).
CALDER: *Antennae with red and blue dots*, 1960, wire and painted metal, 109.5 × 126.5 × 126.5 cm, London, Tate Gallery (John Webb).
CARO: *Deep North*, 1969-70, steel and aluminium, 243 × 580 × 290 cm, the artist's collection (Floyd Picture Library).
CESAR: *Torso*, 1954, welded iron,

77 × 59.5 × 69 cm, New York, Museum of Modern Art, Blanchette Rockefeller Fund.
DAVID SMITH: *Cubi XII*, 1963, stainless steel, height 275.5 cm, Washington, Hirshhorn Museum and Sculpture Garden, Smithsonian Institution.

192-193 Construction
CORNELL: *Bird in a box*, 1943, assemblage, 32 × 29 × 7 cm, Krefeld, Kaiser Wilhelm Museum.
GABO: *Column*, 1923, plastic, wood, glass, height 105.5 cm, New York, Solomon R. Guggenheim Museum.
KIENHOLZ: *Portable war museum*, 1968, mixed materials, 285 × 235 × 960 cm, Cologne, Wallraf-Richartz Museum.
SCHOFFER: *Chronos*, 1962, cybernetic light sculpture, the artist's collection.
OLDENBURG: *Soft blue drainpipe*, 1967, acrylic on gathered canvas, 260 × 188 cm, London, Tate Gallery.

194-195 Relief
GHIBERTI: *The Isaac panel*, from "*The Gates of Paradise*", c. 1425-47, gilded bronze relief, 78 × 78 cm, Florence, Baptistery (Scala).
DONATELLO: *The Ascension with Christ giving the keys to St Peter*, c. 1430, marble relief, 40.5 × 114.5 cm, London, Victoria and Albert Museum.
NINEVEH: *King Assurbanipal killing a lion*, c. 668-627 BC, stone relief (probably alabaster, and originally painted), height 165 cm, London, British Museum.
MANZU: *St Notburga and the beheading of the blessed Engelbert Knolland*, 1958, bronze, Salzburg Cathedral (Foto Oscar Savio).
GUATEMALA: Toltec stela, c. 1000, stone (Werner Forman Archive).
Diagram: Michael McGuinness and Alan Suttie.

196-197 Relief/2
ALGARDI: *The meeting of Pope Leo I and Attila*, 1646-53, marble, height 7.5 metres, Rome, St Peter's (Scala).
MATHURA, INDIA: *Yakshi*, c. AD 100, sandstone, London, Victoria and Albert Museum.
NEVELSON: *Golden Gate*, 1961, gold-painted wood, 240 × 161 × 30 cm, New York, The Pace Gallery.
HANS BRUGGEMANN: The Brodesholm altarpiece, 1515-21, wood, Schleswig Cathedral (Bildarchiv Foto Marburg).

198-199 Sculpture and Architecture
ELURA, INDIA: The Kailasanatha temple, c. 900, rock, height about 29 metres (Michael Ridley).
AUTUN, ST LAZARE: *The Flight into Egypt*, c. 1125-35, stone, Autun Cathedral (Sonia Halliday).
OLYMPIA, GREECE: West pediment, the temple of Zeus, model by G. Treu, original c. 460 BC, marble, 285 cm (P. Grunauer).
LONDON: *Censing angel*, c. 1250, stone, Westminster Abbey (Woodmansterne).
HEPWORTH: *Winged figure*, 1962, aluminium, 5.7 metres, London, John Lewis building (Angelo Hornak).
TULA, MEXICO: *Toltec warrior*, c. 900-1168, stone, height 3 metres, Temple of Quetzalcoatl (Michael Holford).
Diagram: Dinah Lone.

200-201 Sculpture and Architecture
DESIDERIO DA SETTIGNANO: The Marsuppini monument, c. 1453, marble, 6 × 3.5 metres, Florence, S. Croce (Scala).
NICOLA PISANO: The pulpit of Siena Cathedral, 1265-68, marble (Scala).
SOLESMES, FRANCE: *The entombment of Christ*, 1496, stone with traces of paint, life-size or larger, Solesmes Abbey (James Austin; details Caisse Nationale des Monuments et des Sites).
GIUSTI BROTHERS: Tomb of Louis XII and Anne of Brittany, completed 1531, marble, St Denis, Abbey church (Caisse Nationale des Monuments et des Sites).

202-203 Sculpture in its Setting
MOCHI: *Duke Alexander Farnese*, 1620-25, bronze, over life-size, Piacenza, Piazza dei Cavalli (Alinari).
GOERITZ: *The square of towers*, 1957, painted concrete pylons, height 36.5 metres, Mexico, Ciudad (Hamlyn Picture Library).
J. H. FOLEY: *Prince Albert*, 1868-73, marble and gilt-bronze, height 4.2 metres, London, Hyde Park (Angelo Hornak, Spectrum Color Library).
BORGLUM: Mount Rushmore memorial, 1927-41, rock, height of each figure about 20 metres, South Dakota, Mount Rushmore (Keystone Press).
ZADKINE: *The destroyed city*, 1953, bronze, height 6.4 metres, Schiedamse Dijk, Rotterdam

(Keystone Press).
Diagram: Chris Forsey.

204-205 Sculpture in its Setting
BRANCUSI: *Endless column*, 1937, cast iron, height about 19 metres, Romania, Tirgu Jiu (Susan Griggs Agency/Adam Woolfitt).
NOGUCHI: Courtyard, 1960-64, white marble, Yale University (Esto Photographics).
CHRISTO: *Wrapped coast*, 1969, various kinds of plastic, Sydney, Little Bay (Christo).
ROME: "*The Nymph of Subterranean Waters*", from the Fountain of the Naiads, 1900, bronze, Rome, Piazza della Repubblica (Robert Harding Associates).
GIAMBOLOGNA: *Appennino*, 1577-81, brick and stone, height 10 metres, Pratolino, Villa Demidorff (Scala).
ITALY, NEAR NAPLES: *Diana and nymphs*, c. 1770, marble, figures over life-size, Caserta, Villa Reale (Alinari).

206-207 Small Portable Sculpture
ROME: The Portland Vase, 1st century AD, glass cameo, height 25.5 cm, London, British Museum (Michael Holford).
EGYPT: *Negro girl carrying a chest*, c. 1400 BC, hardwood, 14 × 5 cm, London, British Museum.
CHINA: *Buffalo*, c. 15th century, jade, height 16.5 cm, width 28 cm, length 43 cm, Cambridge, Fitzwilliam Museum.
NICCOLO FIORENTINO: *Medal of Giovanna Albizzi*, c. 1486, bronze, diameter 7.5 cm, London, British Museum.
PERSIA: Libation vessel, c. 5th century BC, gold, height 9.5 cm, Tehran, Archaeological Museum (Scala).
RICCIO: *Seated satyr*, c. 1500, bronze, height 10 cm, Florence, Bargello (Scala).
NORTH ITALY: Rooster brooch, 16th/17th century, gold, enamel, blister pearl, diamonds and ruby, 7 × 5.5 cm, Florence, Museo degli Argenti (Scala).
CENTRAL GERMANY: Eltenberg shrine, c. 1150, gilt, bronze, champlevé enamel, walrus ivory, height 54.5 cm, London, Victoria and Albert Museum.
HEINO: *SALT conference medal*, 1969, struck bronze, diameter 7 cm, London, British Museum.
Diagram: Dinah Lone.

Index

Page numbers in **bold** refer to the main entries; *italic* numbers refer to the illustrations.

Credits

The publishers wish to thank the
following people and
organizations for their help in
the research and production of
this book and its three
companion volumes:

A.J. Ayres
Frank Auerbach
John Berger
Ann Blyth, National Gallery,
    London
Susan Bolsom
British Museum, Department of
    Prints and Drawings
Harold Bull
Central Reference Library,
    Westminster
Christo
Geoffrey Clarke
Cooper Bridgeman Library
Anthony Caro
Susie Courtauld
Courtauld Institute of Art
Chris Dale-Green
Graham Darlow
The Fotomas Index
Giraudon
Richard Hamilton
Dr Victor Harris
John Hedgecoe
Jack Hillier
Michael Holford
Angelo Hornak
John Hoyland
Mark Jones
Edward Kienholz
R.B. Kitaj
Felix Klee
Ravi Kumar
Professor Peter Lasko
Leo Castelli Gallery
Edward Lucie-Smith
Professor Norbert Lynton
Dr Valerie Males
The Mansell Collection
Metropolitan Museum of Art,
    NY, Photo Library
Henry Moore
Museum of Modern Art, NY,
    Photo Library
National Portrait Gallery,
    London
Frank O'Shea
Terry Pepper
Photo Bulloz
Benedict Read
René Roland
Peter Sedgely
Professor Aaron Sharf
Ronald Sheridan
Dr Nicola Smith
Claudia Stumpf
Peter Sullivan
Tate Gallery Publications
    Department
Nicholas Turner
Victor Vaserély
Victoria and Albert Museum
Suzanne Walter
Warburg Institute
Werner Forman Archive
Dr Roderick Whitfield
Daphne Wood
J.P. Ziole